AUTHORS OUT HERE

Fitzgerald,
West, Parker,
and Schulberg
in Hollywood

TOM CERASULO

THE UNIVERSITY OF SOUTH CAROLINA PRESS

© 2010 University of South Carolina

Published by the University of South Carolina Press
Columbia, South Carolina 29208

www.sc.edu/uscpress

Manufactured in the United States of America

19 18 17 16 15 14 13 12 11 10   10 9 8 7 6 5 4 3 2 1

Library of Congress Cataloging-in-Publication Data
Cerasulo, Tom.
  Authors out here : Fitzgerald, West, Parker, and Schulberg in
  Hollywood / Tom Cerasulo.
      p. cm.
  Includes bibliographical references and index.
  ISBN 978-1-57003-903-4 (cloth : alk. paper)
  1. American fiction--20th century—Film and video adaptations. 2.
American fiction—20th century—History and criticism. 3. Motion
pictures and literature—United States. 4. Motion picture
authorship—United States—History. I. Title.
    PS374.M55C42 2010
    791.43'6—dc22
                                        2009051098

This book was printed on Glatfelter Natures, a recycled paper with
30 percent postconsumer waste content.

For Celeste

Contents

Illustrations

Acknowledgments

Hollywood films, Hollywood novels, and the books written about them are all the result of multiple collaborators. I am listed as the author of this work, but many individuals and institutions deserve a share of the credit. I first need to thank the Ph.D. program in English of the Graduate Center of the City University of New York for giving me the chance to learn from and with an outstanding group of scholars and friends: Marc Dolan, who helped me draw up the original blueprints for this project; Morris Dickstein, whose solid writing continues to serve as my model; the late George Custen, who showed me that the Hollywood studio system was as fascinating as the movies it produced; and Rob Dowling and Sam Cohen, who have remained terrific early readers and cherished longtime friends.

Along the way I have benefited from the moral support of my colleagues at Elms College, especially Damien Murray. Elms media guys Mike Dialessi and Chris Pelletier provided technical support. For her supply of candy, I must also acknowledge the Humanities Division secretary, Annette Ziomek. This project was researched and written with the help of multiple grants and course releases awarded by Elms College and its alumni association, for which I am very grateful. I am also indebted to the students in my Modern Novel and Hollywood Novel courses at Elms for allowing me to hone my ideas during classroom discussions.

A portion of chapter 1 of this book appeared as "The Magician with Words: Fitzgerald and the 1920s Film Market" in *Studies in American Culture* 30 (October 2007). Parts of the Nathanael West discussion in chapters 1 and 2 appeared as "*The Dream Life of Balso Snell* and the Vocation of Nathanael West" in *Arizona Quarterly* 62 (Summer 2006). I am grateful for permission to include revised versions of these essays here. Jay Martin generously provided permission to reprint the Nathanael West photographs, and I also need to thank him for his definitive biography of West, which first sparked my interest in authors-turned-screenwriters. Sections of the Budd Schulberg material from chapters 4, 6, and 7 appeared in Jay Parini, ed., *American Writers: Supplement XVIII: Charles*

Frederick Briggs to Robert Wrigley. © 2008 Gale, a part of Cengage Learning, Inc. Reproduced by permission. www.cengage.com/permissions.

I wish to thank Jim Denton, Jonathan Haupt, and Karen Rood, as well as everyone else at University of South Carolina Press, for putting this book into the world. I want to thank Ron Mandelbaum at Photofest. I would like to thank my father, Thomas P. Cerasulo, for passing on his love of movies and for comforting me after losses by my beloved New York Giants; my mother, Kathryn Lord, for her generosity and wisdom; my dog, Buster, for making me take a break from writing once in a while; and my partner, Celeste Donovan, for the love and support that sustains me.

Introduction

What shining phantom folds its wings before us?
What apparition, smiling yet remote?
Is this—so portly yet so highly porous—
The old friend who went west and never wrote?

Edmund Wilson, *The Boys
in the Back Room*

ﾂﾉ

In "Mightier Than the Sword," one of the last short stories F. Scott Fitzgerald ever wrote, the veteran screenwriter Pat Hobby comforts an East Coast novelist who has been unkindly treated by a ruthless Hollywood producer. "Authors get a tough break out here," Hobby says, consoling his new friend. "They don't want authors. They want writers—like me" (*The Pat Hobby Stories* 149).

Fitzgerald is the tragic hero of what might be called the Hollywood vampire story. According to dozens of critics—most notably Edmund Wilson, Arthur Mizener, Aaron Latham—and sometimes even Fitzgerald himself, the movie industry broke his spirit and dried up his creativity. This myth of Hollywood as a malevolent entity that feeds on the brains of artists has followed us into the new century. John Parris Springer's 2000 book, *Hollywood Fictions: The Dream Factory in American Popular Literature*, states that in Hollywood Fitzgerald's "career seemed to bottom out" and that his work for the studios "meant the end of the great literary solo flights he had performed" (209, 215). Yet from 1937 to 1940, when his career was supposedly bottoming out, Fitzgerald published more than thirty stories and articles and wrote the lion's share of a new novel.

An examination of Fitzgerald's career as a whole shows no great chasm between his pre-Hollywood career and his last years in Los Angeles. In both "halves" there is an eagerness to be popular and reach a wide audience. In both there is a desire to be, in Fitzgerald's words, "endorsed by the intellectually elite" (*Letters of FSF* 151), an artist whose place in history is assured. In both his willingness to use his cultural capital to champion writers he liked and respected is apparent—from Dorothy Parker, Ring Lardner, and Ernest Hemingway in the 1920s to Nathanael West, John O'Hara, and Budd Schulberg in the 1930s. In both Fitzgerald experiences vocational anxiety, yet continues to practice his craft and producing good work. In short Hollywood was not the setting for F. Scott Fitzgerald's failed second act; it was part of the same successful performance.

Authors Out Here reconsiders the Hollywood vampire myth by tracing the careers of an interrelated group of authors with literary aspirations—those who sought lasting elite cultural status, endeavored to create works possessing intellectual prestige, and conducted commercially risky experiments in content and/or form—who wrote for and about the movies during the studio era. Using an interdisciplinary approach that considers literature and film and takes into account both text and context, I examine how these authors contributed to the motion-picture industry and how the motion-picture industry contributed to these authors. Such writers came to Hollywood for one reason—the money—but they eventually discovered other reasons to stick around. I argue that rather than destroying their talent, time spent in Hollywood actually benefited artists such as F. Scott Fitzgerald, Nathanael West, Dorothy Parker, and Budd Schulberg. Hollywood provided the financial, creative, and social resources they each needed during a complex moment in American cultural life. My discussion of the production histories of films such as *A Star Is Born* (1937), *Three Comrades* (1938), and *On the Waterfront* (1954) demonstrates the contributions these writers, who had all established themselves in other genres, were able to make to the art of the motion picture. I argue that Hollywood was good for these artists, and these artists were good for Hollywood. But this reciprocal relationship was far from painless.

The role of the artist in society has undergone several historical and institutional shifts, ones that place the position of the literary writer in Hollywood into relief. In the years before the Renaissance, artists were viewed as craftsmen who produced objects dictated to them by the gods. Creativity could emanate only from the heavens. When sculptors and poets began being recognized as the originating sources of inspiration, a patronage system developed to cultivate these artists. Now *craftsmen* referred to those who made useful things, while artists were free to explore the themes and forms suggested to them by their genius. But there was a catch: the work these artists produced could not directly challenge the ruling class, for fear of losing their financial support. With the emergence and spread of a commodity economy, the artist was gradually liberated from direct dependence on a definite group, but now was now forced to depend indirectly on a larger, unknowable force—the market. Art could be sold to whomever paid most, but to cater that art to that buyer would be to give up a new sense of creative autonomy. By the second half of the eighteenth century, the urge for writers to resist the market and stand apart from society needed to be weighed against a pressure to be accepted and make a profit.

The desire to personalize and control artistic creation, to become an author, emanates from a Western culture idea of individualism, and the resulting belief in a literary work as intrinsically and exclusively centered on the expression of a singular genius reached its full flowering during the Romantic period. This conception of authorship still remains strong. Modernist novelists such as James Joyce and Gustave Flaubert may have argued for the absence of the author, but their statements on the matter, that the artist "must be everywhere felt, but never seen" (Flaubert 230) and must remain "within or behind or beyond or above his handiwork, invisible, refined out of existence, indifferent, paring his fingernails" (Joyce 181), still reveal an egocentric authorial presence exhibiting a godlike, monotheistic control at the moment of conception. Even the theorists Roland Barthes and Michel Foucault became famous authors by problematizing the very notion of the autonomous author. Their words on killing the author so that the reader may be born carry the power of authority, individuality, creativity, and originality.

But screenwriters under the studio system were denied the wielding of such prestigious authorial powers. As opposed to the novelist, who legally owned the material produced by his or her singular imagination, the Hollywood scriptwriter was called upon to work with existing materials owned by someone else and help craft them into a marketable commodity ultimately built by many hands. As Pat Hobby's statement in "Mightier Than the Sword" makes plain, writers and those they worked under, movie producers and directors, battled not only over creative control of individual texts but also over notions of authorship and authority in general. As salaried employees crafting screenplays for Hollywood film, a collaborative mass medium in which words were not primary and writers resided somewhere toward the bottom of the middle of a hierarchical system, many authors were forced to question the very foundation of their callings.

This self-examination, which necessitated viewing themselves more as economic beings working in the United States and less as artistic figures residing in an imaginary republic of letters, was often unsettling for them. But a recognition that they were workers in the culture industry was never artistically devastating, and it was never a vocation killer. In fact, looking at the careers of Fitzgerald, West, Parker, and Schulberg as they unfold over time reveals another shift in the vocation of authorship, from a late modernist pose of the disaffected genius who stands outside of society to a later role as an engaged laborer in industrial America. This realization that they were creative workers also served to inspire some of their best creative work.

Yet the notion persists among literary critics, most of whom have a professional stake in preserving the virginal aura of literary production and a few of whom love a sordid plot of decline, that Hollywood was a glitzy siren luring artists to commit intellectual, aesthetic, and spiritual suicide in Los Angeles swimming pools. Real writers must protect themselves from the call of the marketplace. Do not get greedy and try to amass both commercial capital and aesthetic capital. To sell out, to acknowledge you are selling anything, is to enter a devil's bargain and to be cast out of the Eden of pure literary production. In such highbrow formulations Hollywood takes the fall as a symbol of all that is wrong with an uneducated, fickle, homogenizing mass culture of consumption. Trying to work both sides of the art and commerce divide, desiring both money and prestige, will turn the noble, special author into a common, workaday hack. In this illusory zero-sum game, which divides up cultural regions the way the movie studios divided up theater territories, an acknowledgment of the successes authors achieved in Hollywood might risk a devaluing of their literary reputations (as well as invite a challenge to the critic's own evaluative authority to distinguish between elite culture and mass culture). But I argue that art and commerce are inexorably linked. There is no natural divide. Authors who want to be read and want to live by their writing have always—and will always—concern themselves with questions of marketing and audience.

Tom Dardis's *Some Time in the Sun* (1976) went a long way toward dispelling the persistent myth, fueled by Edmund Wilson's 1941 essay "The Boys in the Back Room," that moving to Los Angeles ruined Nathanael West and Scott Fitzgerald. Although both novelists complained that screen writing led them astray from their "real" work, their contracts were often for short periods of time. Neither was an especially prolific novelist before settling in Hollywood, and both made a good deal of money writing for the movies at a time when their fiction was not selling. As Dardis points out, West's *The Day of the Locust* (1939) and Fitzgerald's *The Last Tycoon*

(1941), written during their time in Los Angeles, are now widely regarded as among their better books.

But in his effort to paint bright portraits of individual authors through carefully selected anecdotes highlighting their California years, Dardis elides the larger picture of a moment of cultural crisis in the writing vocation. An unabashed movie fan, he focuses on the product and ignores much of the process. While Dardis is correct in stating that Hollywood did not destroy writers, it did make them face head-on their status as workers toiling in an ungenteel marketplace. Concerns about holding on to an identity as a "serious" artist in an age of mass culture, worries that began even before they signed screen-writing contracts, only intensified once inside the studio gates.

The generation of authors that forms the body of *Authors Out Here* grew up alongside the American film industry—Dorothy Parker was born in 1893, the same year that Thomas Edison's Kinetoscope was introduced to the world. As these artists came of age, many wore their distaste for the movies like an elite badge of honor, intellectuals distancing themselves from commercial culture. Coeval critics such as Van Wyck Brooks, in *America's Coming of Age* (1915), and H. L. Mencken, in *The American Language* (1919), popularized the highbrow/lowbrow distinction that used the language of taste (and a bit of amateur phrenology) to talk about class. But as writers bemoaned the waning cultural importance of literature in a market flooded with commodities, many secretly envied film's power to reach the masses and its wonderfully democratic possibilities. In the 1920s, shortly before writing his editor that "lowbrows go to the movies" (*Letters of FSF* 168), Fitzgerald told friends that Hollywood was the future. He and his contemporaries began to recognize that motion pictures would allow them to reach larger audiences than the theater or books ever could. The screen writing was already on the wall.

Soon hundreds of eastern authors would also have an economic motive for boarding the Super Chief cross-country train to Los Angeles. When the Depression hobbled Broadway and the New York publishing industry in the 1930s, Hollywood, with its need for spoken dialogue, allowed starving playwrights, literary journalists, and novelists to transform themselves into screenwriters with a paycheck. But, as Richard Fine points out in *West of Eden* (1993), a history of writers in Hollywood during the Depression, this new role came with a price.

Accepting a studio contract put authors into a structure and hierarchy where time, function, and productivity were measured and used to gauge success. Fine explains: "Writers were not destroyed by Hollywood in the

1930s. But the profession of authorship as they knew it was certainly under attack" (159). Movie producers divided up labor in such a way that the guiding vision behind individual films remained their own, as did legal ownership of the scripts. Screen credits were sometimes withheld out of spite or granted to friends and lovers on a whim. Multiple writers were often assigned to the same script, a policy that infuriated many "name" authors. As Parker once remarked of a screenwriter she considered her literary inferior, "If he's a creative writer, I'm Marie of Rumania" (qtd. in Schwartz 124). But movie producers believed that the product was too expensive to be left in the hands of effete, dillydallying artists, and writers who smelled of the highbrow were often paired with industry insiders or junior apprentices. Budd Schulberg, the son of a movie mogul—and therefore both a neophyte and an insider—was called upon to babysit Fitzgerald during a 1939 screen-writing trip to the campus of Dartmouth, a journey fictionalized in Schulberg's novel *The Disenchanted* (1950).

I contend that working in Hollywood not only made writers further question their professional roles; it also deepened their anxiety about their cultural roles. Fitzgerald felt that Walter Wanger had brought him to Dartmouth merely to show him off as a fancy new employee. Among many Hollywood executives, a dismissal of high culture was often paired with a reverence for the cultural prestige it carried. In the absence of possessing artistic credibility, many film executives settled for possessing the possessors of this quality. Jack Warner bragged to visitors to his lot that Warner Bros. had hired America's most celebrated novelist, William Faulkner, "for peanuts" (qtd. in Hamilton 200). Books, movies, and the people who write them have both an economic value and a cultural value, and these exchanges are rarely equal. Name authors such as Fitzgerald and Parker at times were worried that they had cashed out their status as artists at too low a price.

And yet despite their fears and misgivings, working for the movies was beneficial for the four writers whose careers and relations to Hollywood form the narrative arc of *Authors Out Here*. West and Fitzgerald, by their own admission, were not successful screenwriters. Yet the job provided them with financial support and allowed them to study at its epicenter the theme of American dreaming and its discontents that runs throughout their fiction. Furthermore, as their letters show, even before their Hollywood novels, even before their first trips to the studios, Fitzgerald and West were questioning the notion of the author in twentieth-century America, questions still relevant today in an age of Web-based hypertext, online publishing, ever-sprouting creative writing programs, and ever-declining audiences for literary fiction: Why do I create? Who is listening? What makes what I have to say unique? What does it mean to call myself an author?

This book examines how these issues play out in their early fiction—from West's sculptor who does not sculpt in "The Impostor" (circa 1926) to Fitzgerald's writer who does not write in *The Beautiful and Damned* (1922); from authors in search of audiences in West's *The Dream Life of Balso Snell* (1931) and Fitzgerald's "Crazy Sunday" (1932) to an audience in search of an author in West's *Miss Lonelyhearts* (1933); from a psychiatrist who plays at being a writer in Fitzgerald's *Tender Is the Night* (1934) to a writer who plays at being a psychiatrist in *Miss Lonelyhearts*—culminating in discussions of West's *The Day of the Locust* and Fitzgerald's Pat Hobby stories (1940) and *The Last Tycoon*.

Instead of viewing their fiction written in Los Angeles as revenge tracts, as many critics have done, I view them as sites of negotiation. These texts, as well as Schulberg's *What Makes Sammy Run?* (1941) and *The Disenchanted*, do not condemn Hollywood; they try to come to terms with it. Bruce L. Chipman's *Into America's Dream Dump: A Postmodern Study of the American Novel* (1999) views the subgenre as an exploration of cultural wastelands populated by archetypal "cheaters" and "seekers." Despite the promises of the word *postmodern* in the title, Chipman tills the same old unfruitful ground. He writes: "Hollywood, the place where dreams are mass produced, is the incarnation and culmination of the American Dream and, ultimately, the symbol of its betrayal; the Hollywood novel reflects this deterioration from Utopian promise through decadence to nightmare and apocalypse" (197). To Chipman, as to Edmund Wilson, Hollywood is the great American signifier for depravity, a stand-in for a déclassé medium, a corrupt place, a miserable state of mind. But Hollywood in the novels of West, Schulberg, and Fitzgerald does not function as a catchall symbol of dissolution. Their examinations of issues of film spectatorship and cinematic grammar, in fact, offer some of the earliest examples of American film theory. They also have much to say about the manufacture of films.

Just as high culture involves more than the production of rarefied masterpieces—those masterpieces must also be marketed and sold—mass culture involves more than the consumption of industrial goods. These books depict Hollywood as a company town where groups of people work hard and things get made. Most Hollywood novels are not oppositional; they are dialectic. They satirize the film industry, sometimes even savagely. But they also carefully examine studio society and American society at large, trying to figure out the writer's place within both.

For example, despite popular belief, Fitzgerald's Pat Hobby stories are neither jeremiads nor mere potboilers. Not only are they more objective about the film industry than they have been given credit for, but Fitzgerald also revised them many times and had definite ideas on the order in which they should be published. While it is true that Fitzgerald, like Pat and his colleagues, had his share of troubles as a screenwriter, many of these difficulties were of his own devising. Of the four authors I consider, Fitzgerald was the one most invested in the romantic notion of the artist as solitary man of genius. His collaborators often resented his claims to superior taste and judgment, especially since his scripts, many of which have now been published, tended to contain screen-writing no-no's such as facial expressions, long passages of narrative, and flowery dialogue. Throughout Fitzgerald's movie-writing career, his scripts were criticized for not being filmic enough, for lacking a feel for screen rhythm, and for having a tin ear for the sound of spoken dialogue. In the film *Beloved Infidel* (1958), based on Sheilah Graham's memoir of her years as Scott's companion, a movie executive looks at one of Fitzgerald's scripts and shakes his gray head in frustration. "How do you photograph adjectives!?" he finally exclaims, echoing the sentiments of many of his real-life counterparts in studio front offices.

Fitzgerald always worked hard on his scripts, and was paid well for them, even if they were not produced. For him the movies filled the financial gap left when the short story market weakened. Fitzgerald not only came to appreciate the possibilities of reaching a larger audience afforded by film, but also went on to explore the application of cinematic techniques to animate his fiction. And although he never got the hang of screen writing, the unfinished *The Last Tycoon* and the underrated Pat Hobby stories, written while under Hollywood contract, show his powers as a fiction writer had not been left on the cutting room floor.

Unlike Fitzgerald and Parker, who had tasted commercial success in the literary marketplace of the 1920s before losing it to the Depression, and Schulberg, who had a surprise best seller with *What Makes Sammy Run?*, West, whose career was confined to the 1930s, was unable to support himself as a writer outside of Hollywood. Because his name meant nothing outside of a small circle of artists and intellectuals, he had difficulty breaking into the "major" studios (MGM, Paramount, Warner Bros., Twentieth Century-Fox, and RKO) or even the "major minors" (Columbia, Universal, and United Artists). When he finally did, it came as a relief. "Thank God for the movies," he told friends (qtd. in Martin 341). Fellow screenwriter Wells Root told an interviewer that West "was happy to be out here and making money so he could write more novels. He was quite the reverse of some of the writers who came out here and thought they were slumming" (Server 178). In addition to a paycheck, the movies provided him with a golden opportunity to pursue further his career-long examination of the role of the artist in a market flooded with commodities. In college West began affiliating himself with the avant-garde, cultivating a pose of "art for art's sake" and adopting an air of disinterestedness. Yet *The Dream Life of Balso Snell*, his first novel, concerns writers in search of an audience. Behind the flippancy of this self-described "protest against the writing of books" (qtd. in Siegel 4) lurks West's anxiety about the position of the artist in society and a fear of mass culture, a theme that culminates in his last novel, *The Day of the Locust*.

As West's Hollywood years exemplify, screen writing provided these authors not only with subject matter and financial support, but also with a network of social support. An important segment of the audience for writing is other writers, and during their years in California these four artists championed each other's work and offered peer approval, encouraging each other to keep writing during a time when all questioned their literary vocations. In the back room of a Los Angeles bookshop run by a hard-drinking Texan named Stanley Rose, artists such as Parker, Faulkner, Schulberg, John O'Hara, Dashiell Hammett, West, and Fitzgerald often gathered after a day put in at the studios. West was never commercially or critically successful, but within this group that met to drink and talk, he was accorded the highest respect. As a "writer's writer," known by those in the know, Nathanael West was an inside celebrity. Typifying what the sociologist Pierre Bourdieu would call a "loser wins" situation, West was considered a big man at Rose's bookshop in part *because* he was so unappreciated by the larger culture and the marketplace. His novels had value for being valueless. So instead of destroying him, Hollywood can be said to have subsidized Nathanael West's fiction financially and emotionally. And by lending his time and his name to the long battle for recognition of the Screen Writers Guild (SWG)—as did Parker and Schulberg—West returned the favor by helping to buoy a unionizing movement fighting for writer solidarity.

A vocal leader in the SWG and well connected in publishing circles, Dorothy Parker was a valuable ally to other Hollywood authors and screenwriters. Like Fitzgerald, who had recommended her to Maxwell Perkins when she was considering writing a book of fiction, she was extremely supportive of younger and less-established colleagues. She provided jacket blurbs for *The Day of the Locust* and *What Makes Sammy Run?*

and reviewed both books favorably. Despite the fact that Parker was well treated and highly paid by the studios, she supported the SWG and fought for rights that would have their greatest effect on the least-fortunate members of her profession. In 1941, nine years after the struggle had begun and one year after West's and Fitzgerald's deaths, a minimum fee scale was instituted, and the guild was given jurisdiction over screen credits. In this respect not only was the film industry good for writers such as West, Parker, and Schulberg, but these writers were also good for the film industry.

Where Fitzgerald's and West's talents were best suited to writing *about* Hollywood, I argue that Parker and Schulberg did some of their best work writing *for* Hollywood. Like other laborers with a sense of craft, they learned to take pleasure in the work itself; the satisfaction of writing well eventually became its own reward. But they also experienced recognition for their screen writing. Both received Academy Award nominations—Parker for *A Star Is Born* (1937) and *Smash-Up: The Story of a Woman* (1947) and Schulberg for *On the Waterfront* (1954)—and both successfully navigated the rough waters of the studio system to bring their words to the screen.

Parker's urbane wit and ability to think on her feet, honed around the Algonquin Round Table in the 1920s, led to her reputation as the best "pitcher" on the MGM lot in the 1930s. Since reading is time-consuming, many movie executives preferred scripts and story ideas to be talked out to them, and Parker was adept at getting her ideas across in meetings and making sure her contributions made it into the final product. Her legendary genius for bon mots, which did not translate well into longer forms such as the novel, proved to be ideally suited for the stylized, rapid-fire patter of 1930s sound film, and her sharp voice can clearly be heard in film classics such as *A Star Is Born* and *Suzy* (1936). Often teamed with her husband, Alan Campbell, who worked on structure as she worked on dialogue, the duo manufactured scripts quickly and effectively. Like Parker and Campbell, many screenwriters found that forming partnerships—with other writers or with directors—increased their chances of getting their scripts produced and receiving screen credits. Because of ego clashes, some of these duos were partners in name only: Horace McCoy and William Lipman hated each other so much that one would write during the day shift and the other would take the night shift so they would never have to see each other. But other partnerships were more symbiotic. Frances Goodrich / Albert Hackett and Howard Hawks / William Faulkner are notable examples. Another is the collaboration between Elia Kazan and Schulberg.

As the title of his autobiography, *Moving Pictures: Memories of a Hollywood Prince* (1981), attests, Schulberg, the son of one of the founders of the American film industry, grew up as California royalty. The summer before he left for college at Dartmouth, his mother, a Hollywood agent, helped him sell a screen treatment. Therefore, unlike the other three authors featured in this study, Schulberg's life as a professional writer began in the movies. After graduating and publishing a few short stories, he returned to Hollywood to work in the family business, gathering up material for his fiction and building friendships with Fitzgerald, West, and Parker before going into eastern exile again in the 1940s.

When the prodigal son returned in the mid 1950s, the studio system was dissolving and independent production was taking over. Kazan and Schulberg partnered up, and they created *On the Waterfront* and *A Face in the Crowd* (1957) to great acclaim. Both films were adapted solely by Schulberg from his own original stories—something that would not have been allowed under the studio system at its height. Therefore, while he may not be the "auteur" of these movies, I argue that his mark on them can clearly be seen. In a manner that was not possible under the factory-like conditions of the studio system, a Taylorized filmmaking process where the screenwriter stopped working when the project began shooting, Kazan and Schulberg collaborated every step of the way—from preproduction, to production, to postproduction—to create these movies.

Schulberg's writing career spanned more than seventy-five years. He died in 2009. Because he lived so much longer than West, Fitzgerald, and Parker—and as a "Hollywood prince" had an insider's view of the rise and fall of the studio system—biographers and film historians were eager to hear him reminisce. He was an often-quoted source in examinations of his canonized friends. Yet Schulberg's fiction itself has received little critical attention, perhaps with good reason. In the final analysis, he was more successful writing stories for Hollywood than about Hollywood. *What Makes Sammy Run?* and *The Disenchanted* are interesting attempts to document the rewards and punishments of screen writing, but both suffer from one-dimensional characters and a plodding style.

As Fitzgerald learned, script writing and novel writing are different skills, and what plays on the page does not always play in front of the camera. Obviously the reverse also holds true, as can be demonstrated by Schulberg's misguided novelization, *Waterfront*. Schulberg's strength was for screen writing, not for prose fiction. He excelled at giving structure to scripts, something his friends Fitzgerald and West struggled with. More important, as a Hollywood insider he knew the complicated process of how movies actually get made—what would work and what would not, what was possible and what was not. He was able to write directly *to* the screen instead of blindly *for* the screen.

Many writers eventually realized that trying to understand the movie business was more important than vilifying it. All four of the authors featured in *Authors Out Here* used their observations as subject matter, and all four did some of their best work while under contract to the studios. Along the way these authors donated their support to others working in Hollywood—writers like them. Time spent in Los Angeles benefited Fitzgerald, West, Parker, and Schulberg. Rather than being destroyed by the movie industry, their careers were invigorated by it.

1

Ain't We Got Funds?

MARKETS AND
VOCATIONS IN
THE 1920S

I want to be one of the greatest writers who have ever lived.
Don't you?

F. Scott Fitzgerald to Edmund Wilson

Some of us view with a peculiar thrill the prospect that Los
Angeles may become the Boston of the photoplay.

Vachel Lindsay, *The Art of the Moving Picture*

"They came pouring in, mostly illegible scrawls," B.P. would tell
me, "written on everything from postcards to butcher paper.
Everybody who paid his nickel to see one of our shows thought
it was easy money to dash off a movie."

Budd Schulberg, *Moving Pictures:
Memories of a Hollywood Prince*

ℬ

The term *author* implies a claim to authority. To promote his upcoming book *This Side of Paradise*, the novelist F. Scott Fitzgerald, a former Manhattan ad man, sat down for an interview with himself in March 1920. He submitted a transcript of this phony conversation to his publisher's marketing department, but Scribner's ultimately decided not to use it. The reasons why can be deduced. At the time Fitzgerald was simply one more young man with an ambitious debut novel. With a catalog that included titles by august names such as Henry James and Edith Wharton, Scribner's might have believed that no one would want to listen to a beginner talk about the state of American literature and the profession of

F. Scott Fitzgerald in the 1920s. Photofest

authorship. Scribner's was a noble, conservative house. It sold books; it was not in the business of selling authors. Overconfident Fitzgerald pronouncements such as "The wise writer, I think, writes for the youth of his own generation, the critics of the next, and the schoolmasters of ever afterward" (*Letters of FSF* 459) might even have put some potential readers off.

The Magician with Words

When *This Side of Paradise* was released, some critics found it pedantic, and others noted that it was full of typographical errors, but Scribner's quickly found that the public certainly did care what Fitzgerald had to say. The idea of a distinctly American literature, free from its European antecedents, was beginning to take hold in the popular imagination. In the

1920s there would be an increased interest in American writers, especially photogenic ones, and much of the positive buzz over Fitzgerald's novel was about the young author, not the book itself. A reporter who had interviewed Scott described him as "an actor . . . vivacious, imaginative, forceful, slightly unbalanced. The latter is his chief charm" (qtd. in Bruccoli and Bryer 416). The media ate up Fitzgerald's showmanship and his sense of style. Like his new friend Dorothy Parker, whom he had met through Robert Sherwood, Fitzgerald was now a New York celebrity, the toast of the town in the great city he referred to as "the land of ambition and success" (*Correspondence* 38). One afternoon Parker saw a taxi driving down Fifth Avenue with Fitzgerald sitting on the roof waving to pedestrians. "Everyone wanted to meet him," she told Zelda Fitzgerald's biographer Nancy Milford (67). A short time after that taxi incident, Parker wrote a bagatelle for the *Saturday Evening Post* making fun of Fitzgerald's shameless self-promotion: He did not invent youth, "but he was well up in the van when it came to cashing in on the idea. . . . He has the nicest, most reassuring way of taking it all cozily for granted that not a man or a woman and but a few children in these loosely United States could have missed a word that he has written" ("Professional Youth" 14).

This Side of Paradise made Fitzgerald famous, but it is a myth that it also made him rich. His royalties for the novel, which took about thirty-six months to write, amounted to less than ten thousand dollars (*As Ever* xvii). The book did not pay for Scott and Zelda's wedding, but it represented to them, and to the public at large, that Fitzgerald had a promising literary career ahead of him. In this way the capital gained from the novel was more cultural than financial, more symbolic than concrete. On a deeper level than the monetary, writing and selling *This Side of Paradise* solidified Fitzgerald's self-identity. In "The Crack-Up" he writes of the months before it was published: "While I waited for the novel to appear, the metamorphosis of amateur into professional began to take place . . . the stitching together of your life in such a way that the end of one job automatically becomes the beginning of the next" (*Crack-Up* 86).

According to William Charvat, until the early nineteenth century, writing in the United States was seen as a hobby, a pastime for a gentleman amateur—especially since lax copyright laws made it pretty much impossible for an author to make a living (292–93). But Fitzgerald's statements on writing, many of which were collected by Matthew J. Bruccoli and Judith Baughman in *F. Scott Fitzgerald on Authorship*, reveal he was no gentleman amateur. With his talk of consecration by "the schoolmasters of ever afterward," he certainly felt the pull, described by Raymond

Williams in *Culture and Society,* between the artist as genius and the author as professional. Yet the instrumental value of authorship was as important to Fitzgerald in the early 1920s as its expressive value. Scott was largely in the writing business to make money and win people over. From the inception of his career, he promoted himself and his work, studied the different segments of the market for this work, and developed strategies to exploit each of these markets.

Popular myth has it that prostituting his talent in Hollywood in the 1930s destroyed F. Scott Fitzgerald. But from the beginning of his career, he had targeted the movie business as a potential route to fame and fortune, a route mapped out—complete with warnings about dead ends—in the pages of his 1922 novel, *The Beautiful and Damned.* Fitzgerald may have lived as a celebrity novelist during the 1920s, but he never made his living that way. Popular culture—primarily the film industry and mass-market magazines—picked up most of his tabs.

Scott and Zelda, an artist in her own right, courted celebrity. The scrapbooks they kept, portions of which were later published by Bruccoli, Scottie Fitzgerald Smith, and Joan Kerr under the title *The Romantic Egoists* (1974), demonstrate just how much press attention the Fitzgeralds received in the 1920s, and just how much they enjoyed receiving it. Years later Zelda wrote to Scottie, her daughter: "Daddy loved glamour & I also had a great respect for popular acclaim" (qtd. in Mellow 491). Shortly after their wedding, the couple began serving up autobiographical slices of their lives to mass-market magazines such as the *Ladies' Home Journal, Cosmopolitan,* and the *Saturday Evening Post.* Like the puff profiles of movie stars that had begun appearing in fan magazines in the 1920s, these pieces by the Fitzgeralds were more likely to focus on how swell it was to be famous rather than on the rigors and intellectual rewards of being a creative artist. And although they often carried both of their names, they were likely to have been written solely by Zelda.

Scott's letters make it apparent that he saw himself primarily as a novelist, working in the genre that the great Henry James had argued could give authors the artistic status of painters and sculptors, but just as textbooks subsidized Scribner's literature list, it was money from articles, short stories, and films—not novels—that paid most of Fitzgerald's enormous bills in the 1920s. Scott always kept his eyes on the cash box but never wanted to appear to be doing so. In this way he resembled Scribner's itself. Mark McGurl writes that "the book publishing industry has been perhaps unique in American capitalism in the degree to which it has touted itself as a 'bad business' with relatively tiny profit margins, a labor not of capitalist greed but of cultural responsibility and love" (14). Fitzgerald relied on his tenacious agent, Harold Ober, to make the money deals with the magazines and the studios, but he insisted on working with the people at Scribner's directly.

Biographical accounts such as Aaron Latham's and Arthur Mizener's unfavorably compare the men of letters Fitzgerald dealt with at the New York publishing house with the producers he believed constantly undercut him in Hollywood, and in *West of Eden*, Richard Fine does a good job of establishing that author/publisher relations in the 1920s were generally cordial: "Once in New York, authors discovered a world where, in and out of the business office, a writer was a person of consequence . . . a world which usually afforded him at least a modest living and invariably the less tangible but no less cherished rewards of prestige, respect, and celebrity" (41). But even a marriage as seemingly perfect as the Fitzgerald/Scribner's union had its rough patches.

Maxwell Perkins, Fitzgerald's legendary editor, may have believed in his author from the jump, but his bosses upstairs were not so sure. James L. W. West's *The Making of "This Side of Paradise"* shows that Scribner's thought interest in Fitzgerald was a passing fad, and they originally published the book in eleven small printings—waiting for each to sell out completely before going back to press—rather than in two or three larger ones, a strategy that cost the novelist sales, sleep, and money (111–15).

That Fitzgerald wrangled a large income and gained exposure from the popular-magazine market throughout the 1920s is a fact universally acknowledged—and usually forgiven—by observers of his career. But to see the author as a 1930s Hollywood sellout is to ignore the fact that he had been selling to the movies since the early years of his career in New York City and Long Island. He viewed the film industry as a rich source of income and, later, a medium with artistic promise, and he was not alone in this among respected writers.

Poet Vachel Lindsay's 1915 book *The Art of the Motion Picture* had called for writers in the new century to "lay hold of the motion picture as our national text-book in Art as Boston appropriated to herself the guardianship of the national text-books of literature" (*Prose* 307). With this Emersonian call for the Whitman of the silver screen, Lindsay seems to be anticipating a second American Renaissance. But this time Boston would not be the epicenter, nor would New York. Hollywood was the new cultural wellspring for the aspiring man of letters.

William Dean Howells, Stephen Crane, George Bernard Shaw, James Joyce, Sigmund Freud, and even Count Leo Tolstoy were other early believers in cinema's potential. And reciprocally the film industry was beginning to see the potential rewards of beckoning literary artists into the fold. In 1919 Sam Goldwyn had a studio but no stars. To distinguish his films in the crowded marketplace and to raise the cultural status of the film medium itself, he started the "Eminent Authors" project and recruited celebrity writers such as Gertrude Atherton, Rupert Hughes, Elmer Rice, Edward Justice Mayer, and Rex Beach.

That same year, in the months before *This Side of Paradise* was published, Fitzgerald had submitted several scripts to D. W. Griffith, whose studio had just given Dorothy Parker her first film credit, for *Remodeling Her Husband* (1920). Henry Dan Piper writes that Fitzgerald "had tried unsuccessfully to persuade D. W. Griffith that the craft of movie making itself was a wonderful subject for a picture. According to Fitzgerald, Griffith had laughed at him" (137). Of course history, as well as the hit film *Merton of the Movies* (1924), soon proved Fitzgerald correct. Whereas the audience for books has little interest in reading about the mechanics of the printing press and the valiant efforts of those brave souls working in permissions, moviegoers are fascinated with the filmmaking process and relish a glimpse of a movie camera filming a movie camera filming a movie.

Fitzgerald's letters show that he also tried pitching his movie-about-movies idea to Metro Pictures, but they passed as well. Although the industry was still young, it already possessed the lure of money and glamour, and it was tough to break in. But that did not stop aspiring wordsmiths from all walks of life from trying. In the late 1910s and early 1920s, the studios began being deluged with movie ideas and original stories from amateurs and professionals alike.

Charlatans quickly schemed to prey upon these movie hopefuls. Newspaper ads for sham correspondence courses and thin pamphlets gave the false impression that those with no writing skills, no knowledge of the film medium, and no connections within the industry could make a fortune selling ideas to the movie people. These ads, like motion pictures themselves, were aimed primarily at housewives. Unlike would-be starlets, who had to get a babysitter (and often a transcontinental train ticket) before pounding the pavement in make-up and heels, aspiring film play writers were assured by these ads that they could work at home at the kitchen table and jot down screen stories in their spare moments before making dinner or after the kids were asleep.

Professional writers also felt the financial lure of the film medium. During the period there had been increases in federal legislation protecting authors' rights to their royalties and ownership of their works. Motion pictures foreground their status as commercial enterprises, and it did not take long for fiction writers such as Fitzgerald to realize that a lucrative market had just opened up for them. If they could not sell originals, they could surely make money off the work they'd already done.

The year *This Side of Paradise* was published, the Fitzgerald story "Head and Shoulders" was filmed as Metro's *The Chorus Girl's Romance* (1920), and "Myra Meets His Family" was transformed into Fox's *The Husband Hunter.* Shortly thereafter two more of his early stories, "The Off-Shore Pirate" and "The Camel's Back," were also snapped up by the studios. Fitzgerald thought he saw a gold mine. In a March 1920 telegram to fiancée Zelda, he boasts of his newfound ability to support her: "I HAVE SOLD THE MOVIE RIGHTS OF HEAD AND SHOULDERS TO METRO COMPANY FOR TWENTY FIVE HUNDRED DOLLARS. I LOVE YOU DEAREST GIRL" (qtd. in Milford 58). Despite the legend, Fitzgerald did not turn to the movies as a humiliating last resort; he had been courting them the whole way along.

However, Fitzgerald also felt pressure in the early 1920s to publish big, ponderous books in order to prove to himself that he was an author rather than a media personality. He had enjoyed the fame and the whirlwind of parties that had followed *This Side of Paradise,* but, writes Mizener, "Fitzgerald's writer's conscience, his serious ambition, began to assert itself; what that conscience thought of Scott and Zelda Fitzgerald was to come out in his next novel" (147). From the very beginnings of his career, not just in Hollywood in the 1930s, Fitzgerald was questioning what it meant to be a "serious" author. Success in the commercial sphere often means limiting stylistic and thematic experimentation in favor of the tried and true, with the hopes of attracting more readers and making more money. But some other writers aim for a more restricted audience. They care most about the aesthetic value of their work and write for an elite audience made up of peer authors, educated critics, and artistic foundations. Here the rewards are largely, often purely, symbolic. But they can last a lot longer than the money will. Although it would have been a safer financial bet, Fitzgerald did not want to write a sequel to *This Side of Paradise.* He wanted to try something else. The 1922 New York novel *The Beautiful and Damned,* serialized in *Metropolitan Magazine,* was his attempt to mimic the type of literary naturalism favored by Mencken, George Jean Nathan, and other influential critics young novelists wanted to impress.

Playing off of Wharton's title *The House of Mirth,* Fitzgerald considered calling the book "The House of Pain," an appellation some readers may think fitting. Not much happens in *The Beautiful and Damned.* Its theme is the meaninglessness of life. Anthony Patch, the unsympathetic protagonist, a Wall Street trust-fund baby, grows increasingly bitter over the course of 450 pages as he waits around to inherit money. The fullest character in the book is the celebrity author Richard Caramel. As Pat Hobby would be later, Caramel is the type of mediocre writer and New York media personality Fitzgerald was afraid he had settled for being.

Fitzgerald's anxiety about selling out was beginning to nag at him. In 1922 he had some gag stationary printed up with letterhead that read:

> F. SCOTT FITZGERALD
>
> HACK WRITER AND PLAGIARIST
>
> ST. PAUL
>
> MINNESOTA (*Correspondence* 107)

As if poking fun at himself were not enough, Fitzgerald has his characters doing it, too. At one point in the novel, Caramel dismisses *This Side of Paradise* as trite (*Beautiful* 421). Caramel, like Fitzgerald, is the author of a novel that has caught on with America's youth. But his talent has shrunk in inverse proportion to his prosperity. *The Demon Lover*—another working title for the novel we are reading—is his only good book. Through Caramel, who has devolved into writing prose as sweet and unnourishing as his name, Fitzgerald releases his own demons. Unfortunately, and a bit ironically, *The Beautiful and Damned* is a shoddy realist novel written by an author whose skills lay in romantic lyricism. Disappointed in how it had turned out, Fitzgerald wrote to the author Thomas Boyd, "I shall never write another document novel. I have decided to be a pure artist + experiment in form and emotion" (*Correspondence 126*). Although it outsold *This Side of Paradise,* and in fact outsold every subsequent Fitzgerald novel during his lifetime, *The Beautiful and Damned* remains the type of book Caramel might write in order to please the critical establishment and remarket himself as a "serious" writer.

Caramel's friends believe he is popular because he has more talent than he does smarts. His golden prose hides the flimsy content lying beneath it. Speaking in passive-aggressive hypotheticals, Anthony tells him: "Suppose, for instance, I have more wisdom than you, and less talent. It would tend to make me inarticulate. You, on the contrary, have enough water for your pail and a big enough pail to hold the water. . . . the more narrowly you can look at a thing the more entertaining you can be about it" (36). Later Caramel justifies his movie-friendly short stories—full of "kissing, shooting, and sacrificing"—by arguing, "Wasn't it true that men who had attained real permanence from Shakespeare to Mark Twain had appealed to the many as well to the elect?" (222). It sounds like a rationalization, but it nonetheless makes the point that just because something is popular does not necessarily mean it is no good. Caramel believes that as a professional writer he contributes to society. He relies more on technical know-how than on inspiration from the muses, believes in the market as an indicator of value, and feels a responsibility to his reading public. In a novel filled with nihilists, Caramel voices that life and work are not meaningless.

During a discussion about the function of the artist in society, Anthony Patch, the author of several unwritten books, hypocritically declares: "Every writer writes because it's his mode of living" (37). Richard Caramel may not be meeting his early potential, but at least he supports himself with his craft. He is a professional writer who actually writes. Patch, on the other hand, is a poseur. Being a writer is not his mode of living; it is a title he hides behind. Because there is no system of credentials for becoming a writer, as there is for, let's say, becoming a medical doctor or Catholic priest, it is easy for Patch to declare himself open for business. But that is as far as it goes. Nothing ever pours out. He lacks the discipline to do any actual writing.

His wife, Gloria, has a similar get-artistic-quick scheme. She wants to act in the movies, and tells her husband she is trying to get famous for his own good: "I hate to see you go to pieces by just lying around and saying you ought to work. Perhaps if I did go into this for a while it would stir you up so you would do something" (215). Although only in her twenties, Gloria thinks her looks are fading, and she wants her beauty preserved on celluloid. She is not a writer, or painter, or composer, or a trained actress, so her face is probably her best hope at artistic immortality. But her dreams are thwarted when she screen-tests for the ingenue and instead lands the part of the middle-aged dowager.

Anthony does not fare much better in his profession. His workday consists of sitting at his desk in a smoking jacket, sharpening pencils, drinking tea, and staring at the wall (211–12). He has vague literary pretensions, and flips through books with titles such as *Success as a Writer Made Easy*, but he is more interested in looking in the bathroom mirror than in looking inside himself for material. Anthony has gravitated toward the arts because he finds the idea of a straight job distasteful, and writing looks as though it is easy. Running out of money, he is suddenly forced to start producing pages. But writing, like tennis playing or most other human activities, requires practice to be done well. The prose that comes out of Anthony consists of "wretched and pitiable efforts to 'write down' by a man who had never before made a consistent effort to write at all" (303). Caramel tries to help him out by telling him to concentrate on short stories if he wants to make some quick money, and advises him to make them plot driven, "cheerful and on the side of the heaviest artillery" (301). That way, the movies—represented in the novel by producer Joseph Bloeckman, a hard-working class striver who stands in moral contrast to Anthony's laziness and class privilege—might buy the rights to them.

Fitzgerald had some experience with this market strategy himself. The working title for *Tales of the Jazz Age,* a collection of his stories published the same year as *The Beautiful and Damned,* was "In One Reel." In part Fitzgerald promoted his early short story collections as catalogs of properties available for filming, just in case the movie people had missed them the first time. The narrator of the story "Dice, Brassknuckles, and Guitar" offers his opinion on how his protagonist should be filmed: "Now if this were a moving picture (as, of course, I hope it will be some day) I would take as many thousand feet of her as I was allowed—then I would move the camera up close and show the yellow down on the back of her neck where her hair stopped and the warm color of her cheeks and arms" (*The Price Was High* 48). Fitzgerald's ledger, which lists all his work and all income generated from it, records that in 1922 Warner Bros. paid $2,500 for the rights to *The Beautiful and Damned.* The author had no input on the movie made from his novel, and he was not quiet about his dislike for how it had turned out. As he wrote a friend, "If you want a good laugh see the screen version of the B+D" (*Correspondence* 120).

In 1923 Fitzgerald thought he saw his chance to be the creative force behind a film. He was approached to write an adaptation of *This Side of Paradise* for a motion picture in which he and Zelda would star. He received three thousand dollars and was excited by the possibility, but the project fell through. Later that same year, from New York, he wrote the intertitles (the text inserted between moving images in silent films) for a Paramount / Famous Players–Lasky film based on Wharton's novel *The Glimpses of the Moon* and was the scenarist for a production of *Grit* starring Clara Bow.

A scenarist was the writer who provided the original screen story during the silent era. Before the financial and technological demands of sound forced the American film industry to adhere to a more corporate model, job titles and division of labor were often arbitrary. The first screenwriters were not really screenwriters at all, at least not in the way playwrights were playwrights. The first "screenwriters" were studio clerks with good imaginations, former newspaper reporters who could work quickly, copywriters who could come up with snappy bits of prose, and people on set who had good ideas in the midst of filming. None of them thought of

Fitzgerald posed as a writer at work. Photofest

themselves as creative geniuses who would use the medium to bring their personal visions to the screen.

Movie historian Pat McGilligan writes: "Before 1926, at least to judge by the official credits, there were no screenwriters. The expression per se scarcely existed. . . . There were subspecies of gag writers, continuity writers, treatment writers, scenarists, adapters, titlists, what-have-you" (1). Fitzgerald's first stab as a scenarist was not a critical success. Alan Margolies, who has done valuable work on Fitzgerald's pre-Hollywood film career, quotes from a review of *Grit* that singles out Fitzgerald's contribution as "a rather weak and poorly developed crook theme" (71).

Despite dipping into the movie business, Fitzgerald saw himself primarily as a novelist—not as a scenarist, titlist, or what have you. Although famous throughout the 1920s, Fitzgerald was surprisingly never a best-selling novelist. As he often boasted to interviewers and friends, since the release of *This Side of Paradise* he had supported his family solely by writing, a quantifiable marker of an author's success. But this support did not derive from novels.

Disappointed in the sluggish market performance of *The Great Gatsby* (1925), Fitzgerald laid out a revised career plan to Perkins: "I shall write some cheap ones [short stories] until I've accumulated enough for my next novel. When that is finished and published I'll wait and see. If it will support me with no more intervals of trash I'll go on as a novelist. If not, I'm going to quit, come home, go to Hollywood and learn the movie business" (*Letters of FSF* 180). Fitzgerald talks as if the movie business was as far away from the literature business as the cereal business, but, again, subsidiary rights—and hastily written short stories such as "The Camel's Back"—helped keep him afloat in the earlier part of the decade. While his stab at a money-making play, *The Vegetable* (1922), had not worked out, *This Side of Paradise* and *The Beautiful and Damned* were both sold to the film industry, and while *Gatsby* as a book barely broke even, Harold Ober had quickly set up deals that would make it generate twenty thousand dollars of extra income on the stage and on screen.

Two years later, in 1927, Fitzgerald was trying to ingratiate himself into the Los Angeles film community. In addition to picking up a truckload of money as a screenwriter, he was also hoping to collect material for a Hollywood novel. This new project, set on the Riviera, concerned a troubled young motion-picture technician named Francis Melarky who murders his mother. Fitzgerald told Ober to start fielding offers from the studios, and in January 1927 Scott made his first trip to Hollywood. He was paid a $3,500 advance to write a treatment for United Artists called *Lipstick* that was attached to "flapper" star Constance Talmadge. If the screenplay was accepted, he would collect another $12,500. The film story was not accepted, however, and after spending three months going to parties, pulling pranks with Zelda such as grabbing the purses of their guests and boiling them in a pot, drinking and dining with Hollywood power players, making a screen test, and flirting with the ingenue Lois Moran, Fitzgerald returned home having spent more than the $3,500 he had made.

Reflecting on the experience a decade later, Fitzgerald, who could elevate contrition to an art form, told his daughter what went wrong: "At that time I had been generally acknowledged for several years as the top American writer both seriously and, as far as prices went, popularly. . . . Hollywood made a big fuss over us and the ladies all looked very beautiful to a man of thirty. I honestly believed that with *no effort on my part* I was a sort of magician with words—an odd delusion on my part when I had worked so desperately hard to develop a hard, colorful prose style" (*Letters of FSF* 16).

While Fitzgerald may have at one time been the most popular serious writer in America, it is doubtful that he was ever generally regarded as the most serious. To many literary critics of the time, even to his pal and "intellectual conscience" Edmund Wilson, he was just too popular and too sentimental to be taken too seriously. Wilson found Fitzgerald's writing too emotional, too slick, and not detached enough. In many letters he appears to stop just shy of telling Fitzgerald that he will never be a great author because he writes like a girl: "You might become a very popular trashy novelist without much difficulty," he had warned his friend in the mid 1920s (qtd. in Bruccoli, *Some Sort* 274). Fitzgerald wanted to be both popular *and* serious, but for Wilson popular was trashy and Fitzgerald was a dope. A slight that has been attributed to both Edna St. Vincent Millay and Wilson compares Fitzgerald's heaven-sent, poorly executed talent to "a stupid old woman with whom someone had left a diamond" (*Letters of FSF* 332). It is the modernist flip side to T. S. Eliot's judgment of Djuna Barnes: "never has so much genius been combined with so little talent" (qtd. in Field 222).

Fitzgerald's letter to Scottie is valuable in that it shows that he realized early on that writing for the screen would not be easy, and that it had been conceited of him to believe it would be. The *Lipstick* treatment is full of belabored slapstick and overly broad comic types; it is the kind of "slumming" screenplay—highbrows imagining what lowbrows might like to see—that the author himself would later deride in *The Last Tycoon*. Like many of the participants in Goldwyn's "Eminent Authors" project, most of whom could not adapt to the medium (or chose not to), Fitzgerald had tried to write down to the screen and had produced an unacceptable piece of work.

The letter also demonstrates Fitzgerald's career-long examination of—and his reflections on—his own talent, fame, and work ethic. As a young man, he had fought "desperately hard" to become a professional writer, to master his own distinctive style, and to develop a literary reputation. The *Lipstick* experience taught him that he would have to approach film writing the same way. By regarding the screenplay as a easier form to master than the novel and, like a gullible customer of a screen-writing correspondence course, not thinking he would need to break a sweat to succeed at it, Fitzgerald had committed a hubristic, Anthony Patch–like error, one to which he freely admitted. This feeling that he could write film scripts in his sleep, his ability to make his stories and novels sprout new profits through subsidiary rights, and his nagging fear that—like Richard Caramel in *The Beautiful and Damned*—he was some sort of literary idiot savant might explain Fitzgerald's "delusion" that he would be "some sort of magician with words" when it came to writing a movie about a magic tube of lipstick, but Hollywood films themselves deserve part of the blame. American films depend upon an illusion of effortlessness. As critics David Bordwell, Janet Staiger, and Kristin Thompson point out, Hollywood's "invisible style" hides the fact that the movie is something made, something created with hands and hammers and machines. If Fitzgerald truly were a "magician with words," the scripts really would write themselves "with no effort on his part."

The screenplay genre also did not play to Fitzgerald's strengths. Good film scripts are about structure, not lyricism. The archetypal Hollywood narrative of the studio era begins with a sympathetic protagonist with a goal, introduces an opposing force to that goal, proceeds by gradually escalating the struggle, and ends by resolving the conflict. Such a template streamlined production and provided a basis for judging screenplays. Everything that did not contribute to building and resolving conflict was extraneous. Fitzgerald's self-proclaimed "colorful prose style," one that favors description over dramatization, was a liability in Hollywood. In *The Beautiful and Damned,* Joseph Bloeckman appears to be commenting on the very text he is in when he remarks: "So many novels are all full of thoughts and psychology. . . . It's impossible to make much of that interesting on the screen" (96). The movies want plots first, he tells Caramel and Patch.

Even Fitzgerald's most ardent admirers admit his novels reveal him to be a better stylist than a constructionist, a "weakness" the 1922 review of *Grit* had singled out. Only when the plot is in place, only when the film's outline is traced, can the coloring begin. In cinema the image, not the words, must be colorful, and those on set—during the studio era that group did not include the writer—see to that. The 1927 trip had taught Fitzgerald his first major lesson about writing for Hollywood: screen writing does not require less effort than fiction writing; and it demands a different set of skills. He may have been a seasoned novelist, but working behind the scenes had taught him that he was only an apprentice screenwriter.

Nonetheless Fitzgerald had spent the 1920s playing the role he had written for himself in his youth: an author who was beloved, famous, and rich. This member of the "Lost Generation" had actually found his calling early. His first story, "The Mystery of the Raymond Mortgage," had been published when he was thirteen. In college he told Edmund Wilson that the only names we knew from the Elizabethan Age were those of authors. In 1929 he wrote to Ober: "America will from now on give about ½ its book-buying ear to serious people" (*As Ever* 158). Fitzgerald believed in the writer as the last best hope for humanity; he believed in what John Guillory derides in *Cultural Capital* (1995) as the "fantasy . . . that literary culture is the site at which the most socially important beliefs and attitudes are produced" (152). Yet Fitzgerald's first trip to Hollywood— perhaps a better candidate for Guillory's above-mentioned "site"—had tempted him with the possibility of becoming even more celebrated, even more influential, and even more flush.

The Occasional Writer

In March 1920, the month Fitzgerald became a published novelist and sold his first screen property, Dorothy Parker became an unemployed magazine writer. The twenty-seven-year-old was fired from *Vanity Fair,* a magazine that covered the avant-garde for the middle class. Throughout the nineteenth century, magazines had been a genteel extension of the publishing industry, but by 1920 they had become a medium funded by advertisers. Parker had angered powerful clients with her scathing drama reviews, and her bosses let her go. In a show of solidarity, colleague Robert Benchley resigned. The incident and its participants were newsworthy enough to be reported in the *New York Times* and the *Herald Tribune.*

Parker and Benchley formed the core of the Algonquin Round Table, a circle that grew to include—in various permutations—Robert Sherwood, Alexander Woollcott, S. N. Behrman, Harold Ross, Harpo Marx, Franklin Pierce Adams, Edna Ferber, Heywood Broun, Donald Ogden Stewart, and Marc Connelly. Lots of anecdotal history has been written about the group, but whether or not they consciously stood for any cause, movement, or position is up for debate. Parker biographer John Keats claims: "They were not in revolt against society. They merely felt superior to it" (73). Critic Arthur Kinney calls these writers "a mutually supportive society for high standards of language in an increasingly popularized world of journalism" (11), but they all—even Harpo—did far more talking than typing. In the final tally, the group's reason for gathering together seems to have been to provide a permanent excuse for not picking up a pen.

Benchley once said: "It took me fifteen years to discover that I had no talent for writing, but I couldn't give it up because by that time I was too famous" (qtd. in Frewin 46). More urbane than cerebral, Benchley and company were known for their quick mouths rather than their deep thoughts. Franklin Pierce Adams, known as FPA, kept his friends in the news by celebrating their exploits in his popular "Conning Tower" column. The syndicated column was also used to launch attacks on other writers. FPA printed lists of the misspellings in *This Side of Paradise,* making Fitzgerald angry and ashamed (*Correspondence* 63). But the group was not solely reliant on self-promotion. Looking for a quip or a quote, other journalists would show up at the Algonquin Hotel around lunchtime to see what the tablemates were saying and to garner their opinions. Janice Radway and Lawrence Levine have charted the emergence of a middlebrow culture industry, "devoted to the business of commodifying and marketing taste" (Radway 248), making elements of elite culture available to a wide group of readers. If the celebrities of Hollywood were popular idols of glamour and consumption, the celebrities of the Round Table were middlebrow idols of wit and sophistication. The group fit the reading public's image of how New York writers should look, speak, and behave—it mattered little that none of them did much writing. They were famous.

"Men seldom make passes at girls who wear glasses"; "one more drink and I'll be under the host"; and "you can lead a horticulture but you can't make her think" are among Parker's most famous zingers, but her literary ambitions were broader than just being known for talking wise. In her long career she wrote poems, humor pieces, reviews, articles, and stories. Her biographer Marion Meade reports, however, that her ultimate goal was to write a novel, since "real writers, in her eyes, seldom limited themselves to short fiction" and she "needed to prove she was a real writer" (195). A public figure in the commercial realm, Parker's career as "a real writer" was, nonetheless, very important to her. Her poems and autobiographical monologues create a layered, palimpsestic "Dorothy Parker" who may have been outwardly, stereotypically feminine and accommodating, but who deep down had no fear of ambition and competing in a man's world of high art. In the poem "Fighting Words" Parker warns potential suitors they can criticize her personality; "But say my verses do not scan / And I get me another man!" (*Portable* 114).

Unlike the canonical poets of modernism, most of whom cultivate difficulty in their work, Parker's verses do scan, and they rhyme, and they are funny. They also contain world-weariness and an air of self-deprecation. Many of them find the speaker tired of love, life, and literature. Short poems such as "A Well-Worn Story" and "Two-Volume Novel" display her comic compressions of the protracted, literary love plot. Why write (or read) a five-hundred-page novel when a few lines will do? Why even bother with the poem? If you have read one love poem, dear reader, you have read them all. Lauren Berlant locates Parker's poems "outside of mass culture by virtue of their manifest self-reflexive seriousness, inside of mass culture by virtue of the venues where the middlebrow find their art, and in the thick of low things to the degree that they are doggerel that loves and cultivates failure: the love sonnet as wisecrack" (227).

One reason Parker has never received much critical attention as a serious writer is because much of her writing is so ambivalent about serious writing. Her celebrity was not a result of her accomplishments; it was the result of a carefully crafted persona of the blasé. Her popular fame as a writer was a product of her distanced pose of appearing to be unconcerned with seeking either popular fame or elite immortality. A "New Woman" not bound to the ethic of care, a woman writer who was one of the boys, Parker used magazines, the theater, and the newspapers to reach a huge audience. In 1922, for instance, she published short articles in popular magazines such as *Ainslee's, Life,* and *Ladies' Home Journal,* sang on stage with her friends in the revue *No Siree,* and published her first book, an extended humor piece written in collaboration with FPA titled *Men I'm Not Married To, Women I'm Not Married To.*

Her volumes of poetry made the bestseller lists in the 1920s, an impressive feat in any decade. But literary fiction was where Parker's real interest lay. "Such a Pretty Little Picture," which appeared in the December 1922 issue of H. L. Mencken and George Jean Nathan's *Smart Set,* is a representative example of her early stories. Kinney believes that Parker's fiction owes something "to her friend Scott Fitzgerald's use of setting and to his ability to choose details that at once will reveal and satirize his characters" (118), but she had been doing it longer than Fitzgerald had, and it was one of the things she did best. Through free indirect discourse, Parker's stories usually crumble the facade between how things appear and how they really are. In "Such a Pretty Little Picture," she focuses on a loveless suburban marriage that everyone mistakenly believes is perfect: "Adelaide Wheelock's friends—and she had many of them—said of her that there was no nonsense about her. They and she regarded it as a compliment"; "The lovely light was kind to the cheap, hurriedly built stucco house, to the clean gravel path, and the bits of closely cut lawn" (*Complete Stories* 4, 11). Mencken, no friend of the folks he called the "muddlebrows" and the "booboisie," was likely attracted to the story's attack on the hypocrisy of the average American. The *Smart Set* did not pay very well, around fifty bucks, and with the departures of Mencken and Nathan in the mid-1920s it would soon become a middlebrow magazine filled with the type of formulaic "success stories" that it had been created to oppose;

but appearing in it was a prestigious feather in Parker's hat. In later years she would say of the story, "its mother thinks it's the best thing she ever wrote" (qtd. in Meade 100).

Parker was often at her most productive when writing with others, although such output did not hold the same literary cachet as the singly authored work. In 1925 she contributed chapter 7 to a Fitzgerald-influenced group novel called *Bobbed Hair* that was serialized in *Collier's* magazine. Another collaborative venture of hers that year was "Business is Business," written with George S. Kaufman. Here Parker and Kaufman had found a way to reach both the stage and the screen audiences simultaneously—though you would have to dig pretty hard to find this out. Like the early poems she considered too saccharine, the author dropped the piece from collections of her work. Parker's biographers (Frewin, Keats) and chronologists (Breese, Calhoun) mistakenly list "Business is Business" as Parker's first original film script, but a look at the June 2, 1925, review in the *New York Times* reveals the work to be a live action play, performed in movie theaters, about a shoe manufacturer with a get-rich-quick scheme. Movie theaters in the 1920s wanted to provide their patrons with "an evening's entertainment," and at higher-priced houses in major American cities it was not uncommon to put on a play to warm up the crowd for the feature that followed.

Plays were one thing, but Hollywood films left Dorothy Parker cold. Where Fitzgerald was willing to study movie writing in the late 1920s, Parker could not be bothered. She had no interest in the medium. The crackly quality of sound film hurt her ears, and the other moviegoers bugged her. As she wrote in the *New Yorker* in November 1927: "I attend no movies, for any motion-picture theater is as an enlarged lethal chamber to me" (*Portable* 465). A few months after these words appeared, however, MGM hired the woman their press release mistakenly called "the author of 'Too Much Rope,' the popular novel" (qtd. in Meade 197). *Too Much Rope* was a book of collected poems, one probably unread by the studios.

Earlier in the decade, her colleague Robert Sherwood had visited Hollywood on assignment for *Life* magazine, looking for glamour and scandal. What he found was a "normal community inhabited by regular people who go about their business in much the same manner as do people in Emporia, Pawtucket, Little Rock, and Medicine Hat" (qtd. in Fine 59). Hollywood had bored Sherwood, and it would bore Parker as well. Arriving in Los Angeles in the spring of 1928, she signed a three-month contract with MGM at three hundred dollars a week, was told she'd be writing dialogue for a project called "Madame X," and was pointed toward her office. She received no further instructions. According to Parker, after two weeks or so of doing nothing she sought out the film's producers. They did not know who she was or what she was doing there. Meade writes: "Other writers seemed reluctant to visit her cubicle. She felt isolated. When a sign painter arrived to letter her name on the door, she felt like bribing him to print GENTLEMEN instead" (198).

It seems fitting that Parker did no writing during her first screen-writing project. Unlike Fitzgerald she never saw herself as a magician with words. She made no secret of the fact that writing was difficult for her: "I can't write five words but that I change seven" (qtd. in *The Writer's Quotation Book* 47). When she missed deadlines, a regular occurrence, her excuse was often that "someone else was using the pencil" (Silverstein 32). Although Parker did not like the paperwork, she did, however, like being a writer, and nowhere in the American 1920s were writers more valued than in New York City, a place she returned to after skipping out on her screen-writing contract several weeks early. Van Wyck Brooks writes: "There had never been a time and a place so favorable to literary growth. . . . the reverence that religion had once absorbed was redirected towards artists, who were regarded as saints" (*Days of the Phoenix* 164). Hyperbole aside, the writer now possessed a special aura—if not quite a halo.

Parker had felt isolated in Hollywood, but back in Manhattan, among her writer friends, she felt part of a community. Drawn to the limelight of café society and to fancy things, her main objective during the Jazz Age was, she said, "to be smarty" and "cute" (qtd. in Frewin 57). But Parker's mind was as sharp as her tongue. She was an excellent book reviewer, despite cultivating a myth of being a lazy writer and a lackluster reader. Her "Constant Reader" column for the *New Yorker,* the metropolitan magazine famously "not edited for the old lady in Dubuque" (or Emporia, Pawtucket, Little Rock, and Medicine Hat), found her often failing to finish the book she was reviewing because it bored her. If she liked the book, however, she finished it and could be vigorous in her endorsement of it. While she was often dismissive of her own career and her own writing, she took the writing of others very seriously.

Parker's *New Yorker* columns possess the world-weary, sophisticated voice that is part of her image—and the magazine's image as well—but they also show what a fine (and funny) literary judge she can be. Nancy Walker writes that Parker "derives her authority precisely from seeming not to be one at all, projecting personae composed of enthusiasms, prejudices, and personal quirks" (7). Parker's judgments could often be scathing;

she tore apart Elinor Glyn and said that reading A. A. Milne's *House at Pooh Corner* (1928) made "Tonstant Weader Fwow up" (*Portable* 518), but her praise for work that met her high standards—André Gide, Ernest Hemingway, Upton Sinclair—was often effusive. In a television documentary on Parker, the writer Fran Lebowitz said that Parker's "best stuff" was her novel reviews and that writing intelligently about books is "really a much rarer talent than being a good short story writer" (*Would You Kindly Direct Me to Hell*).

Parker is not generally regarded as a good short story writer. Regina Barreca writes in her 1995 introduction to the author's *Complete Stories:* "Parker has been slammed for at least thirty years. One recent critic complains that Parker had 'no disinterestedness, no imagination,' and another bows low to introduce Parker with the gallant phrase 'The span of her work is narrow and what it embraces is often slight'" (x). Although Barreca takes more umbrage at the second critic's comment, which talks about the work in a typically gendered way, the first critic's barb, which talks about Parker's creative intelligence, is actually the more cutting. Nevertheless, masterpieces can result when the scope of the work is narrow and what it embraces is slight. Jane Austen, one of the most celebrated writers of our time, spoke of "the little bit (two inches wide) of Ivory, on which I work with so fine a brush" (469). But *disinterestedness* and *imagination* are critical buzzwords designating elite artists, and pointing to the absence of these qualities is the critic's way of calling Parker a hack.

Parker's most famous short story is "Big Blonde" (1929). It is also arguably her best. Like most of her fiction, it examines the gap between private and public roles, especially those played by women. Unlike most of Parker's fiction, however, "Big Blonde" contains a fully realized character who changes over time. The price Hazel pays for dropping the "good sport" act (*Complete Stories* 105) is loneliness. The story moves through dramatic action rather than Parker's usual condescending tactic of using the dramatic monologue to force her characters to hang themselves with their own rope. "Big Blonde" is emotionally moving without being as blatantly manipulative or overly sentimental as most of Parker's other work. We sense the pain behind Hazel's "good sport" mask without feeling as though we are being solicited to do so.

"Big Blonde," which appeared in the February 1929 issue of the small circulation magazine the *Bookman,* won the O. Henry Award for best short story of the year. FPA, of course, publicized the prize in his column. Amid the buzz over the story, Fitzgerald—who earlier in the decade had brought Hemingway to Scribner's—urged Maxwell Perkins to hurry up and offer

Parker a book contract for the "novelette or novel" she was writing because "just now she's at a high point as a producer and as to reputation. . . . I wouldn't lose any time about this if it interests you" (*Letters of FSF* 215). Scribner's extended an offer to Parker to send them the novel, the working title of which was "Sonnets in Suicide; or The Life of John Knox." But there was a problem. There was no novel.

Literary Tourists

In American literary history, the 1920s have retained the glow of a golden age, a banquet of writers surrounded by other friendly, supportive writers. Parker publishes articles increasing Fitzgerald's fame; Fitzgerald puts Parker in touch with Scribner's. Budd Schulberg writes of the tight-knit literary community of the Lost Generation: "In the Jazz Age it was still literary etiquette for a young man of promise to send politely autographed copies of his new book to Edith Wharton, T. S. Eliot, or other established literary figures of his day. There was every sort of exchange, from Scott Fitzgerald's genteel tea-time encouragement from Edith Wharton and Eliot, to his Long Island drinking bouts with Ring Lardner" (*Four Seasons* 3).

Throughout his life Schulberg maintained a yearning for the 1920s, a decade he spent as a minor. Reading *Moving Pictures: Memories of a Hollywood Prince,* his autobiography of his childhood and adolescence, one gets the feeling that there was a literary party going on in the 1920s, and Budd was stuck sitting inside his mansion at the kids' table.

What goes unmentioned, however, is that the most notorious part of Wharton's genteel encouragement of Fitzgerald was praising him for bringing to life the "perfect Jew," Meyer Wolfsheim, in *The Great Gatsby,* an anti-Semitism their tea-sipping tablemate Eliot also shared, as did those in the United States, described by Neal Gabler in *An Empire of Their Own: How the Jews Invented Hollywood,* who resented families such as the Schulbergs with all their movie money.

In the mid-1920s the rising star at Paramount was Schulberg's father, B. P. Schulberg. A New York transplant who had moved to Hollywood earlier in the decade, after most of the industry had already done so in the 1910s (partially for the weather and the available land and partially to avoid the long arm of Edison's camera patents), the senior Schulberg was arguably the most intelligent producer in town. Writer Herman Mankiewicz, a member of Parker's Manhattan circle, grumbled about him: "He's read too goddamn many books" (qtd. in Gabler 203). Schulberg had also written one, adding to the growing shelf of screen writing / get-rich-quick textbooks. An aggressive businessman, a compulsive gambler, and a philanderer who slept with actresses such as Sylvia Sidney and, according to Dorothy Parker biographer Leslie Frewin, writers such as Parker (211), the elder Schulberg was nonetheless the highly literate and cultured man that MGM's head of production, Irving Thalberg, who had others do his reading for him, often got credit for being.

Literature was held in the highest regard in the Schulberg home. According to Budd, Sunday afternoons at their Hollywood mansion would find his father reading Charles Dickens, Herman Melville, Leo Tolstoy, and Fyodor Dostoyevsky to his children (Vonnegut 96). Budd's mother, Ad, who would later become a literary agent, paid her kids a quarter for every book they read. Budd told Kurt Vonnegut in an interview for the *Paris Review*: "Sonya, my youngest sister, said in our house the typewriter stood where a piano might be in other homes. We'd just sit down at the typewriter and run off a couple of scales—stories" (97). Budd Schulberg was encouraged to be a writer in the way that other parents pushed their offspring toward professions in finance, medicine, or law.

A vocal stammer led Schulberg to become a good listener and to gravitate even more strongly toward the quiet pastimes of reading and writing. But he was also getting a valuable education in the family business. While still a child, he began honing his gift for plot structure by sitting in on his father's script sessions and story conferences. Programmed since birth to be an author, Budd could not grow up quickly enough.

Like Schulberg, Nathanael West was another aspiring writer of the 1920s feeling the pain of coming of age too late. A transfer student from Tufts University—where he enrolled by doctoring his lackluster high school record and flunked out by refusing to attend classes—West, whose given name was Nathan Weinstein, had gotten into Brown University by stealing the credits of another man with the same name. Luckily this other Weinstein was a good science student, leaving his namesake free to concentrate on the humanities. In describing this period, Jay Martin, West's biographer, paints a portrait of the artist as a young aesthete. West's generous allowance from his parents, who were then enjoying the flush of prosperity in the building trade, allowed him to buy good clothes and all the books he wanted. He wore beautiful clothes, dabbled in Catholic mysticism, and founded a society of intellectual elites, a group that often went to the movies to laugh at the sad parts and cry during the funny parts. West could not decide whether he'd rather be a painter or a writer, but he knew he did not want to work for a living. Joining his father's construction business held no appeal for him.

For many American artists of the period, the road toward becoming a man of letters ran through Paris, the literary and cultural capital of France, and West prepared for his trip abroad not by studying travel guides but by reading fictional accounts of expatriate life. In August 1926 Nathan Weinstein legally became Nathanael West, and two months later, with a new name on his passport and an early draft of the novella *The Dream Life of Balso Snell* in his suitcase, he sailed for France on a trip funded by his uncles. For the rest of his life, West would mythologize this trip, telling friends and acquaintances made-up stories about fleecing American debutantes who were fresh off the boat, working as a gentleman detective for a rich family, engaging in sex marathons with exotic women, and living in abject poverty.

Although James F. Light's 1961 *Nathanael West: An Interpretative Study* led the way for future scholars, it prints many such West lies as fact. The truth, as Jay Martin uncovered, was that during his time abroad West mainly went sightseeing. Martin depicts West in Paris as more of a tourist than an expatriate. The young author hung around far more than he wrote. He spotted Hemingway wearing yellow gloves and a homburg. Another day he got a quick glimpse of Eliot. A friend arranged for him to meet Henry Miller, but the two bored each other. When West was not writer-watching, he frequented a parlor where nude models casually walked around a furnished room, seemingly oblivious to the paying customers staring at them.

Asked about Jazz Age expatriate life in Paris, Archibald MacLeish once remarked: "There was no 'community' in the sense in which you, I think, are using the word. No Americans-in-Paris community. That notion is a myth concocted after the event by critics with fish to fry. There was the literary-tourist world of the Dome and the Rotonde, but no work came out of that" (Plimpton 278).

This "literary-tourist world" is featured in an unpublished piece of fiction by West titled "The Impostor," a send-up of artists, like Fitzgerald's Anthony Patch, who make no art. The story's narrator arrives in Paris and quickly discovers that all of the artists are poseurs, and that all of the good artistic poses have already been taken. The only products these artists create are themselves. After hiding in his hotel for a week, not daring to show himself "at the Dome for fear of making a bad impression" (*Novels* 411), the narrator decides that his costume will be a business suit; he will be the crazy bohemian who looks respectable. Dorothy Parker explores the same theme in her poem "Bohemia," with its exasperated cry: "God, for a man that solicits insurance!" (*Portable* 223). With a working stiff on her arm, the speaker can distinguish herself from the others in her sophisticated, artistic circle.

Decked out for Wall Street, the narrator of "The Imposter" soon realizes that posing as someone who has dropped out of the economy is a full-time job: "We came to the business of being an artist with the definitions of the non-artist and took libels for the truth. In order to be recognized as artists, we were everything our enemies said we were. . . . In those days, if not these, art critics, like Hollywood directors, insisted on typecasting" (*Novels* 411–12). The binaries between high culture (art critics and museums) and mass culture (Hollywood and magazines), and between art and commerce, are inevitably collapsed in West's fiction. He never lets us forget that culture—even "elite" culture—is an industry. Foundations and museums, supported by the radical bourgeoisie, offer funding to those who simply look and behave like artists. Magazines and newspapers boost their circulation by covering—and offering publicity to—those artists who behave outlandishly (Scott and Zelda) or say outlandish things (Dorothy Parker). The public may not know art, but they know what they like their artists to be like.

Although it quickly devolves into an expatriate version of the movie *Weekend at Bernie's,* with much of the humor centering on a corpse that a sculptor lugs around in order to show to his financial backers that "all modern sculpture is wrong" (416), "The Impostor" demonstrates that Nathanael West had learned the lesson that Fitzgerald and Parker had figured out already: "make it new" is not only a modernist call, it is a marketing call as well. Cultural artistic movements exist to make people buy new culture; even if the new culture has echoes of an ancient culture. If "all modern sculpture is wrong," somebody better keep paying until we get it right again. Artists fashion their works—and their artistic personas—with markets in mind. Fitzgerald had caught on with the youth of his generation; Parker had caught on with aspiring sophisticates; but West was still trying to find a place to fit in.

Of these three authors, West was the one most interested in exploring the artifice of the artist in his fiction. Following the lead of "The Impostor," in future novels *The Dream Life of Balso Snell* and *A Cool Million* West depicts avant-garde writers who realize that cultivating the myth of the reclusive bohemian has mass appeal. There is money in disinterestedness about money, and sometimes the best market strategy is pretending to have no strategy at all.

But West really had no strategy, hidden or otherwise. Fitzgerald and Parker had expensive tastes that often exceeded their incomes, but the profession of authorship, as they practiced it throughout the 1920s, had given them the financial freedom to command their own time. West did not have this luxury. With the building trade slowing down to a halt, his family could not afford to support him anymore, and he returned from France in January 1927 in need of a steady job. Through an aunt he was hired as the night manager of the Kenmore Hotel on East Twenty-third Street; later he took a position at the slightly more upscale Sutton on East Fifty-sixth. The work was not terribly taxing, and he was able to get some writing done in his office. He was also able to lend a hand to some of the literary friends he was making. By providing free rooms to writers such as Lillian Hellman, Dashiell Hammett, James T. Farrell, and Erskine Cald-well, West supported the arts and began accumulating favors and goodwill.

He began spending the majority of his time in the company of other writers. Along with friends from college, including his brother-in-law, S. J. Perelman, the aspiring author explored Greenwich Village, running into E. E. Cummings and Edmund Wilson. Through Perelman, who had begun writing for the *New Yorker*, he was also introduced to Dorothy Parker and other contributors to the magazine. Unlike Parker's midtown circle, which wore their love of money on their sleeves and had the clothes to prove it, the downtown crowd had the air of pursuing art for art's sake. West was attracted to the Village community. As with Paris, however, he had arrived too late. The real action was already over. A hotbed for pro-gressivism and experimental lifestyles and literature in the 1910s, by the late 1920s the neighborhood had begun to gentrify. Bohemian-themed restaurants opened for business, catering to tourists and slummers.

Walking through Greenwich Village seems to have taught West that once big business finds something original, they reproduce it as quickly as possible. In another unpublished story, "Mr. Potts of Pottstown," West's American hero arrives at the Swiss Alps expecting a natural high, a peak experience. But when he sees a boy from home dressed as a yodeler, he gets him to confess that Switzerland has become "nothing but a fake, an amusement park owned by a very wealthy company. The whole show is put on for the tourist trade—lakes, forests, glaciers, yodelers, peasants, goats, milkmaids, mountains and the rest of it. It's all scenery" (*Novels* 441). This story demonstrates its author's reservations about multinational capitalism, but at this early point in his career West, although left-leaning, was not as politically active as many of his peers. When Mike Gold tried to inspire him to write for Socialist magazines such as the *New Masses* in the late 1920s, he was not interested. At this point he wanted to make some money as a writer, not write about how money was unequally distributed.

West was working on two novels simultaneously—with no luck in attracting publisher interest in either one. In late 1929, with a first draft of *Balso* completed and work on *Miss Lonelyhearts* under way, he began making plans to join his fiancée, Parker's *New Yorker* colleague Beatrice Mathieu, in Paris. On his visa he even optimistically listed his occupation as "writer." But cold feet had gotten the better of him. He canceled his ticket and broke off the love affair. Martin quotes from a letter to Mathieu in which West tells her he cannot go to Paris because he is "yellow. . . . to try and earn a living writing, hacking, I'd rather work in a hotel" (119–20). His college dreams of the life of an expatriate hack no longer seemed so romantic.

Being a domestic hack, however, was a different story. As he sat at his desk at the hotel, collecting a steady paycheck, West began thinking of ways to make some quick bucks as a writer without actually having to write anything. To this end he cut up an old pile of *Field and Stream* magazines and pasted paragraphs together in new combinations. He then submitted the resulting "new" articles back to *Field and Stream*. For the literary market, he rearranged passages from Flaubert into free verse and then mailed them out to editors under his own name. That these scams might also be viewed as Dadaist artistic statements must have sweetened the potboiling for West, but neither "found" project found a buyer. His first professional publication, in 1929, came from selling a Bret Harte parody to a magazine that had been founded by Bret Harte.

Throughout the 1920s West, like many aspiring artists, had flirted with taking an alienated stance and turning his back on money, prestige, and acceptance from an audience—at least for show, as in his story "The Impostor." Perhaps disinterestedness was the best way to elicit interest. Then again, maybe the whole writing game was not worth it. Maybe he should try painting again. He was a member of the New York literary community—a community that F. Scott Fitzgerald partied through, Dorothy Parker ruled over, and Hollywood prince Budd Schulberg yearned for—but now he was not sure if the life agreed with him or not. Could his prose provide him with a living? Was he a writer who managed a hotel or a hotel manager who wrote on the side? Either way, he was seriously considering becoming a candy manufacturer.

2

Dream Lives

FITZGERALD
AND WEST IN
1931–1932

If you read the lives and letters of writers, you will find that
virtually every one of them was often a victim of moods of
depression and that they had many anxieties about their own
writing. Joseph Conrad used to read Flaubert and he would
feel that there was no use.

   James T. Farrell, *The League of Frightened Philistines*

He had had what were considered nice assignments since his
arrival six months before and he submitted his scenes and
sequences with enthusiasm. He referred to himself modestly as
a hack but really did not think of it that way.

   F. Scott Fitzgerald, "Crazy Sunday"

A work of art is the unique result of a unique temperament.
Its beauty comes from the fact that the author is what he is. It
has nothing to do with the fact that other people want what
they want. The moment that an artist takes notice of what other
people want, and tries to supply the demand, he ceases to be
an artist and becomes a dull or amusing craftsman, an honest
or dishonest tradesman.

   Oscar Wilde, "The Soul of Man under Socialism"

තු

At the end of 1931 Nathanael West was an Ivy League–educated young
man with a beautiful fiancée, a host of literary friends, a debut novel

recently published by a respected house, and another, more ambitious book nearing completion. If, from these angles, the portrait resembles the Scott Fitzgerald of exactly a decade earlier, a closer look reveals a different picture. *This Side of Paradise* is a Kunstlerroman, the story of an artist finding his powers and making his way in the world; West's *The Dream Life of Balso Snell* is an anti-Kunstlerroman, the story of the futility of the literary vocation. *This Side of Paradise,* originally called "The Romantic Egoist" (*Letters of FSF* 137–38), celebrates the uniqueness of self; *Balso Snell* calls the concept of a unified self into question. The publishers behind these two novels were also worlds apart. Scribner's carried a long and impressive publishing history before releasing Fitzgerald's debut. Contact Editions, the Paris-based press Robert McAlmon had founded in the 1920s, had published a distinguished list of high modernist books over the decade, including works from Ernest Hemingway, Djuna Barnes, William Carlos Williams, Gertrude Stein, and Ezra Pound. But the Contact Editions that published *The Dream Life of Balso Snell* was run by two bookstore clerks who had borrowed the name from McAlmon. West's book was their first title, and it would also be their last.

A peek at Scott Fitzgerald's life in the closing days of 1931 might also reveal a misleading picture. Many Fitzgerald critics write about this time as if the author's career, finances, talent, and hopes had been lost in the stock market crash. James Mellow's biographical portrait of Scott and Zelda, for instance, devotes 350 pages to the 1920s and only 100 pages to the 1930s. Biographer André Le Vot's gloomy chapter titles for Fitzgerald's life circa 1931 and 1932 are "The Beginning of the End" and "Illusions and Depressions."

It had been six years since *The Great Gatsby*, so the story goes, and throughout the late 1920s Fitzgerald had been working sporadically on the project that would become *Tender Is the Night*. But his chronic drinking and Zelda's madness kept getting in the way. Le Vot relates that when the sirens of Hollywood called, Fitzgerald felt compelled to answer: "His moral conscience would be stronger than his artistic conscience. He would prostitute his talent and kill himself doing it to pay the bills for Zelda, Scottie, and himself" (263). This Hollywood trip, like the last, says Le Vot, was a failure: "he had again been humiliated" (264). When Fitzgerald returned east, he immediately got to work on a fictionalized account of the humiliation he had suffered.

But Le Vot has it wrong. Fitzgerald had not been humiliated in Hollywood; he had humiliated himself, as both the genesis of "Crazy Sunday" and the short story itself make plain. If it comes as a surprise that West's first novel tarnishes its own unique aura as a first novel, it may also come as a surprise that "Crazy Sunday," the story of Fitzgerald's 1931 Hollywood trip, is not an outright attack on the movie colony. In fact it celebrates the graciousness and creativity of many of the artists working there. Furthermore, contrary to popular myth, Fitzgerald was not aching for film money in the early 1930s—although he certainly would be later in the decade. He often called himself a poor custodian of his own talent, but he was an excellent record keeper and archivist. In his ledger Fitzgerald carefully traced his submissions, publications, and payments. The ledger details that 1931 was financially his best year ever. He made $37,599, $31,500 of which came from short stories, and $5,400 of which came from screen writing. (Novels, book reviews, and other "literary" work accounted for less than a thousand dollars of his income.) He had some debt, but with Zelda stabilized and out of the expensive Swiss sanitarium, even without the film work Fitzgerald would have had a prosperous year, so it cannot be said that he went to Hollywood for the money alone. He did not really need to, as Le Vot puts it, "prostitute his talent" for the film industry. Fitzgerald could have stayed home and written short stories for that. As he had recently told Hemingway, "The *Post* now pays the old whore $4000 a screw" (*FSF: A Life in Letters* 169). Maybe Hollywood would put him in a more comfortable, more artistic position.

A First Novel Written against the Writing of First Novels

Even if the professional author F. Scott Fitzgerald were in fact prostituting his writing talent to the *Post*, making a fortune by providing entertainment to a large audience, he'd still be in better shape than the writers who populate Nathanael West's *The Dream Life of Balso Snell*. The novel is a portrait of a young artist discovering his powerlessness. The title character, a lyric poet, takes a nightmare tour through the bowels of the Trojan Horse, meeting a series of failed and frustrated wordsmiths along the way. Each surrealistic episode underscores the futility of the literary vocation and gleefully mocks the pipe dreams of amateurs who aspire to wealth and immortality.

Fittingly, it might seem, *Balso* has usually been written off by critics as a freshman effort best left forgotten. Over the years even the author's most enthusiastic readers have dismissed it. Daniel Aaron, who was at the vanguard of the West revival of the mid–twentieth century, calls *Balso* "a privately printed little exercise that never should have been printed at all" (114). Anna Weinstein, West's own mother, claimed that "all it says is 'stink, stink, stink'" (qtd. in Martin 227). Deborah Wyrick, one of the book's few defenders, sums up the novel's customary place in the West corpus: "Critics agree that it is formless, chaotic, a juvenile pastiche of bathroom jokes, college magazine parody, and borrowings from contemporary avant-garde authors" (157).

Echoing West's own claim that he had published the novel as "a protest against the writing of books," Wyrick then goes on to make a case for *Balso* as a Dadaist minor masterpiece: "West's aesthetic sensibilities transform ugly material into a beautiful composition . . . that, by its very artistry, celebrates that which it wishes to destroy" (164). Wyrick seems to believe that the author set out to create a bad book but was too talented to pull it off. Jonathan Veitch has offered a similar view of *Balso* as satisfyingly subversive, arguing that the novel "undertakes not just a disavowal of high modernism and the idealism of its art-for-art's sake aestheticism, but a critique of nothing less than the grand tradition of Western culture upon which it depends. That critique results in a thorough housecleaning, an operation that will dispense with everything from Plato to Picasso" (27). Wyrick and Veitch see the novel as a bomb hidden within a piece of art, much like the ancient Trojan Horse itself.

As a form of cultural protest, West's bomb is a dud. But the novel should not be summarily dismissed as worthless juvenilia, either. The form and content of *Balso* are shaped more by West's professional fears, inexperience, and feelings of cultural belatedness than by his disgust for the literary bent. *Balso* deserves our attention today not for the artistic myths it weakly tries to dispense with, but for what it keenly reveals about the vocation of authorship in general and the apprenticeship of West in particular.

When the novel's title character proclaims, "Interesting psychologically, but is it art? I'd give you a B minus and a good spanking" (22), he could be speaking about the book itself. In its randomness and frenetic pacing, in the pretentious way it attacks literary pretension, in its questioning of the belief that art can edify, *Balso* reads more like an anxiety (of influence) dream than an assault on the Western canon. The primary target of the author's satiric attack is not literature; it is his own desire to write and publish. West's book is not "a disavowal" of high modernism; it is a late entry within it. In *Balso* West is stumbling toward finding his writing voice amid a chorus of louder voices. He is also worrying out loud if a Depression-era audience for serious literature will still be out there to listen when he does.

According to biographer Jay Martin, by 1931 West had already been working on a version of the manuscript for nine long years. While shopping

Nathanael West in 1931.
Photograph courtesy of Jay Martin

Balso to publishers, he knew it was inferior to the new project he was working on, *Miss Lonelyhearts* (Martin 120), but the hotel clerk wanted his name on a book jacket as soon as possible. After receiving numerous rejections from other houses, West hoped that his friends at Contact Editions could help him out (*Novels* 813). David Moss and Martin Kamin were bookstore owners who wanted to branch out into publishing. It was a business plan that was a throwback to another era, and it was one that could never work on a mass scale.

Throughout the eighteenth century and most of the nineteenth, it was common for American publishers to do their own printing and selling. But since then the process had become much more complicated, and labor had been divided. Companies such as Fitzgerald's publisher, Scribner's, had long ago distanced themselves from direct contact with the cash register and printer's ink. By 1931, in order for a book to get from writer to reader, it usually had to travel through agents, primary readers, acquisition editors, copy editors, proofreaders, typesetters, promotion staff, sales staff, wholesalers, and bookstore owners. The route for getting *Balso* to market was much simpler. West had no agent yet, and Contact Editions had no editorial staff. Moss asked William Carlos Williams, another friend of the bookshop and its owners, to critique West's manuscript, and on the strength of his favorable report it was accepted. West agreed to subsidize the novel's publication. It was not technically vanity publishing, but it was close. Of the run of 500 copies, West guaranteed the sale of 150 units (Martin 124–25).

As soon as the book hit the shelves, West, like the debut novelist Fitzgerald, began practicing the art of authorial self-promotion, ghostwriting an advertising leaflet for the book that marketed the novel's author as—and here, in their branding strategies, is where West and Fitzgerald part company—"vicious, mean, ugly, obscene and insane" (*Novels* 397). He thought a little scandal might stir up interest in him, if not for the book, and he nudged his friends into firing off letters to literary magazines complaining about the scathing reviews the novel was receiving from the philistines in the New York City press. These reviews, of course, were nonexistent. Nevertheless the press run of *The Dream Life of Balso Snell* sold quickly, making it a best seller of sorts, not surprising since the author himself had purchased many of the books. At the end of the decade he would still have some left (Martin 124). The limited press run, with numbered copies, assured that the "art" book would never be mistaken for a mass-produced commodity and would be consumed by a restricted audience of those in the know (that is, friends and family of West, if not a discriminating reading public of intellectuals).

The first numbered copy, signed by West, had gone to his fiancée, the model Alice Shepard, to whom the book is dedicated (Siegel 5). This is not the gesture of someone making a social statement "as a protest against the writing of books"; it is the behavior of someone who believes in the Romantic cult of the author. The custom of signing a book, declaring intellectual ownership of everything contained within the covers that separate it from other texts in the world, cements its authorial claim to be an original work of art produced by a single mind. But the book's contents belie this philosophy. Some of its writer characters steal, mimic, and appropriate the work of others; a few characters wonder where literature ends and they begin. West's novel shows the creative unconscious to be a place already colonized, a wellspring already muddied by the footprints of others. The novel makes the point that the texts produced by authors are not the products of individual creators alone. All writing is the result of a variety of factors: the psychological and emotional state of the writer, the writer's ideas of what writing is and what it does, the writer's notions of audience, the political and social environments in which the writing occurs, the aesthetic and economic pressures that encourage (or retard) the process, and other variables. Books are written by authors who intend to inscribe meanings into the texts they produce, of course, but these authors are also people who exist in historical, psychological, and cultural frameworks and contexts. *Balso* reminds us that all discourse is, at least in part, socially constructed.

Like West himself every writer character in *Balso* writes toward an unknowable—yet achingly desired—public. The novel is populated by neurotic artists who are always performing, forever marketing themselves, and always working an angle. Like a hotshot screenwriter at a pitch meeting, the holy man Maloney the Areopagite launches into a "short précis" of his story idea (11) concerning a new angle on the Christ saga. A small boy tells Balso "for a dollar I'll sell you a brief outline of my position" on life (23). But as West's friend and former lover Lillian Hellman claims in her autobiography: "Writers care less for dollars than for attention" (30). This is certainly true of the contents (and of the publishing history) of *The Dream Life of Balso Snell*. For West's performers it is more important to fill the seats than to charge a high admission price. Balso, like his creator, is a struggling writer who dreams of getting his voice recognized over the barking of competing authorial voices. This battle exists on two fronts: in the writer's head and in the frenzy of the marketplace.

The artists in *Balso* want to make their indelible, original marks on the world, but the canvas is already filled with the scribbles of others. As one character puts it: "There was a time when I felt that I was indeed a rare spirit. Then I had genuinely expressed my personality with a babe's delight in confessing the details of its inner life. Soon, however, in order to interest my listeners, I found it necessary to shorten my long out-pourings; to make them, by straining my imagination, spectacular. Oh, how much work goes into the search from the odd, the escape from the same!" (25).

The artists in *Balso* want to be listened to; they need to prove to themselves that their lives have meaning. If they cannot be original, they can at least be shocking. The book is filled with images of body fluids, extreme violence, and dysfunctional sex. Earlier in the novel the same poetic, sensitive, "rare spirit" reveals his habit of writing "while smelling the moistened forefinger" of his left hand, fresh from his ass (14).

The Trojan Horse intestines Balso Snell travels through are inhabited solely by "writers in search of an audience" (34), and B.S. quickly realizes they are all full of shit, himself included. He is constantly being forced to read their tales, to pay them attention, to pay them money, to listen to streams of nonsense. The writers "come to the paper with a constipation of ideas—eager, impatient. The white paper acts as a laxative. A diar-rhoea of words is the result" (15). They tell themselves, quoting the Irish novelist and wit George Moore, that "art is sublime excrement" (9), but crap begets crap. Instead of D. H. Lawrence's notion of the artist's beatific self-regeneration, we get the Phoenix Excrementi, a race of men, invented by Balso, who eat themselves and are reborn from their own feces.

West's vocational fears are dramatized in a series of similarly grotesque scenes—the bookish spinster Miss McGeeney offers sexual favors in return for editorial advice; St. Puce the Flea takes up residence in Christ's armpit as an embedded journalist; a vengeful hunchback and a rapacious herma-phrodite, transmogrifications of characters we have already met, also make appearances. Like a set of Russian dolls of the unconscious, every writer Balso meets in his nightmare morphs into another writer who engenders still more writer characters. There are dreams within dreams; stories within stories; journals within journals; discourses within discourses. Everyone is a figment of someone else's imagination and ego. Everyone in the novel speaks and writes in voices that are not their own.

West's novel serves to remind us that behind every name on every book cover stand multiple sources and influences both implicit and explicit, a complex web of intertextuality. To take one example, Beagle Darwin's let-ters, in which he imitates Hemingway without mentioning him by name, are written by McGeeney, who vocalizes her desire to imitate Henry Field-ing. John Gilson, a type of Arthur Rimbaud–like prodigy West both sati-rizes and envies, has been so influenced by Dostoyevsky that his prose sometimes hiccups into the voice of a ready-made Raskolnikov. Not only do writers weigh themselves against their contemporaries, *The Dream Life of Balso Snell* demonstrates, but those serious about their art often also measure how they stack up against those who have come before. With no clear set of objective criteria to go by, no system of separating the hack from the maestro, this self-examination can be unnerving.

In *Balso* West foregrounds his anxiety of influence in an attempt to move past it. The book documents his struggle to wrest himself away from the strong voices of his literary mothers and fathers. It also announces that he is ready to start making some noise of his own. West may be late in get-ting to the overcrowded avant-garde ball, but he wants his presence to be felt. Although the book was printed in New York City, its original title page read "Paris," which connected it to Contact's first incarnation and to the royal line of modernism. Similarly a letter West's friend Julian Shapiro wrote to the Paris-based literary magazine the *New Review,* defending the book from scathing reviews that did not exist, cleverly uses shaky logic and some quick name-dropping to put the book in good high modernist company: "Mr. Pound recently wrote in one of your issues that Mr. Joyce had complained that no reviewer had ever said he enjoyed *Ulysses*. Well, the same's true here. West's book is at least funny, but no one has written about that" (47).

This statement manages to have it both ways. It compares the novel to a twentieth-century masterpiece (on the wide basis that no critic said it was pleasurable reading) and elevates *Balso* above it because, unlike *Ulysses*, "West's book is at least funny." Shapiro is claiming that West mixes the highbrow intellectual seriousness of Joyce with a dash of lowbrow comedic entertainment, and, in fact, many of the attempts at humor in *Balso* come at Joyce's expense. Parodies of the master begin and end the novel. Before entering the Trojan Horse, Balso delivers a Stephen Dedalus–like prayer: "O Beer! O Meyerbeer! O Bach! O Offenbach! Stand me now as ever in good stead" (5). In the sex scene / wet dream that closes the novel, Miss McGeeney swoons in a Molly Bloomian reverie: "Moooompicher yaaaah . . . yes, yes. Drag me down into the mire, drag. Yes!" (53). Stein, Charles Baudelaire, Dostoyevsky, Hemingway, Freud, Rimbaud, Jonathan Swift, J.-K. Huysmans, Maksim Gorky, François Rabelais, and other writers are roasted by the first-time author as well.

With its numerous "found" (or stolen) passages and narrative disjunction, *Balso* backs up critic Louis Menand's claim that "when we examine a modernist literary work as an instance of modernist theory in practice, we can never quite be certain whether we are looking at an example of the critical prescription being applied successfully or an example of the disease the prescription is supposed to cure" (113). Self-reflexively announcing its claim to modernist literariness, West's book challenges the reader to catch as many of its arcane references as possible. That way both writer and audience can compare college educations and share a smug sense of intellectual satisfaction. The parodies serve to display West's irreverence, but their main purpose is always to assert his authority. By mocking *A Portrait of the Artist as a Young Man* and *Ulysses*, the novel tries to hollow them out. West's derision of artists such as Joyce, Stein, and Rimbaud— all of whom his friend Edmund Wilson helped canonize in *Axel's Castle*, published the same year as *Balso*—are bold challenges to be included in the top ranks of a newly institutionalized literary pantheon. In an effort to find his own voice, West apes the styles of precursors and contemporaries.

These efforts will start paying dividends in his later novels, books more accomplished than this one. The hard-boiled prose of Hemingway and Hammett that Beagle burlesques in his second series of letters—passages where the attitude is tough and the description is spare—later becomes the comic tone of *Miss Lonelyhearts*. And the notes of the mock-heroic struck during Balso's journey sound a lot like *A Cool Million*. West's fear of mass culture, lurking throughout *Balso,* eventually reaches hysteria in *The Day of the Locust.* Throughout his debut novel, despite its choir of voices, the individual timbre of much of West's recognizable style is present, especially his flair for mixing highbrow allusions and gross-out comedy. But more important, within the pages of *Balso* West begins to explore many of the issues that would shape his later work and career, particularly the role of the artist—and his art—in an American society that could not care less about either. Audiences in West's books do not want to be edified; they want to be entertained—and quickly.

Instead of being pristine and timeless monuments, books in *Balso* are transitory and decaying, read not by scholars and young aspiring writers but by people looking for "pornography and facts about strange diseases." Every tome, says library employee / child prodigy John Gilson, eventually ends up smelling "like the breaths of the authors . . . like a closet full of old shoes through which a steam pipe passes" (17). It is all disposable, all trash. Each time someone gives Balso something to read, he scans it quickly and tosses it away.

West's anxiety that the market was already flooded with books unpurchased and unread was justified. O. H. Cheney's 1931 economic survey of the American publishing industry, for example, called for a cease-fire in the "excessive numbers of titles" (89) being released. Because there were so many titles to choose from, many books and their authors were going unread. People were reading more than ever before, and more was being written than ever before, but this did not translate into sales for experimental fiction such as *The Dream Life of Balso Snell,* especially during a time of economic depression, when the avant-garde suffers the most from lack of sponsors. The early 1930s was a tough time to begin a career as a literary novelist, especially since the chasm between middle-class and highbrow reading tastes was growing evermore vast. There was no national reading audience. As Stein pronounced in *Everybody's Autobiography,* only in the nineteenth century could an author reach a wide public and make a good living writing. In the eighteenth century there were too few readers, in the twentieth there were too many, and "too few is as many as too many" (100). The spread of literacy had created a public that can read novels—but will not. Elsewhere Stein describes her ideal reading audience as "writers, university students, librarians and young people who have very little money" (*Alice B. Toklas* 244). Stein, speaking in the voice of Alice B. Toklas speaking in the voice of Gertrude Stein, only desires readers who can appreciate reading.

It is not unusual to find an aspiring author of the early twentieth century who has no faith in the mass public, but *Balso* appears to catch West already having a tough time believing in either art or the artistic vocation. The sensory experience of madeleines launches Marcel Proust's hero into an imaginative reverie; West's aesthetes smell their shit off their fingers in a futile attempt to keep their self-indulgent writing grounded in an outside reality. The effete artists in *Balso*—especially the young men—are objects that can relate only to themselves. They have lost touch with the masculine workaday world. Sounding like a Catholic School gym coach, the book's title character offers his fellow writers the following advice: "Don't be morbid. Take your eyes off your navel. Take your head from under your armpit. Stop sniffing mortality. Play games. Don't read so many books. Take cold showers. Eat more meat" (13). West seems disgusted with the life of the artist even before having a chance to live it fully. His metaphors show art to be a giant waste of time: it is chronic masturbation, walking around with your head up your ass, spitting in the wind.

An early draft of the novel opens with Kurt Schwitters's Dadaist motto: "Tout ce que l'artiste crache, c'est l'art" (qtd. in Martin 125). This sounds liberating, especially in French. After all if everything the artist spits out is art, so is *Balso*. You do not need to break a sweat, and if you do, well, you can call that art, too. But West is also aware of the pitfalls inherent in the German artist's proclamation. If everything the artist expectorates is art, does not that mean everyone is an artist? Especially since there are no rules on who can call themselves one. After all anyone can write, paint, or compose a "modern" piece that makes no sense. As in West's story "The Imposter," if everyone is an artist, then no one is an artist.

One way to achieve separation from the audience in the cultural field is through outright disdain for them. The artists in "The Imposter" mock their benefactors. A playwright in *Balso* conceives of a production during which "the ceiling of the theatre will be made to open and cover the occupants with tons of loose excrement. After the deluge, if they so desire, the patrons of my art can gather in the customary charming groups and discuss the play" (28). Displaying contempt for your audience will only make them love you more. Keep biting their hands, and you will keep getting fed.

West's work cleverly parodies the vapid bohemian type he vowed he would never become. In *The Beautiful and Damned*, writers write because it is "their mode of living," the way they make their money. In *Balso*, on the other hand, Beagle Darwin writes because "literature has deeply dyed" his brain "its own color" (42). His fellow writer John Gilson knows that art is probably a dead end, yet "because of some great need I am forced to make the attempt" (17). As it is with his characters, writing was not simply a way for West to try to make money; it was his vocation and identity. He was compelled to write despite economic uncertainty, audience apathy, and frequent episodes of doubt bordering on self-disgust. West was well aware that public recognition usually never comes—if it does, it is usually after death.

A letter to the editor that appeared in the October 20, 1931, edition of the *New York World-Telegram* gives us even further insight into West's vocational philosophy:

> I have had some experience with the little magazine and think that such a statement as the one recently made by Mr. Frank Shay in connection with *Contempo* ought not to pass unchallenged. When he wrote about "panhandling magazines," he was taking a crack at one of the few decent things in American letters. Apparently he is unacquainted with their sponsors and ignorant of the purpose they serve.
>
> As to the sponsors, it would be hard to find greater idealists in the literary world. Invariably they have spent money and given time to what they knew from the start was to be a losing venture. As to purpose, the little magazine in the past has found audiences for such writers as Sherwood Anderson, Ben Hecht, Ernest Hemingway. . . .
>
> Surely the unpaid writer for that type of magazine has little to complain of, since he and "litrachoor"—but never the sponsors— get anything out of it. (*Novels* 769–70)

The letter writer seems to believe that the less the financial return, the greater the nobility of the artistic venture. The little magazine West claims experience with, the place of authority he speaks from, is the second coming of the 1920s Paris literary journal *Contact,* which was gearing up to put out its first new issue under the sponsorship of Moss and Kamin. The rebirth of *Contact* would be taking place without the assistance of one of its founding editors, Robert McAlmon, but the other, William Carlos Williams, had accepted Moss and Kamin's offer to run the magazine. Because he had been impressed with *The Dream Life of Balso Snell,* Williams had asked West to assist him in reviving the journal (Martin 144). This was the opportunity—and the validation—West had been waiting for. With supporters such as Williams, Hammett, Wilson, Parker, and, later, Fitzgerald and Faulkner, he was cementing a reputation as a writer's writer, an artist recognized by his peers.

The readers most coveted by the writers in *Balso* are other writers, since they are the ones most likely to keep a literary reputation alive. Miss McGeeney wants to write the biography of the man who wrote the biography of the man who wrote the biography of the man who wrote the biography of the man who wrote the biography of James Boswell (30). She hopes another writer will take the hint. In the case of West, recognition from an esteemed author such as Williams and an invitation from him to join a rejuvenated literary magazine made the young author feel like part of something. Martin writes: "It is true, certainly, that by virtue of the publication of a book by Contact Editions, West could claim a very distinguished and special place in the literary fellowship. But the associate editorship of *Contact* was even more tangible evidence that he was gaining a special place among his fellow writers" (144).

On the one hand, concepts of the "literary" are subject to cultural and historic fluctuations. Although it has connotations of the elite, the respectable, the refined, the noble, the sophisticated, the inspiring, the best that has ever been thought and said, and so on, the term *literature* has no essential qualities and is not an objective category. Yet writing labeled "literary" has worth beyond the commercial, however that worth is defined, that sets it apart from its opposite, "trash," which is not worth keeping.

A writer who aspires to write literature hopes to stick around. By compiling a historical bibliography of the little magazine, West placed *Contact II*—and by extension, himself—into a distinguished literary tradition. It is also worth pointing out that the "little," when referring to "little magazines," does not refer to payment or paper size; it refers to the number of readers being targeted. Such magazines often enjoy a literate and sophisticated reading audience, but it is usually one that consists almost solely of other struggling writers.

West's early career demonstrates that the writing profession really is not a profession at all. Authors do not share a specialized body of knowledge, a common educational background, a code of ethics, or a system of peer review and self-regulation. However, with a newly released debut novel and an editorial position at a literary magazine that had introduced many Americans to modernism, it can be said that he had now become a member in good standing of the club.

But could he make a living? Was there still money in modernism? Through fortunate timing a commitment to pure art had paid off for Joseph Conrad, Lawrence, and Joyce. But the Depression was now in full swing. As scholars such as Lawrence Rainey and Joyce Wexler have demonstrated, such modernists as McAlmon and Stein paid bills and promoted experimental literature through inherited or family money. West had no trust fund. He would be doing most of the actual labor in putting *Contact II* together—the running around, the calling, and the collecting. And he'd be doing it all for free. But it was not about the money for West. Even though he could not support himself with literature, he was a published author who was quickly developing a reputation as a writer's writer, an artist whose poor sales his friends took to be evidence of the purity of his intentions. With each new commercial failure, West would become an even greater success.

Trying to Adapt

In October 1931, the month that West was asked to work on the literary magazine *Contact II* for free, F. Scott Fitzgerald was offered $750 a week to work at the Hollywood studio MGM. A year earlier Fitzgerald "had a hunch that the talkies would make even the best selling novelist as archaic as silent pictures" (*Crack-Up* 78), and he wondered if screen writing could help him reach a larger audience. The medium's power and influence could no longer be denied, and a tour of duty in Los Angeles would provide him the added benefit of soaking up material for his new book—if he ever finished writing it—which throughout its false starts had dealt with Hollywood to varying degrees. When MGM came calling, Fitzgerald decided to do what any professional writer would do—he tested his market value by holding out for more money. That November he accepted a $1,200-a-week Hollywood contract, placing the author on one of the top rungs of the screenwriter pay scale (*As Ever* 178–80).

Upon his arrival in California, Fitzgerald was assigned to work on *Red-Headed Woman,* a project being adapted from Katherine Brush's best-selling novel. MGM, the "Tiffany Studio" that touted itself as the richest and most prestigious outfit in town, had the desire and the capital to pursue "presold" properties, such as Brush's, that had first been successful in other media. It made good market sense. Films adapted from novels, plays, and short stories had a built-in audience of those who had enjoyed the originals, and a larger potential audience of those who recognized the title of the source material. Most authors, like Fitzgerald himself, were happy to sell the screen rights to their fiction, and equally happy to disown what had been done to them. This also made good market sense. Novels and short stories carried the outward signature of one name alone, so most of the praise or blame for these products was directed at the author. But adaptation allowed for scapegoats. If the adaptation was successful, the author of the source material could claim all the credit. If not,

Fitzgerald joked with his aunt and uncle, "you can always say, 'Oh, well, the movie is in a different spirit from the way it was written!'" (*Letters of FSF* 466).

But not all authors were as willing as Fitzgerald to separate themselves from film adaptations of their work. A 1931 court case that pitted Theodore Dreiser against Paramount Pictures illustrates the extent to which studios controlled the properties they bought, and how little they cared about the alleged sacrosanctity of source material. Dreiser was deeply unhappy with the film that had been made from his *An American Tragedy* (1925). He had liked the script prepared by Sergey Eisenstein in the late 1920s, but B. P. Schulberg had found it unfilmable. The new creative team assigned to revive the project, Dreiser believed, had bastardized his novel. A psychological study of a man's decline had been turned into nothing but a morality tale, and Dreiser wanted to stop the picture from being released. With the courtroom as his stage, the publicity-loving author rose to his feet, banged his fists on the desk, and hollered that art and the artist were under attack. After telling him to sit down, and then telling him again, the judge ruled in favor of the studio, declaring: "In the preparation of the picture the producer must give consideration to the fact that the great majority of the people comprising the motion-picture audience will be more interested in justice prevailing over wrongdoing than that the inevitability of Clyde's end clearly appear" (qtd. in Swanberg 454).

The judge's words are true enough. But producers and adapters have more to consider than the sophistication levels of the respective audiences for motion pictures and print literature; they must also take into account the differences in the two media. Adapting a work of literature often necessitates cutting everything that does not drive the story forward. Moviemakers and moviegoers alike are likely more interested in *what* happens to Clyde than they are in *why* it happens. In a visual medium, action sheds light on character—not usually the other way around. Novels can be contemplative, but films should be immediate. Individual readers consume a novel at their leisure, with time in between each word, sentence, or chapter to stop for reflection. But films (at least in the days before home entertainment systems) unfold all at once and must move an audience as a group.

The Dreiser affair makes clear that studio properties were produced and marketed toward attracting the largest audience possible. In 1931 that audience appeared to be shrinking. Hollywood was beginning to feel the Depression. More than 60 percent of the American population, about seventy million people, still went to the movies every week, but that was ten million fewer than the year before. The price of an average ticket had fallen from thirty cents to twenty cents, but films themselves were getting more expensive to make (Balio 13). With sound becoming standard, and times getting tougher, Hollywood felt it could no longer afford to aim films at narrow markets. Many more people had heard of *An American Tragedy* than had read it, and these people could not care less if it was faithful to the book. Like *Sister Carrie* (1900) before it, the novel had a reputation for being "lurid," and that was enough to arouse public curiosity about the film version.

Red-Headed Woman had a similar risqué appeal. MGM cast Jean Harlow in the title role, and Charles Boyer would play the chauffeur she gleefully runs away with after leaving a wake of destruction behind her. At first Fitzgerald seemed like a good choice to write the screenplay, since Brush's source novel imitates his themes and style. It is filled with gin-soaked "New Women" who sin without being punished and contains lyrical passages that simultaneously deride the rich and glorify them. Sam Marx, the young story editor at MGM, admired Fitzgerald and hoped he could provide characterization for the script and something even more important—spoken dialogue.

Since 1927, the year *The Jazz Singer* was released and the last time Fitzgerald had been in Hollywood, sound had become standard. To help decide who would be speaking and what they would say, the studios began offering contracts to "talk men" from the East Coast—novelists, dramatists, magazine writers. As he began working on the *Red-Headed Woman* script, Fitzgerald hoped that this screen-writing experience would be more satisfying than the previous one. But as he recalled to his daughter, Scottie, years later: "Far from approaching it too confidently I was far too humble. I ran afoul of a bastard named de Sano, since a suicide, and let myself be gypped out of command. I wrote the picture and he changed as I wrote. I tried to get at Thalberg but was erroneously warned against it as 'bad taste.' Result—a bad script" (*Letters of FSF* 16–17).

If novelists expected deference and hero worship in Hollywood, they were soon disabused of that notion. Old screen-writing hands such as Marcel de Sano, who had recently been promoted to director, often resented newcomers such as Fitzgerald. Accepting a studio contract also placed authors into a structure and hierarchy where time and function were measured, institutionalizing a creative process. Writers, used to being on their own, were asked to assume work roles that served studio needs. They found themselves within an industry that had divided its labor and routinized its work sequences. Each studio was organized around hierarchies of power designed to squeeze maximum value out of employees and the physical plant itself. Writers were often expected to punch clocks and put in a full day. If the typewriter stopped clacking, if you took a few moments to think over the next plot point or bit of dialogue, a producer might poke his head into your office and ask why you were not working. Jack Warner at Warner Bros. believed his writers were lollygaggers and often used binoculars to spy on them from his office window.

At MGM, where Fitzgerald worked, the atmosphere was more genteel, but the product was more expensive, and therefore more hands were involved in assembling it—beginning with the script. Aaron Latham writes of the *Red-Headed Woman* screenplay: "All that remains of the work which Fitzgerald did for Thalberg is an unfinished seventy-six page script, the one de Sano reworked" (63). Fitzgerald claimed in his letter to Scottie that he himself "wrote the picture." But even had he worked on the script solo, it still would have only been a blueprint for the picture. Fitzgerald struggled with the fact that scripts are sketches, parts of a larger whole, invitations to collaborate rather than stand-alone works of art.

In addition to having difficulties with the screenwriter's craft, he also had troubles with the screenwriter's function. Fitzgerald had learned his lesson in the 1920s about how much practice and study it would take to write a good screenplay, but he would never learn to be a team player or respect a chain of command. It is somewhat ironic that he would think of going to Thalberg to complain, and that he would come to admire him so much. As the head of production at the richest studio in Hollywood, Thalberg was the architect of the MGM screen-writing system that Fitzgerald so hated, a system soon adopted on the other lots. The policy of multiple writers working on a single script—in collaboration, in competition, in pieces—was Thalberg's idea. He believed that pitting writers against one another caused them to do their best work. Once an individual or a team produced a finished script, that script, in whole or in part, was often sent to other writers to be rewritten. The rule of thumb appeared to be that the more people working on a film, and more money spent on it, the better the finished product.

Producers, working with relative independence but ultimately accountable to a central producer such as Thalberg at MGM or Jack Warner at Warner Bros. or Darryl Zanuck at Fox, often took the best from each contributor and put together the shooting script. Here the writer's contribution ended. Once the film went into production, writers were assigned to another project or fired. Following the same pattern, once the movie was shot and moved into postproduction for editing, the director was usually shuffled to another soundstage. The studio system operated like an assembly line, and in 1931, the year that Ford made its twenty millionth car, the film production machine was humming. That this system resulted in many wonderful films and a studio lot that was busy 168 hours a week there is no doubt. But behind the practical efficiency lay a will to power. Screen credits were sometimes withheld out of spite or granted to secretaries or lovers on a whim. In an attempt to make the assignment of credits more fair, writers such as John Howard Lawson and Dudley Nichols tried to start a union in late 1931, but the producers quickly crushed it. Executives wanted labor divided up in such a way that the guiding vision behind individual films remained their own. Fitzgerald could not have gotten "gypped out of command" on the Jean Harlow picture. He was never in command.

What Fitzgerald claimed he most hated about screen writing was having to collaborate. But what he really hated was being forced to work under or alongside men he considered his intellectual inferiors. He had been collaborating his entire career, lest we forget that commercial book publishing is a group enterprise. Maxwell Perkins had convinced him to rewrite the first-person narration of *This Side of Paradise* using the third-person point of view, and under Perkins's guidance the character of Jay Gatsby had become rounder and more prominent (James L. W. West, *Making of "This Side of Paradise"* 56–60, 90–97). In addition Fitzgerald often benefited from the advice of other writers. Scholars such as Matthew J. Bruccoli, Nancy Mitford, and Andrew Turnbull have documented the influence that Ernest Hemingway, Edmund Wilson, and Zelda had on Fitzgerald's work. But for the most part, Fitzgerald viewed these people as his peers. Most of his film collaborators, as his letters show, he considered to be beneath him, believing his taste and judgment were superior to theirs.

Fitzgerald thought he saw a kindred spirit in Irving Thalberg, a former "boy genius" like himself. No Hollywood producer's instincts and judgment were more respected than Thalberg's. He and his wife, the actress Norma Shearer, were the closest thing to Hollywood royalty. One Sunday after a week spent on *Red-Headed Woman*, Fitzgerald went to an afternoon tea party at their home. What happened there would inspire the story "Crazy Sunday."

Nervous about making a bad impression, he began throwing back cocktails. Things devolved after that. Fitzgerald made fun of actor Robert Montgomery's riding breeches. He then told Shearer he wanted to sing his "Dog" song. Ramon Novarro agreed to play the piano. According to writer Dwight Taylor, who had accompanied Fitzgerald to the party, the crowd "gathered in a half circle near the piano, but not too near, their faces devoid of expression, like people gathered at the scene of an accident" (*Joy Ride* 243). Fitzgerald's song was not funny. At first the group listened politely, but after the second verse, they grew restless. Taylor recalls that Lupe Velez and John Gilbert booed. Some people slipped away, and others soon followed. Thalberg stood across the room, saying nothing. Fitzgerald realized what an ass he'd made of himself, and left the party (244).

The following day, nursing a hangover and a bad case of regret, he went to the studio commissary and found himself sitting next to Daisy and Violet Hilton—Siamese twins. The Hilton sisters, along with their cast mates—pinheads, dwarves, human skeletons, and giants—were on the MGM lot filming *Freaks*.

After lunch Fitzgerald returned to his office. Waiting for him was a telegram from Norma Shearer that lifted his spirits. It read: "I THOUGHT YOU WERE ONE OF THE MOST AGREEABLE PERSONS AT OUR TEA" (*Correspondence* 282).

A week later Fitzgerald was fired. Latham, among others, implies that the screenwriter was let go because of the tea-party incident, but this seems unlikely. He had been hired for six weeks, and after five it must have been clear that the script needed some new blood. That is how the system operated. Fitzgerald was replaced on *Red-Headed Woman* by Anita Loos. Already a fifteen-year veteran of the young industry, Loos had a reputation for working quickly, coming up with witty dialogue, and getting a "woman's touch" into her scripts that would appeal to the all-important female audience (who made up the bulk of moviegoers). Thalberg told Loos that "Scott tried to turn the silly book into a tone poem" (Loos 34). The writer had tried to be an author. The employee had tried to be an artist. Loos received solo screen credit for *Red-Headed Woman*.

Fitzgerald started writing a story about the experience in early January 1932, but what emerged was not the poison-pen letter to Hollywood that might have been expected. In "Crazy Sunday" his admiration for Thalberg shines through, as does his unwavering belief in the cult of the artist as singular genius. Miles Calman, a prototype for Monroe Stahr of *The Last Tycoon*, is a maestro trying to remain free from the sticky web of industrial bureaucracy—a desire clearly not shared by company man Thalberg, Calman's real-life counterpart. Like Cecil B. DeMille or Frank Capra, Calman is a director who serves as his own producer. He has no supervisor. The vision behind his films is his own, and he has so far been able to fight off interference from Louis B. Mayeresque front office executives such as "old Beltzer" (*Stories of FSF* 411). Like Thalberg and Stahr, Calman is sickly and exhausted, but he refuses to stop working. He must push himself toward greater and greater artistic achievements. When this Hollywood Icarus dies in a plane crash (as Stahr was ordained to do in the unfinished *Tycoon*), the screenwriter Joel Coles ruminates on his legacy: "He was the only American born director with both an interesting temperament and an artistic conscience. Meshed in an industry, he had paid with his ruined nerves for having no resilience, no healthy cynicism, no refuge" (416).

Lacking the "healthy cynicism" of West, or even the unhealthy cynicism of Parker, Fitzgerald, like Calman, had invested himself heavily in the idealistic belief of the artist as hero. Calman is an artist with the popular touch, much as Fitzgerald viewed himself. Few fiction writers are as autobiographical as Fitzgerald. In the story "Crazy Sunday" he unabashedly sprinkles his own experiences, seasoned with those of his friends, among the characters. Just as Fitzgerald would use Hollywood prince Budd Schulberg as a model for the character of Cecilia in *The Last Tycoon,* the screenwriter Coles in "Crazy Sunday" has Dwight Taylor's youth and show business lineage. Taylor was the son of the star Laurette Taylor, and Coles had grown up in the entertainment industry as well: "His mother had been a successful actress; Joel had spent his childhood between London and New York trying to separate the real from the unreal, or at least to keep one guess ahead" (403). Coles writes continuity, which means he works at making all the cobbled pieces of the script fit together. Those assigned to continuity need to have the ability to translate narrative into cinematic terms. It is a marketable skill, but not a very creative one. Despite this, on the whole, Coles likes screen writing.

Accompanying Coles to the party is the "heavy drinking, highly paid," and profligate Nat Keogh, a man with Fitzgerald's curriculum vitae and spending habits. But it is Joel who makes a fool of himself by performing an inappropriate song at the tea party. This writer among actors then proceeds to impersonate the ethnic accent and comic malapropisms of a respected movie executive. The silence Joel receives from his audience, writes Fitzgerald, is "the resentment of the professional towards the amateur, of the community towards the stranger, the thumbs down of the clan" (407). Despite Joel's slipup, all is forgiven. Like a magical do-over, "Crazy Sunday" transforms Fitzgerald's frustrating screen-writing trip into a fictional one where the writer gains the respect and affection of the patriarchal producer and sleeps with his beautiful, nurturing wife. The Oedipal scene that ends the story could not have been scripted any better: when Calman dies, Stella runs into Joel's arms for comfort.

The Dream Life of Balso Snell shows West dramatizing his vocational fears in the form of a series of nightmarish scenes; "Crazy Sunday" reads like a laborer's daydream of being invited to move into the CEO's mansion. Yet the two works have a lot in common, especially where the role of the creative artist in society is concerned. In Fitzgerald's "Crazy Sunday," the writer Joel struggles to "separate the real from the unreal" by staying "one step ahead" (403). In Nathanael West's *Balso,* John Gilson writes in his journal: "If only I could discover the Real. A Real that I could know with my senses. . . . I must devote my whole life to the pursuit of a shadow. It is as if I were attempting to trace with the point of a pencil the shadow of the tracing pencil" (*Novels* 14–16). Robert Emmet Long writes of West's novel: "The pretension of art to know what reality is, and thus to raise man above the disorder of his condition, is rejected as a deception and illusion" (34). Artists are supposed to see things that the general public cannot, and they are supposed to see the truth behind those things. But in "Crazy Sunday" Joel gets pulled into the center orbit of the couple he is observing and has to fight hard to separate fact from fiction. When they hear the news of Calman's plane crash, Joel and Stella wrestle with the possibility that the director might have staged it: "This is part of his scheme. He's torturing me. I know he's alive," Stella says. She looks at the telegram "as though it were a black lie," and Joel wonders if Calman is "really dead" (*Short Stories* 416–17). As in West's *The Day of the Locust,* those who produce artifice often find themselves struggling to distinguish the real from the illusory.

"Crazy Sunday" and *Balso Snell* are both populated by frenzied artists who are always performing, forever pitching, always working an angle. Joel tells Stella: "Everybody's afraid, aren't they? . . . Everybody watches for everybody else's blunders, or tries to make sure they are with people that'll do them credit" (404). In the following passage, Fitzgerald lets us eavesdrop on the drone of "shop talk," the Hollywood version of West's "diarrhoea of words": "There was the endless detail of script revision— 'Instead of a lousy dissolve, we can leave her voice on the sound track and cut to a medium shot of the taxi from Bell's angle or we can simply pull the camera back to include the station, hold it a minute and then pan to the row of taxis'" (411).

Today's audiences are familiar with terms such as *dissolve* and *pan,* but in the manner that the more arcane literary references in *Balso* are meant to shut the reader out, this cinema argot seems meant to stupefy 1930s readers. Fitzgerald supposes we will not be able to make heads or tails of it, and the phrase "endless detail" trivializes the work being done.

But just as West's literary parodies serve to display his erudition and authority, the above passage shows Fitzgerald announcing that he is picked up something about sound-film grammar and the concept of asynchronous sound. Fitzgerald and other novelists working as screenwriters in the 1930s needed to learn to take into account things such as mise-en-scène, gesture, music, sound, camera angle, and length of shot. Taken out of context, it is impossible to get the total picture and know what would work best for the scene the screenwriters in "Crazy Sunday" are discussing, but the last option, the "pull back, pause, and pan," is the most seamless way to join the scenes in that it requires camera movement instead of a continuity edit. Furthermore if it can be done "simply," it probably means it is the right way to convey the visual information within Hollywood's "invisible style." But perhaps more important than all this, the passage shows Fitzgerald thinking about ways to move from scene to scene in a filmic manner.

In addition to marking an advance in Fitzgerald's film sense, "Crazy Sunday" continues a darkening in the tenor of his writing that had begun in stories such as "One Trip Abroad" and "Babylon Revisited." This change in tone was not good for Fitzgerald commercially, but artistically it produced some of his best work. Few are better at writing about disappointment, disillusionment, and loss. Here he describes a 1931 trip to the roof of the Empire State Building: "Full of vaunting pride the New Yorker had climbed here and seen with dismay what he had never suspected, that the city was not the endless succession of canyons that he had supposed but that it had limits—from the tallest structure he saw for the first time that it faded out into the country on all sides, into an expanse of green and blue that alone was limitless. And with the awful realization that New York was a city after all and not the universe, the whole shining edifice that he had reared in his imagination came crashing to the ground" (*Crack-Up* 32).

This note of wistfulness in the author's prose was increasingly being viewed by magazine editors as too somber and unglamorous. After years of crafting stories for quick market sale, Fitzgerald appeared to be writing from his heart rather than his checkbook. Ober was still placing most of his work, and he supported the darker direction Fitzgerald's fiction was taking, but it was getting harder to find a home for it. "Crazy Sunday" was no exception. *Redbook* passed on the story. The *Saturday Evening Post*, once Fitzgerald's cash cow, rejected it on the grounds that its ending was too unexpected. *Cosmopolitan*, owned by William Randolph Hearst, also declined (Piper 167). Finally George Jean Nathan and H. L. Mencken's current magazine, the *American Mercury,* took the story, falsely promoting it—on Fitzgerald's advice—as a piece written for *Cosmopolitan* that was killed by Hearst because of its unflattering portrayal of his colleagues in the movie business (*Correspondence* 295).

The *American Mercury*—like West and Williams's *Contact II*—was free from the pressure of having to appease conglomerates and soap advertisers. Consequently, though, neither magazine operated at a profit nor neither paid its authors very well. Fitzgerald received two hundred dollars for "Crazy Sunday," a fraction of what he usually commanded for a piece. Yet he did not seem to mind. He believed the story to be of the first rank. He thought it was "litrachoor," as West's letter in defense of little magazines had accented the word. "It's a little too good for the popular magazines," Fitzgerald wrote to Mencken about the story (*Correspondence* 295).

Both *Contact II* and the *American Mercury* enjoyed a literate and sophisticated reading audience—one that consisted almost solely of other writers. Mencken's editorial policy of bashing the middle class, coupled with a high cover price, assured that his audience in the Depression heartland would be small. The mission of *Contact II* to publish a distinctly American modernist literature—and its inability to define exactly what that meant—assured that it would have trouble attracting contributors, not to mention attracting readers. After three issues the magazine folded—but not before publishing several excerpts from the novel that soon would become West's *Miss Lonelyhearts*. Williams wrote *Contact II*'s eulogy, saying that it had at least "given birth to at least one excellent writer who would not otherwise have had means to develop. *Contact* has produced N. West. Now it can die. . . . [West's writing] would offend the paying subscribers if it appeared in the large monthly magazines. Which makes one wonder if they will ever let it enter their consciousness" ("A New American Writer" 49–50).

Gertrude Stein reports that Elliot Paul, the editor of the modernist literary magazine *Transition,* used to say: "If ever there are more than two thousand subscribers, I quit" (*Alice B. Toklas* 240). Williams implies that *Contact II* can die because if it got too popular, the wrong type of people, the ones who subscribe to the large monthlies and are most in need of having their eyes opened, might start reading it. In its difficulty, in its danger of offending a mass audience who will never see it, West's writing makes for good avant-garde literature but for bad business. Stein, who felt misread by the mass audience, wrote, "My sentences get under their skin, only they do not know that they do" (*Alice B. Tolkas* 70), but West was not getting anywhere near the consciousness (or the living rooms) of the reading public.

The publisher Contact Editions and the magazine *Contact II* had given birth to an excellent new author, but both of these parents were now dead, and neither had left West a financial inheritance. To make matters worse, his hotel job, his security blanket, was in jeopardy. With no "paying subscribers" for his novels and stories, the very fear he had tried to face in *The Dream Life of Balso Snell* come to life, how would West survive? A flippant letter he had written to Williams in May 1932 as they were putting together the final issue of the magazine would prove to be a harbinger of things to come: "Business is lousy and my company is close to bankruptcy. New money has to be raised or I guess I'll have to go to Hollywood or start a Brook Farm experiment and wait for THE REVOLUTION" (*Novels* 776–77). In December 1932 West and some friends bought an eighty-three-acre farm in Erwinna, Pennsylvania. West planned to live there and devote himself to writing full time.

3

Activists, Artists,
and Actors

SEARCHES FOR
AN AUDIENCE
IN 1933–1934

It is simply that having once found the intensity of art, nothing
else that can happen in life can ever again seem as important
as the creative process.

> F. Scott Fitzgerald, 1934 letter to H. L. Mencken

To write. To set one word beautifully beside another word.
The privilege of it. The blessed peace of it. Oh for quiet, for
rest. . . . You writers—you don't know.

> Actress character Lily Wynton in
> Dorothy Parker's "Glory in the Daytime"

ℬↄ

In the preface to a mid-1930s reprinting of *The Great Gatsby* by the
Modern Library, F. Scott Fitzgerald singles out Nathanael West as a
promising young novelist whose career is in trouble because of critical ne-
glect and "from sheer lack of a stage to act on" (vii). Fitzgerald's theater
metaphor reminds us that professional writing is a performative act and
that authors are entertainers. Like the actors who populate Fitzgerald's
Tender Is the Night (1934), Dorothy Parker's "Glory in the Daytime"
(1933), and West's *A Cool Million* (1934), writers need audiences. They
also need backers to provide them with a means to reach these audiences.
Unable to support himself as a novelist, West resorted to plan B. It was
a backup plan shared by Fitzgerald and many other novelists of the
1930s—going to Hollywood and writing the screenplays for B movies.

The typical writer of the 1920s had viewed himself as an independent economic agent who worked solo and lent out products and creative services to "backers" such as the print industry, the theater industry, and the film industry. But in the period of 1933–34, as the Depression reached its lowest point and labor issues were on America's mind, screenwriters were starting to realize that they were workers. The structure of the studio system gave all the financial and creative power to studio heads and almost no power to anyone else. After all, despite being engaged in healthy competition, the studios were, according to authors Larry Ceplair and Steven Englund, "one large family financed by the same banks, taking the same risks, making the same product with the same conventions, interchanging a stable corps of artists, battling common enemies, and adopting standardized policies in a whole range of areas, from foreign and domestic public relations and marketing to labor contracts and trade union policies" (1–2). The moguls worked in oligopilistic concert with each other and would present a unified front when challenged by outsiders. Writers were figuring out they had better stick together, too. With the "them" clearly defined as the men in the front office, a new "us" emerged among Hollywood screenwriters that traversed gender, economic, and cultural lines. Whether Ivy League educated or without formal schooling, whether celebrated novelist or struggling gag man, Hollywood screenwriters were finding common ground. In March of 1933, Section VII of President Roosevelt's National Industrial Recovery Act was passed. This granted American workers—even "white-collar" creative workers who were engaged in labor that was by nature more mental than manual—the right to organize and bargain collectively, opening the doors for a screenwriters' union. The unionizing zeal of West and Parker—and the professional support offered by Fitzgerald to them both—demonstrates that many Hollywood writers in the mid-1930s were actively engaged in responding to crises in the profession of authorship.

As Parker and West were beginning to fight for the newly formed Screen Writers Guild, on a different front Fitzgerald was continuing to offer aid to his fellow writers. After Ring Lardner's death in 1933, Fitzgerald, who was living in Baltimore and readying *Tender Is the Night* for publication, wanted to assure his friend's place in literary history. He published an emotional tribute to Lardner in the *New Republic*. The tragedy of Lardner's death, according to Scott, was that he had failed to live up to his artistic promise. He had aimed too low, disparaged his own work, and spent too much time helping others. In this way the elegy reads like a cautionary self-portrait. The usually acerbic Parker wrote Fitzgerald that it was "the finest and most moving thing I've ever read" (*Correspondence* 318).

Shortly afterward Zelda's paintings were shown in New York. Parker attended the opening and purchased two of her watercolors. The rest of the week, Scott and Dorothy spent a good deal of time together in Manhattan, drinking and reminiscing about the 1920s (Mellow 427; Meade 235). In addition to mutual friends (such as Lardner) and a bent toward pouring their innermost thoughts and emotions into their writing (unlike Lardner), they shared a love/hate relationship with the rich, a tendency toward self-pity, a tragic view of life, and a fear that they were squandering their talents. Ever generous with his praise and help, Fitzgerald reminded Parker of his promise—the same one he had delivered on for Lardner and Hemingway in the 1920s—that when she wrote the novel she was planning he would make sure it got to the right people at Scribner's (Kinney 27).

Parker's Waltz

Parker's novel was stuck in the planning stage. By her own admission, she was a painfully slow worker, someone who began editing a line before she was even done writing it. *After Such Pleasures,* a 1933 compilation of her short fiction, demonstrates why her gifts may not have been ideally suited to the longer form of the novel in the first place. Although some works in the collection, such as "The Waltz," "Horsie," and "Sentiment," stand out, and the author's narrative voice is charming in short stretches, stacking one story upon another like this reveals her limited range and leanings toward sentimentalism. Piece after piece recounts the self-pitying, sharp-tongued, boozy despair of discarded women. Lynn Bloom writes of the strictures of Parker's brand of fiction: "Such narratives, with their fixed perspectives, exploitation of a single petty issue, and simple characters, have to be short. To be any longer would be to add redundance without complexity, to bore rather than to amuse with verbal pyrotechnics" (5).

Many of the stories in *After Such Pleasures* were first published in the *New Yorker* as what the magazine called "casuals," implying that they could be read quickly, were not supposed to be taken seriously, and were intended to evoke a tiny chuckle before the reader turned the page. James Thurber, another creator of "casuals," told the *Paris Review* about an awkward encounter with the novelist Thomas Wolfe: "Wolfe once told me at a cocktail party I didn't know what it was to be a writer. My wife, standing next to me, complained about that. 'But my husband *is* a writer,' she said. Wolfe was genuinely surprised. 'He is?' he asked. 'Why all I ever see is that stuff of his in *The New Yorker*'" (qtd. in Plimpton 132). Genuine writers published books, preferably really long novels, Wolfe believed. He was not alone.

By collecting her "casuals" into a book, Parker conferred an aura of legitimacy to them. In titling that book *After Such Pleasures,* a nod to John Donne's poem "A Farewell to Love," she marks a personal and national end to the frivolity of the 1920s, a time that seemed like such fun at the time, and announces that she and the country are ready to knuckle down and do some serious work. Furthermore, quoting a metaphysical poet admired by modernist masters such as T. S. Eliot increased her chances of being included one day among their illustrious literary company.

The more successful stories in *After Such Pleasures* achieve their power, as "Big Blonde" had in the 1920s, through their ability to pick apart the discrepancy between private and public female selves, between inner rebellious cynicism and outward passive compliance. In "The Waltz" a young woman's gracious comments to her dancing partner belie her bitter interior monologue:

> *Oh, no, no, no. Goodness no. It didn't hurt the least bit. And anyway it was my fault. Really it was. Truly. Well, you're just being sweet, to say that. It really was all my fault.*
>
> I wonder what I'd better do—kill him this instant, with my naked hands, or wait and let him drop in his traces. Maybe it's best not to make a scene. I guess I'll just lie low and watch the pace get him. He can't keep this up indefinitely—he's only flesh and blood. Die he must, and die he shall, for what he did to me. (*Complete* 210)

Critic Emily Toth writes of the story: "Parker's satiric target is neither the clumsy young man nor the bruised young woman, but the social roles they are locked into—in short, the affectations and hypocrisies of a patriarchal society" (77).

But if we look more closely, it is a little tougher than that to separate the dancer from the dance. Toth fails to mention that the waltzer goes on waltzing. "Oh, they've stopped, the mean things. They're not going to play any more. Oh, darn. Oh, do you think they would? Do you really think so, if you gave them fifty dollars? Oh, that would be lovely. And look, do tell them to play this same thing. I'd simply adore to go on waltzing" (*Complete* 212). Perhaps the public self reveals the dancer's true feelings, and the inner voice is the one that should be regarded with suspicion. Could it be that the woman is enjoying herself, despite herself? In the illuminating "Verbal Subversions in Dorothy Parker: 'Trapped Like a Trap in a Trap,'" a deconstructive reading of the story, Paula Treichler identifies "a series of verbal redundancies that play upon each other . . . the language does not mock social realities but affirms them" (56). After the song is over, the young woman has her chance to stop dancing, but she does not.

Treichler's close reading of the story can easily be extended to Parker's own writing career, especially her waltz with a frequent partner she considered clumsy and beneath her—Hollywood. East Coast bashing of the movie business was already becoming old hat by the mid-1930s. In a 1934 article in the *New Yorker,* Algonquin Round Table member S. N. Behrman "took issue" with friends such as Edmund Wilson, Moss Hart, and George S. Kaufman. Behrman writes, "Satirizing of Hollywood is now firmly entrenched as one of the most thriving branches of the national literary industry" (30–35). Parker was no exception. In the mid-1930s she told Nathanael West she hated writing for the movies (Martin 209), the same thing she told anyone who would listen. Yet she continued to do so, despite being financially solvent. In this way the waltz represents Parker's social dance—one that shares many of the same steps as Fitzgerald's— between high culture and popular culture, between being recognized by the many and appreciated by the cognoscenti, between starving for art and consuming as conspicuously as possible. Hollywood was the stage where these performances of vocational selves were often illuminated in bright lights.

Gary Cross has described the "bargain" entered into by American workers as the United States shifted from a producer economy to a consumer economy. In exchange for ceding workplace control to managers, employees gained higher wages and were granted increased leisure time to buy things (20). The studios gave writers more money for their writing than it usually commanded but less control over the form and content of that writing. For many authors it was a thorny bargain. Parker lived in high style in Hollywood, despite grumbling about the place and the producers (managers) she encountered there. As novelist John O' Hara wrote to Fitzgerald: "I stayed with Dottie and her husband when I first came out here. They have a large white house, Southern style, and live in luxury, including a brand new Picasso, a Packard convertible phaeton, a couple of Negroes, and dinner at the very best Beverly Hills homes. Dottie occasionally voices a great discontent, but I think her aversion to movie-writing is as much lazy as intellectual" (*Selected Letters of JOH* 116).

Yet Parker was a whiz at film writing. While occasionally a liability on the printed page, her tendency to mix the maudlin and the amusingly acrid was a good fit for 1930s romantic comedies such as *Here Is My Heart* and *One Hour Late.*

The strength of Parker's writing, related to her gift for humor, lies in her ability to capture people's voices. She worked on dialogue for *Here Is My Heart* (1934)—a film in which Bing Crosby disguises himself as a waiter in order to win the love of a princess played by Kitty Carlisle—without screen credit. That we think we hear her smart mouth in some of the comebacks of Carlisle's character, as we might in Gail Patrick's vitriolic barbs at her husband in *One Hour Late* (1934), does not provide hard evidence that she wrote these particular lines, but it does give us a clue as to why she might have been hired to do so.

Parker often worried that her famous wit locked her into a persona, which threatened her individualization and agency. In her story "The Garter," she offers a mocking self-portrait of the celebrity Dorothy Parker: "Oh, have you met Dorothy Parker? What's she like? Oh, she's terrible. God, she is poisonous. Sits in the corner and sulks all evening—never opens her yap. Dumbest woman you ever saw in your life. You know, they say she does not write a word of her stuff. They say she pays this poor little guy, that lives in some tenement on the lower East Side, ten dollars a week to write it and she just signs her name to it" (*Complete* 101). Here Parker pokes cynical fun at her image as a celebrity author famous for her cynicism. Just as comedians are often asked by strangers in public places to "say something funny," she is expected to entertain and perform at all times. In the voice of her detractors, not only does she not deserve her fame as a literary wit, but worse, the woman does not even write her own material.

On the other hand, her public role as the prototype of the Parker type was also her greatest commodity. Characters based on her abound in the books and plays of her friends. In 1934, for instance, Kaufman's stage version of *Merrily We Roll Along* and Charles Brackett's novel *Entirely Surrounded* featured smart-alecky Parker clones (Silverstein 11). If you were a movie producer who wanted characters spouting Parkerisms, it made sense to hire Parker to write them. Her renowned gift for blending schmaltz and sass made her a speedy generator of spoken dialogue, and she was rewarded well for her services—just as guys who knew how to script a good food fight or women who could chart the rise of a beautiful orphan girl were rewarded for theirs.

The Paramount Pictures salary of five thousand dollars a month given to her and husband, Alan Campbell—but mainly to her—made her one of the highest paid screenwriters in Hollywood (Meade 242). Often enlisted to punch up or fix up poor scripts, Parker and Campbell were a potent rewrite team. Married when Dorothy was around forty years old and Alan

Dorothy Parker in 1934. Photofest

was just shy of thirty, they would rack up fifteen screen-writing credits during the first five years of their marriage. From the outside it may have looked as if Campbell was riding on Parker's mink coattails, but the truth was that he did the majority of the work. An actor who wrote short stories good enough to be published in the *New Yorker*, he proved adept at script construction. His job was to build structures to house Dorothy's dialogue. In Campbell, Parker had found a good collaborator.

The pair knew how to handle the bosses as well, a skill Fitzgerald found it hard to master. Writers often dreaded story conferences, where ideas and plot points and scenes that had taken days to come up with and map out were shot down with a few words from a producer. For a writer who felt that the bosses were idiots—a writer such as Fitzgerald—story conferences were often torture. By all reports Parker felt that movie executives were intellectually beneath her, but she did not let it show. She invested her talent in her scripts but, unlike Fitzgerald, not her sense of self. Parker's ego was fragile when it came to her fiction and poetry, but she felt less possessive of her script contributions. She would knit during story conferences, playing the role of pleasant middle-aged lady as Alan pitched their ideas and took notes for rewrites. Still it is hard not to imagine her gritting her teeth and muttering under her breath during her meetings with producers. Beneath her cashmere sweater beat the heart of a leftist radical.

Although she purchased new hats at whim, and she could frequently be found at the ritzy Garden of Allah apartments lounging around the pool with famous old friends Robert Benchley and Alexander Woollcott, Parker did not spend all of her time and money selfishly. Despite her immense financial success—or perhaps because of the guilt associated with it—she lobbied hard to improve the working conditions of less powerful screenwriters. When "Mrs. Parker" spoke, people listened. Her reputation as a famous wit, the label she believed hurt her chances for being regarded as a serious author, made her a powerful organizing voice for the nascent writers union. Although her critics may have seen her as some sort of swimming pool Red or elfin revolutionary, her money and celebrity offered her a platform from which to effect change.

One of the biggest problems the union organizers faced was getting rich and powerful writers, who had the least to gain, to join. Most writers in Parker's income bracket, a very exclusive club, were content to keep a low profile or align themselves publicly with management. In Hollywood writers were often judged (even by other writers) on the basis of their weekly salaries, a factor that served to classify them and, more important to the antiunion studio management, divide them. Budd Schulberg remembers: "You could see it in the commissary—the commissary was fascinating as a sociological study. Where do the $5000 week writers sit? And the $2000 writers? The bit players? The extras?" ("Two Conversations" 117). Salary in Hollywood meant more than how much money you had, it also told you—and those around you—where you stood in your profession.

Parker and West, for example, spent time together with mutual writer friends in New York and were country neighbors in Bucks County, but in the eyes of Hollywood executives they would forever remain acres apart. Parker was famous; her friend West was not. In the minds of studio executives, the reason Parker made more money than West was because she was a better writer; the reason she was a better writer was because she made more money. At Paramount and MGM it was widely believed that the more money you spent on a picture, the better that picture was likely to be and the more money it was likely to make. Why would you hire one $350-a-week writer such as West when you could have three $1,250-a-week writers?

On the other hand, Harry Cohn at Columbia believed that if you worked for him you must not be very good, so he paid guys such as West accordingly. The further down you were in the writing pecking order, the more likely it was that you would be dismissed without prior notice, denied a paycheck, or denied a screen credit. The union wanted to be an advocate for all screenwriters, not just those, like Parker, who would need its protection least. But along the road to reform, the writers union was encountering tenacious opposition from the studios.

In early 1933 carpenters, painters, stagehands, and electricians were among the few unionized studio workers. The rest of Hollywood was an open shop. In the minds of movie producers, allowing manual laborers to join the International Alliance of Theatrical Stage Employees (IATSE) could not weaken the foundations of the studio system. But if writers became unionized, as they had tried to do before in 1927 and 1931, the assembly line could grind to a halt and profits would evaporate. Not only were writers troublesomely intellectual, annoyingly articulate, and dangerously political, but if they were to organize they might be able to gain control of access to screen properties. If screenwriters joined forces with the Dramatists Guild, for example, and a strike was called, source material from Broadway could be held for ransom. In solidarity with other writers, blockades could be put up to stop the flow of novels and short stories into Hollywood as well.

Film producers liked the way things functioned now: screenwriters worked within the walls of corporations, were subject to dismissal at any time and for any reason, did not own their scripts, and had no control over the final product. Unionization might disrupt this imbalance. Besides, the studios argued, there was already a writers' branch in the Academy of Motion Picture Arts and Sciences, the film industry's house union and the sponsor of the Academy Awards. In the minds of writers, however, getting anything done through AMPAS was—in the words many attribute to Parker—"like trying to get laid in your mother's house. Somebody was always in the parlor, watching" (qtd. in Schwartz 13). In March 1933, citing poverty, the studios instituted pay cuts. Writers could not help noticing that the only employees exempt from the cuts were the members of IATSE. On April 8, 1933, the Screen Writers Guild was born. "The writer is the creator of motion pictures!" newly elected president John Howard Lawson bellowed in his acceptance speech. In *The Hollywood Writers'*

Wars, a labor history of the SWG, Nancy Schwartz explains: "One hundred and seventy-three charter members each contributed a hundred-dollar membership fee, with some giving more for their less solvent brethren. . . . the intent of the union, though led by many of these prestigious literary figures [Donald Ogden Stewart, Parker, Dudley Nichols], was really to protect the young, beginning writers" (21, 25).

When salaries were restored a short time later, interest in bolstering the union waned. But a small group of Hollywood writers, most of whom had met back East in the 1920s, kept pressing. They wanted the studios to stop lending out screenwriters without consent. They wanted written notice of termination. They wanted to end the practice of writing on speculation. They wanted fewer hours and higher wages. They wanted notification if other writers were working on the same project simultaneously. They wanted an end to blacklists, such as the one that would appear in 1934 containing the names of writers who refused to "donate" a portion of their salary to Frank Merriam's campaign for governor against Upton Sinclair, the liberal candidate many screenwriters supported. But most important, these writers wanted the guild—not the studios—to decide who would earn screen credit. Money and security were important to these artist-workers, but so were recognition, respect, and acknowledgment.

A few members of the SWG wanted to use the movies, a medium they had once scoffed at as being hopelessly lowbrow, to get radical leftist messages to the masses—despite the insurmountable obstacle that artists in the film industry do not own the means of production. A handful of writers, most notably John Howard Lawson, wanted to use the guild as an offshoot of the Communist Party. But the majority of those in the SWG had the more reasonable goal of forming a professional organization to protect and support the interests of workingmen in general and the Hollywood writer in particular.

The SWG's aims were largely professional and political, but the organization served a social purpose as well. Safe from the eyes and ears of the studios, writers met secretly at each other's homes to plan and talk and eat and drink and commiserate about their writing. The friendships they were developing were genuine, as opposed to the utilitarian friendships anthropologist Hortense Powdermaker found to be the norm in Hollywood. Powdermaker noted that movie workers socialized with either with the people they were currently working with on a specific project or those they wanted something from in the future. You were only as good as your last picture, and moral support was almost nonexistent. If you were having a run of bad luck, whether personal or professional, people stayed away from you for fear of catching it (30). But the SWG and the community of writers it brought together seemed to be an exception. Not every writer in Hollywood wanted to join the SWG, but those that did found in it a spirit of unity. As Schwartz points out: "Apart from the socializing, the move toward unionization gave many writers a sense of commitment and common destiny that they had never before shared. With all the purpose that the 'lost generation' had lacked, the writers had entered the New Deal" (25). The SWG, along with several actors, boycotted the 1934 Academy Awards in protest against the producers' refusal to recognize the union. Such disruptive worker solidarity in the midst of Hollywood's night of self-congratulations infuriated the producers, fueling their determination to crush the guild.

The work these Hollywood writers were doing on behalf of the people in their industry was a local version of the master narrative of the prototypical American writer of the 1930s as charted in Malcolm Cowley's *Exile's Return*. The expatriate aesthete of the 1920s returns home a decade later, contrite and with a new belief that the artist should help his country and its people. Many Depression writers were beginning to realize that the myth of the suffering genius starving for art kept intellectuals at a distance from political, economic, and social concerns.

"Writing to You, a Stranger"

Attempts to bridge this distance between writer and society form the thematic basis for Nathanael West's *Miss Lonelyhearts*. Published in April 1933, the same month the SWG was born, the novel continues the exploration into the laws and limits of the artistic vocation begun in *The Dream Life of Balso Snell*, but it is a much more powerful work than its predecessor. West's savage black humor is present, but so is a new note of empathy, and the result is that we care about the characters in a way we do not in *Balso*. The novel is tight and expertly crafted. Ironically the book is about a writer who cannot find the right words to connect to his readers.

Where West's first novel was concerned with writers in search of an audience, this second novel concerns an audience in search of a writer. The advice columnist Miss Lonelyhearts has no message for those who write to him asking for help. The tales he reads are of illness and lack. With their misspellings and tortured English usage, the newspaper letters show that the suffering of their authors is infinitely greater than their ability to express their inner turmoil. But Miss Lonelyhearts cannot help them. When he tries to construct a cogent response to their pleas, he can only compose in clichés. The cynical writer has been rendered impotent by real feelings.

Miss Lonelyhearts is a writer who has trouble with verbal and written language. In one of the novel's early chapters, he walks through a park toward a speakeasy. West's language in depicting this journey through the wasteland is powerful, evocative, and direct: "the air smelt as though it had been artificially heated"; "mouthfuls of the heavy shade"; "It had taken all the brutality of July to torture a few green spikes through the exhausted dirt." Although West describes airy things—"the gray sky looked as if it had been rubbed with a soiled eraser" and "a newspaper struggled in the air like a kite with a broken spine" (*Novels* 63–64)—the novelist's words remain effective, grounded, and intact.

These vivid metaphors strongly resemble those later used by William Carlos Williams in *Paterson,* published in five volumes from 1946 to 1958. If Williams had used his influence to give a boost to West's writing career, the younger writer had, in turn, started to influence Williams's own writing. This sense of a debt paid had been hinted at in the poet's eulogy for *Contact II.* In fact West's circle of friends all praised this advance in his style. In July 1933 his pals at the journal *Contempo* dedicated an entire issue to discussions of the novel, one hagiography after another attempting to canonize West as a writer other writers should emulate.

West originally conceived of the novel to be "in the form of a comic strip. The chapters to be squares in which many things happen through one action. The speeches contained in the conventional balloons" (*Novels* 401). In this avant-garde book, West borrows from the mass cultural form of the comic strip to examine mass culture itself.

Writing a novel in the form of a comic strip is also his way of announcing that the traditional ways of telling stories—the loose, baggy monsters that are the novels of the eighteenth and nineteenth centuries—are irrelevant to a culture in frenzy. The short chapters of *Miss Lonelyhearts* give the novel a sense of modernist disjunction. The narrative is constantly being cut into sections. The action is always forced into a new panel. Like Parker's waltzer, "enclosed in a circle of her own words" (Treichler 53), the confining "balloons" West creates are language traps for his characters, preventing any clear message from being delivered.

When Miss Lonelyhearts tries to speak to his fiancée, Betty, his tongue becomes a "fat thumb" (*Novels* 71). At every attempt to respond verbally to the world or its inhabitants, the writer finds that "no repeated words would fit their rhythm" (70). He finds that often when he opens his mouth, the words that come out are Shrike's, his editor and surrogate father. Later at the home of the Doyles, a couple who has written to him for help, the newspaperman is awkwardly silent because "when he did speak it would have to be in the form of a message" (114). But the message never comes to his lips. He does not have his minister father's gift of rhetoric, and his "Christ complex," his longing to be the Word made flesh, makes him aware of this void. Miss Lonelyhearts, the college-educated writer and "priest of our time," hears the cries of the faceless masses but can do nothing to hush them. His frequent silences and multiple retreats to the womb of his bed signal a desire to return to an infant state, a time before language.

Although the women of the novel try to "baby" him, they cannot successfully return Miss Lonelyhearts to a sense of wholeness. He grows frustrated with Betty's maternal complacency and his own inability to settle for her narrow view of the world. Betty is a movie stock character, the wholesome girl who will teach the cynical hero how to love. But Miss Lonelyhearts is beyond reformation. He sadistically tugs at her breast before leaving her in tears. Our hero returns to the speakeasy and listens to stories of women writers being violently gang-raped. These tales are told by newspaper men who once "had believed in literature, had believed in Beauty and in personal expression as an absolute end. When they lost this belief, they lost everything" (74–75). Here, as in the previous scene with Betty and in a later scene with Fay Doyle, as well as examples strewn throughout *Balso,* male writers who cannot master words take out their frustration through violence against women, lashing out at an American mass culture that is coded as both feminine and inferior.

The men who write for the newspaper have come to realize that a belief in art, truth, and beauty is useless in a world where young girls are born without noses and husbands try to murder their wives by scaring them to death. Where can hope or escape be found? Hunchbacked women pick romance magazines out of the garbage and spend their last nickels on movie tickets, but Miss Lonelyhearts discovers that "although dreams were once powerful, they have been made puerile by the movies, radio and newspapers" (103). Whether mass culture responds to our dreams or feeds them to us, the result in West's world is the same—disappointment and disillusionment. And as Shrike's mockery of Miss Lonelyhearts's dreams of the aesthetic life (Huysmans-like feasts of licorice and black coffee and painting noble savages on remote islands) makes clear, high culture has already been played out, too.

But as with *The Dream Life of Balso Snell,* West's recognition of the impossibility of the concept of "high culture" remaining unsullied did not necessarily stand in the way of his literary aspirations. In fact he complained to friends that Horace Liveright, publisher of *Miss Lonelyhearts,*

West during his first trip to Hollywood.
Photograph courtesy of Jay Martin

wanted to "advertise the book on a very low level, not as serious literature but as a smutty expose of the columnist racket" (*Novels* 778). As it
turned out, marketing strategies would be the least of West's woes. *Miss
Lonelyhearts* was a victim of the type of rotten luck that befalls its title
character. Liveright declared bankruptcy as the book was being published;
the printing company refused to release 1,400 copies that had not yet
shipped. The novel received good reviews, but there was no product in the
stores to capitalize on them. Harcourt, Brace soon managed to buy the
rights to publish the novel, but by the time they got *Miss Lonelyhearts*
back on the market in June, the buzz had stopped.

While the publication of *Miss Lonelyhearts* had not allowed West to
support himself as a writer, it had brought him to the attention of the studios. The film rights to the novel were sold to Fox, and in late June 1933,
Sam Goldwyn contacted West about working on a script for the Russian
actress Anna Sten, Goldwyn's beautiful, English-challenged mistress. The
Sten project was dropped before any real work was done, but West settled
in Los Angeles anyway and accepted an offer to work at Columbia Pictures in July. Columbia, like Universal, was a "major minor"—a studio

that specialized in providing the richer companies in the oligopoly with B movies for the bottom of double bills. It was not the most prestigious studio in town, but West was nonetheless happy to be there. The $350 a week Harry Cohn paid him at Columbia was big money for the Depression. It was more than West's old $60-a-week salary at the Sutton Hotel, and it was certainly more than he was making as a fiction writer.

However, for any pals back East who still might be under the mistaken assumption that screen writing was a soft racket, and that a smart writer could fake his way through it, West filed this dispatch: "This stuff about easy work is all wrong. My hours are from ten in the morning to six at night, with a full day on Saturday. They gave me a job to do five minutes after I sat down in my office—a scenario about a beauty parlor—and I'm expected to turn out pages and pages a day. There's no fooling here. All the writers sit in cells in a row and the minute a typewriter stops someone pokes his head in the door to see if you are thinking. Otherwise, it's like the hotel business" (qtd. in Martin 205).

West's letter, written shortly before he joined the SWG, demonstrates how the studios often threw writers into screen-writing assignments without giving them any training in film grammar or, as Parker had found out in the 1920s, any real instruction on what exactly it was they were supposed to be doing. Management expected writers to teach themselves to work their part of the studio assembly line and to routinize their own creative process, a difficult task for many used to the world of publishing. In *Books: From Writer to Reader*, Howard Greenfeld writes: "There are no regular routines, as in an office, and it's impossible to order a writer to work a certain number of hours per day or per week and expect that author to obey" (3).

Here, though, West had a slight advantage over some of his screenwriter colleagues. Working an office job in "the hotel business" had taught him to be able to follow a daily routine, and composing his novels while manning the desk had given him the ability to write with people around. After West finished the scenario for the beauty-parlor picture he mentioned, titled "Beauty Parlor," he quickly produced a "treatment" (a detailed scene-by-scene breakdown of the plot). The studio accepted it and told him to begin drafting the screenplay. It looked like West's film career was off to a good, fast start—but Columbia aborted the project. He then went to work on an original story for the screen titled "Return to the Soil," but the studio let that one languish, too. When Columbia let him go in late August, West stuck around Hollywood anyway. He no longer had someone to come home to. His fiancée, Alice Shepard, had broken off their engagement in

1933 after she learned that "West had spent the night with Lillian Hellman" (*Novels* 808). Another reason for West to stay west was to see how the movie version of *Miss Lonelyhearts* was turning out.

Twentieth Century's head of production, Darryl Zanuck, who had begun his career in the 1920s as a writer (most notably for pictures starring the dog Rin Tin Tin), had bought the movie rights to the book for four thousand dollars, but no one is really sure why. Because of the publishing snafu with Liveright, the novel had sold poorly, so there would be little (or no) audience awaiting its adaptation. Like Faulkner's *Sanctuary*, made into a movie in 1933 and advertised with cheesecake shots of Miriam Hopkins lounging on a bed of corncobs similar to the one Popeye rapes Temple Drake with, West's novel had somewhat of a reputation for being dirty in an artsy way, but it is unlikely the studio bought it for this reason. Jonathan Veitch speculates that Zanuck wanted the property for its title or to capitalize on a cycle of newspaper movies (76–77). Zanuck biographer George Custen believes that the novel's good reviews, coupled with West's obscurity, made for a prestigious, affordable film prospect for a young studio on the rise.

The film made from *Miss Lonelyhearts*, released under the title *Advice to the Lovelorn*, has virtually no connection to its source. A novel depicting a journalist's impotence in the face of mass suffering emerges from the film factory as a peppy love story of one fellow's redemption. The movie received dismissive reviews and did not fill many seats. But West had still come out ahead. He had his foot in the door at the studios, and the four thousand dollars he'd received for the film rights to his novel far exceeded his royalties for the novel's dismissal sales.

Besides money, *Miss Lonelyhearts* had also gained West some new fans—one of whom was Scott Fitzgerald. Although Fitzgerald's motives in helping struggling new novelists such as West were undoubtedly genuine, as was his support of established authors such as Dorothy Parker, the complaints of reviewer silence he makes in his 1934 *Gatsby* preface in defense of West are also meant to complain about the indifference shown to his own work. If he was too popular in the 1920s for highbrow critics to take him seriously, in the 1930s he was too irrelevant for Marxist critics to take him seriously. Fitzgerald felt like a forgotten man. His article "Auction: Model 1934" equates glamorous objects from his and Zelda's high life in the 1920s with ancient relics stripped of their value. There is no market for these things now. No one wants them (*Crack-Up* 56–62). Fame can expire quickly, and in the 1930s Fitzgerald was having trouble renewing his contract with the public.

Besides a fellow neglected talent, Fitzgerald may have also seen a disciple in West. Many thematic, stylistic, and dramatic similarities exist between *Miss Lonelyhearts* and *The Great Gatsby*. Both books blend vulgar speech and dialect, poetic description, and passages of dark comedy. Both books depict New York City as a wasteland populated by grotesques and love triangles. Gatsby and Miss Lonelyhearts are both gunned down by "impotent" men. In the novels of both authors, love is essentially yearning and frustration. For both authors America is defined by its cities.

Praising *Miss Lonelyhearts,* a new book, in the Modern Library preface to *Gatsby,* an older book, might have been a way for Fitzgerald to prove to himself that his creative vision and critical judgment still mattered to younger writers and readers. Priced at an affordable ninety-five cents apiece and aimed at a middlebrow audience, the Modern Library series canonized and commodified modernist literature by publishing it amid a list peppered with classics. Inclusion in the series was an acknowledgment that *The Great Gatsby* was a "modern classic," but it also called attention to the fact that Fitzgerald still had not published another novel since.

Whatever Fitzgerald's motives for wanting to help West, a man he had never met, a letter he received shortly after the *Gatsby* preface appeared would test how far he was willing to go with his support. Dated September 11, 1934, it began: "You have been kind enough to say you liked my novel, 'Miss Lonelyhearts.' I am applying for a Guggenheim Fellowship and I need references for it. I wonder if you would be willing to let me use your name as a reference? It would be enormously valuable to me. I am writing to you, a stranger, because I know very few people, almost none whose names would mean anything to the committee, and apparently the references are the most important part of the application" (*Correspondence* 384).

Like the letter writers of *Miss Lonelyhearts,* West had been reduced to contacting a stranger for help. The mean-spirited, unfunny Horatio Alger parody *A Cool Million,* published in June 1934 by the small press of Covici-Friede, had sold poorly, and the reviews, unlike most of those for *Miss Lonelyhearts,* were negative. West tried to tell friends that he had written the book as an inside joke to them and never intended for it to be a commercial property, but his aspirations to be a successful novelist—to live by his writing for a prolonged period of time and produce books the public would buy—makes this hard to believe. As he wrote to Edmund Wilson in the mid-1930s, "I want to write. Why I don't know, but I do" (*Novels* 780). Yet after three novels he had made only $780 in book royalties.

West was not having much success with other genres, either. His agent, Max Leiber, could not place his short stories with the big magazines, and a play he was working on with S. J. Perelman, a satire on the publicity given to a woman writer who confuses her fiction with real life, could not find any backers. Columbia Pictures had bought the rights to *A Cool Million* when it was in galleys (Veitch 105), getting West some cash at a time when he needed it, but no one believed the film would ever get made. It was common practice for the studios to buy properties to avoid other studios scooping them. By warehousing source material, the studios assured themselves of always having projects ready to go in case of strikes, difficulties in finding the right vehicle for a particular star, or sudden upswings in the value of a particular writer's oeuvre. Many of the works the studios bought were not turned into treatments, many of these treatments were not turned into screenplays, and many of the screenplays were not turned into movies. Jay Martin writes: "Even though West kept up his membership in the Screen Writers Guild all through 1934, no Hollywood offer was prompted by the purchase of another unproducible novel" (245).

By applying for a Guggenheim, and badly needing to get one, West was asking for help from the same type of institutions he had skewered in "The Impostor." Fitzgerald was happy to write West the recommendation, but as in the *Gatsby* preface, his letter in support of West's grant application avails itself of the opportunity to take the literary establishment to task: "I have sometimes felt that you have put especial emphasis on poetry while I think that the most living literary form in America at the moment is prose fiction. In my opinion, Nathanael West is a potential leader in the field of prose fiction." Fitzgerald, who feared that he "had been only a mediocre caretaker" of his talent (*Crack-Up* 71), ends the letter with a flippant salute "to the custodians of the great idea" (*Correspondence* 385). Despite the recommendations of Malcolm Cowley, George S. Kaufman, Edmund Wilson, and Fitzgerald—the "most important part of the application"—West did not get the Guggenheim.

The Sweat behind the Spectacle

The novels that West and Fitzgerald were publishing in the mid-1930s did not mesh with a writing climate that was drifting farther and farther left. In a move Michael Denning traces in *The Cultural Front*, critics were calling on authors to publish books that would advance worker's causes. Writers were no longer religious keepers of a flame, "custodians of the great idea," but citizens necessary to American society. West and Fitzgerald were not heeding this proletarian call in their fiction. They were artists before activists, neutral observers rather than partisans. West believed that there ought to be a place for the writer "who yells fire and indicates where some of the smoke is coming from without actually dragging the hose to the spot" (qtd. in Martin 336). Fitzgerald, also a believer in aesthetic distance, claimed that the mark of a first-rate creative intelligence was "the ability to hold two opposed ideas in the mind at the same time, and still retain the ability to function" (*Crack-Up* 69). Like West he had no interest in writing tracts. Like West, and like Parker, he liked money.

Brian Way believes that Fitzgerald took from schools of thought such as Marxism "only what he could use as an artist: a more dramatic sense of economic relations and historical change; fresh metaphors of disaster; a confirmation and toughening of his own observation of manners" (148). In "Fitzgerald's Consumer World," Kirk Curnutt comes closer to identifying Fitzgerald's finely honed double consciousness when it came to capitalism. He writes: "As a topic of literary exploration, the booming marketplace elicited the best in Fitzgerald: its variegated styles and colors invited him to capture the plush and dazzle of its products, while the change in values it engineered incited his instinct to editorialize" (123). Fitzgerald held on long and tight to the idea of the writer inhabiting a world apart.

Both West and Fitzgerald took heat from reviewers on the 1930s left for being self-indulgent. One reviewer of *Tender Is the Night* warned Fitzgerald that the revolution was coming, and when it did he would not be able to "hide from a hurricane under a beach umbrella" (Scribner xii). Marxist critics believed that Fitzgerald wrote about pretty people in a pretty style. Even though many came to see that the novel indicts the rich, not celebrates them, Fitzgerald was still considered far too interested in the inner lives of the wealthy, the glamorous, and the famous—a privileged class of Americans. West was concentrating on the right segment of the population, his *Miss Lonelyhearts* had probed the suffering of the common man, but it was wrapped in a modernist package the common man could not open. Plagiarized in large chunks from Horatio Alger for satiric purposes, *A Cool Million* was a dressing down of the American dream that some reviewers misread as ultimately a celebration of fascism. After its hero, Lemuel Pitkin, is killed by Communist spies, he becomes a martyr for a right-wing uprising, led by former president Shagpoke Whipple, bent on saving the population from sophisticates, cosmopolites, unions, Jews, and Marxists.

No one is spared from West's satire, not even himself. In West the villain is not capitalism running amok, it is the human race. Too pessimistic, goofy, and iconoclastic to be a good lefty, West pokes fun at radical writers and the manifestos they write. The character Sylvanus Snodgrass in

A Cool Million is a frustrated writer who turns to terrorism to compensate for his lack of talent. Because his overblown allegories about bad capitalists have failed to find a public, he has decided to make the public pay. When he lost faith in himself, he made it his mission to undermine the country's faith as well. Snodgrasse's desire for anarchic revenge is cloaked in Communism, just as Shagpoke Whipple's fascist will-to-power is masked by folksy rhetoric. West's politics in the book are neutral, if neutral can mean hating both sides equally. While he aimed to skewer materialism, he wanted the book to make money. Just as *Balso* was a book written as a protest against the writing of books, *Cool* attacks the marketplace and tries to benefit from it.

Fitzgerald's *Tender Is the Night* is also a materially conflicted book. Like *A Cool Million,* it is more influenced by Oswald Spengler's ideas of a once-great civilization breaking down than it is by Karl Marx's ideas of class consciousness. Fitzgerald glamorizes the Riviera lifestyle, but he also shows a growing awareness, aided by his tours in the Hollywood dream factory, of those who work hard so that others can enjoy a life of leisure. There is sweat behind every spectacle. In the most memorable passage from the novel, Fitzgerald writes:

> Nicole was the product of much ingenuity and toil. For her sake trains began their run in Chicago and traversed the round belly of the continent to California; chicle factories fumed and link belts grew link by link in factories; men mixed toothpaste in vats and drew mouthwash out of copper hogsheads; girls canned tomatoes quickly in August or worked rudely at the Five-and-Tens on Christmas Eve; half-breed Indians toiled on Brazilian coffee plantations and dreamers were muscled out of patent rights in new tractors—these were some of the people who gave a tithe to Nicole. . . . She illustrated very simple principles, containing in herself her own doom, but illustrated them so accurately that there was grace in the procedure, and presently Rosemary would try and imitate it. (54)

Although the work done to produce enough commodities to allow Nicole to play the role of cool, graceful socialite is very real, Nicole herself is struggling to maintain a facade of sanity. Rosemary, an actress, might find it easy to imitate her. But much like the cast of writer/performers in West's *Balso,* it would be an imitation of an imitation.

If West, Fitzgerald, and Parker were choosing not to engage economic struggle directly in their fiction, even though they were succeeding in doing so in their lives as professionals, they were continuing to look at the work that goes behind the construction of artifice. In her introduction to Parker's *Complete Stories,* Gina Barreca writes: "The gap between how life is dressed up to appear and what it looks like underneath its fancy trimmings is the gap where interesting writing begins" (xiii). For this reason it is only natural that these authors would begin to drift thematically toward the movies. Their professional contact with Hollywood had put them face-to-face with real models of such artifice—actors.

Screenwriters created dialogue for stars who resided far above them in the studio hierarchy and were often beloved, famous, and rich—all the things Freud said writers dreamed of being. It is tempting to read the actor characters in fiction written by screenwriters as a form of "author's revenge," the same way the Hollywood novels themselves are sometimes read. But if we look more closely at the performer characters created by Parker, Fitzgerald, and West, we see these writers further exploring the questions of art and the function of the artist that had appeared in their work since the beginning of their careers.

There is a long tradition of characters who are other kinds of artists standing in for writers. Parker's "Glory in the Daytime," West's "The Sun, the Radio, and the Gas Station Attendant" and *A Cool Million,* and Fitzgerald's *Tender Is the Night* all contain portrayals of actors. At a time when their creators were struggling with identity issues of vocation and professional matters of career direction, these performer characters are equated with masquerade, decrepitude, and failure. They are products of the worlds they walk through, American mass-culture spaces where the artificial has replaced the genuine, where surface is more important than substance, where everything is expendable.

A Cool Million sets up a visit to a mock 1933 Chicago World's Fair that features a "Chamber of American Horrors: Animate and Inanimate." West writes: "The hall which led to the main room of the 'inanimate' exhibit was lined with sculptures in plaster. Among the most striking of these was a Venus de Milo with a clock in her abdomen, a copy of Powers' 'Greek Slave' with elastic bandages on all her joints, a Hercules wearing a small, compact truss" (*Novels* 223). History is represented as something broken, wounded, traumatized. The animate part of the exhibit continues in this vein. It features a theatrical revue titled "The Pageant of America or A Curse on Columbus," which consists of "a series of short sketches in which Quakers were shown being branded, Indians brutalized and cheated, negroes sold, children sweated to death" (223). Instead of a unified, triumphalist American narrative, we get a choppy, traumatic one. Such events do not fit neatly into America's story.

The novel's subtitle is "The Dismantling of Lemuel Pitkin," denoting that its protagonist will be gradually and systematically torn apart in some way. But you can only dismantle something that has already been built of separate parts. The novel configures the self—body, soul, and mind—as something constructed and artificial rather than unified, metaphysical, or even organic. The one-noted Lem is not really a character at all; he is an innocent straw man to be burned, shredded, knocked unconscious, and stuffed. When he winds up as a stooge in vaudeville, his onstage partners beat him with his own artificial limbs. The actress in West's "The Sun, the Radio, and the Gas Station Attendant" suffers a similar unraveling. Her surgically altered face literally melts off in the daylight.

The crumbling facade of Lily Wynton, "the great lady of our stage" (*Complete Stories* 218), in Parker's "Glory in the Daytime" is more metaphoric but equally as devastating to her audience. Many of Parker's stories, as in "The Waltz" and "Big Blonde," are about women performing an overly accommodating public self. In "Glory in the Daytime," the gentlewoman actress Wynton publicly reveals herself as a raving, needy alcoholic. She refuses to believe that Mrs. Murdoch, a fan who has come to tea, is not a writer, and she implores the housewife to write her a play that will insure that she "will never be forgotten, because of the years I played in your beautiful, beautiful play" (224).

Performers such as actors and symphony members engage in creative activities that rise and fall on their ability to interpret lines and musical notes already committed to paper. Playwrights and composers, on the other hand, engage in creative activities that test their ability to be innovative, to put something new on the paper. Wynton may be correct that art is long and theater fame is short, that a play sticks around forever while a performance in that play does not, but she is mistaken in her belief that writing is soothing. With her talk of the "peace" and "quiet" and "rest" afforded by authorship, she seems to think that writing is a calming, rhythmic, solitary hobby—like knitting or flower arranging. The pressure of the loving public, her fame, and the accolades of the critics are all too much for Lily to bear. When the grande dame drinks herself unconscious, Mrs. Murdoch returns home forlorn, disillusioned at the reality behind her favorite artist.

Tender Is the Night provides still another unmasking of the presentation of self and the illusion of wholeness. Dick Diver's need to be the center of attention and have people adore him contributes to his downfall. His lecture to his friends on World War I, full of modernist despair of a once-whole civilization now hopelessly broken, ends with the following exchange:

> "All my beautiful lovely safe world blew itself up here with a great gust of high explosive love," Dick mourned persistently. "Isn't that true, Rosemary?"
>
> "I don't know," she answered with a grave face. "You know everything." (56–57)

Like the writer and "priest of our time" Miss Lonelyhearts, the psychiatrist/author Dick is a subject presumed to know. Jeffrey Berman writes: "Fitzgerald shared in the myth of the psychiatrist as modern magician . . . invested with the omniscience and omnipotence of a Godlike healer" (66–68). When the actress Rosemary first sees him, he is performing for the glamorous group of his expatriate friends. "Oh we're such actors — you and I" (*Tender* 105), she says to him before they sleep together, and in a later scene he instructs this professional actress that a performer's first duty is to entertain, not to inspire thought or emotion. The star is drawn to his aura of success and confidence.

Linking the fictional worlds of *Tender Is the Night* and *The Beautiful and Damned,* Rosemary is under contract to Films Par Excellence, Joseph Bloeckman's studio. Although Dick considers himself a serious medical scientist, Rosemary urges him toward a career before the camera. He drifts further away from the masculine realm of reason and intellect and toward the feminized consumer world of popular culture. But after an unsuccessful screen test, a tour of a studio backlot containing a cardboard Moby Dick and other discarded objects, an affair with Rosemary in which neither of them turns out to be what they appear to be, and a breakdown in his ability to manage Nicole's presentation of self, he can no longer keep up the act of a man in total control.

A jet-setting psychiatrist—and would-be movie star—Dick is also a published author. He starts out writing pamphlets, which form the basis for his *A Psychology for Psychiatrists,* a successful psychology textbook / self-help manual. His mentor, sounding like Wilson warning Fitzgerald not to become too trashy or too popular, tells him: "I do not like these generalities. Soon you will be writing little books called 'Deep Thoughts for the Layman,' so simplified they are positively guaranteed not to cause thinking" (137).

Diver wants to be more than a pretty-boy pill pusher. His second manuscript is much more ambitious, so much so that Fitzgerald playfully gives us the working title in both English and German. The English will suffice here: "An Attempt at a Uniform and Pragmatic Classification of the Neuroses and Psychoses, Based on an Examination of Fifteen Hundred Pre-Krapaelin and Post-Krapaelin Cases as they would be Diagnosed in the Terminology of the Different Contemporary Schools, Together with a Chronology of Such Subdivisions of Opinion as Have Arisen Independently" (144). This "monumental" tome is his attempt to be taken more seriously by his peers. It is a hubristic stab at knowing everything and becoming the greatest psychiatrist who ever lived. His fellow expatriate, the audience-pleasing, middlebrow author McKisco, another version of the Caramel character, gets little respect in the literary world, and Diver wants to avoid similar, patronizing snickers from his own colleagues.

But the manuscript remains forever unfinished, always "almost in process of completion" (312), and the European psychiatrists Dick admires scoff at his American arrogance for wanting to dominate the field. Fellow doctor Franz "never after believed that Dick was a serious person. And as time went on he convinced himself that he had never thought so" (240). In Dick's quest to have it both ways—celebrity and gravity, freedom and discipline, easy living and hard work—his reputation suffers, and he fades into obscurity, a forgotten man, a victim of his own vanity and self-delusion. The last novel Fitzgerald would ever complete, one into which he had poured a large part of himself over the course of nine years, ends with a fading snapshot of a failed writer who could not control his wife's mental health.

The autobiographical elements are unmistakable. But Fitzgerald, unlike Dick, finished his big, ambitious book—this one. Furthermore, if the novel appears to condemn entertainment culture and assign pandering authors to the dustbin of history, a look at the film adaptation of *Tender Is the Night* that Fitzgerald tried to get Hollywood interested in adds another layer to the picture. In the mid-1930s he was in debt, had domestic troubles, and was worried about his artistic legacy. But he was not done as a writer, and he was not done exploring markets for his writing. As he wrote to Mencken: "I've got to go to New York about trying to capitalize on my novel in the movies" (*FSF: A Life in Letters* 255). Fitzgerald's *Tender* film-script ends quite differently than the novel—with Dick heroically performing brain surgery on Nicole and making her sane again. It is the type of Hollywood ending, with everyone behaving heroically and getting exactly what they want, that the novel had shown to be inauthentic.

Although *Tender* is a thematically cinematic novel, in that a large part of it concerns the film industry, it is more a psychological novel than a dramatic one, and the attempts to translate it for another medium make for strange reading. In the treatment written by Fitzgerald and Charles Warren, reprinted in the appendix to Bruccoli's *Some Sort of Epic Grandeur,* Nicole's insanity results from a bump on the head, not incest (which the Production Code would never have allowed anyway) or mental illness. Warren, an amateur composer, even wrote some songs for the film they were pitching. Warren then went to Hollywood to bring the treatment door-to-door, reporting back to Fitzgerald that "your name is big and hellishly well known in the studios. You rate out here as a highbrow writer, a thoroughbred novelist and not a talkie hack and therefore these people look up to you" (qtd. in Turnbull 248). Surprised he was held in such high esteem, Fitzgerald wrote to Hollywood players such as Sam Marx and George Cukor to try and get them attached to his film version of *Tender Is the Night,* and he once called Thalberg's house drunk to see if Norma Shearer wanted to play Nicole, but Ober eventually told him to stop bothering people, and the project never got off the ground (*Correspondence* 333, 364; Latham 84, 92).

In the mid-1930s Fitzgerald's drinking was increasing, and so was the frequency of Zelda's breakdowns. Taking care of her and supporting her writing (and dancing and painting) were taking a toll on him. He wrote to her doctor in 1934 that his work "was more important than hers by a large margin, because of the years of preparation for it, and the professional experience, and because my writing kept the mare going, while Zelda's belongs to the luxury trade" (*Correspondence* 381). With him paying the bills, Fitzgerald implies, Zelda could afford to indulge her fantasies of the artistic genius whose work is unsullied by market pressures. The professional author had concentrated too hard on the work of a dilettante amateur, and it had contributed to what Fitzgerald saw as his own vocational nosedive.

As his support of other writers shows, Fitzgerald had an immense capacity for largesse, but he had an even larger capacity for self-pity. He would use his feelings of failure as the catalyst for some of his most honest and powerful work. In 1934 he began writing for *Esquire* magazine, which paid $250 per piece. That was less than the $1,000 and more that the *Saturday Evening Post* used to pay, but the essays and stories he would publish in *Esquire,* many about Hollywood, would be some of the finest of his career. In the December 1934 essay "Sleeping and Waking" he is in the clutches of insomnia, tormented by thoughts of "horror and waste— Waste and horror—what I might have been and done that is lost, spent, gone, dissipated, unrecapturable" (*Crack-Up* 67). In such essays Fitzgerald appears to be tying his own depression to the nation's, making the pieces not only autobiographical confessionals but cultural critiques. Hemingway, who usually took pleasure in seeing a friend down, tried to make him snap out of his introspective funk. "You're not a tragic character," he wrote. "Neither am I. All we are is writers and what we should do is write. . . . You are twice as good now as you were at the time you think you were so marvellous" (qtd. in Mizener 260).

4

Producer's Blood

**HOLLYWOOD
TAKES ON
HOLLYWOOD
IN 1937**

Since I had been brought up in the place, I had no illusions about it. I had learned from intelligent producers, like Irving Thalberg, David Selznick, and my own father, that even the wisest of them looked upon the screenwriter as low man on the totem pole.

Budd Schulberg, *Writers in America:
The Four Seasons of Success*

Oh, Joe, can't producers ever be wrong? I'm a good writer—honest.

F. Scott Fitzgerald to Joseph Mankiewicz

Basically the problem of all writers is the same, and always has been. It consists invariably of a struggle between the writer and businessmen, who seek to exploit that which the writer creates for monetary gain. And when, as so often happens, these businessmen gather together, as it were, into combines and corporations, then the individual writer is as helpless against them as a babe in arms.

SWG president Ernest Pascal, "One
Organization for All American Writers"

❧

In 1937 Dorothy Parker, Budd Schulberg, F. Scott Fitzgerald, and Nathanael West were all living in California and were all employed as screenwriters, working under the management of film producers. With greater literary reputations, Parker and Fitzgerald commanded higher weekly salaries than their two younger colleagues, but neither of these famous writers did any significant literary work during this year. Parker was battling fascism, the studio bosses, and corporate capitalism; Fitzgerald was battling alcoholism, the studio bosses, and self-doubt. West and Schulberg, on the other hand, were finding the time, energy, and inspiration to create prose fiction during their off-hours from screen writing. In addition to composing *for* Hollywood in 1937, all four authors were composing *about* Hollywood. West had finished a first draft of a film industry novel, and Fitzgerald was slowly taking notes toward one.

Two Hollywood-on-Hollywood projects that did enter the market in 1937, the film *A Star Is Born* and the short story "What Makes Sammy Run?," offer insider perspectives into what the film industry thinks about when it thinks about itself. *A Star Is Born,* whose script includes contributions by Parker and Schulberg, is a movie about a movie, a self-reflexive work. Schulberg's "Sammy" story, which he would later expand into a novel, draws upon its author's background as a Hollywood prince turned junior screenwriter. The piece is insider's literature written from an outsider's point of view. A New York City journalist who becomes a Los Angeles screenwriter narrates the lives and labor practices of those working in Hollywood. Like *A Star Is Born,* "Sammy" introduces us to workers in Hollywood and examines the effort that goes into creating films that look effortless. Its longer version, *What Makes Sammy Run?,* would even devote several chapters toward dramatizing the internal strife within the Screen Writers Guild circa 1937, struggles for power and authority that Schulberg, Parker, and West witnessed from the front lines.

By the mid-1930s support for the SWG had grown, but the writers and the studios were still far apart from an agreement. To gain leverage with the producers, Hollywood screenwriters had decided to form an alliance with the existing writers' guilds on the East Coast. In the summer of 1935, the leadership of SWG, the Authors' League of America, and the Dramatists Guild had met in Los Angeles. Combined, they represented the majority of professional writers in America. It was agreed that if the screenwriters went on strike, the other guilds would refuse to sell any works to Hollywood. The studios viewed this tactical maneuver, which would have ground production to a halt, as an evil plot by the New York guilds. Fox's Darryl Zanuck complained that such writers "hate moving pictures and hate Hollywood and make fun of it" (qtd. in Schwartz 60). This battle clearly foregrounded the issue of eastern condescension toward the movies—and by extension toward movie producers—perceived or otherwise, but it also demonstrates that without stories as sources and blueprints—indeed, without writers—there can be no narrative film and therefore no Hollywood. This was the stuff of movie mogul nightmares, and they would use all their power to retain control.

Individual writers were powerless against large corporations, but by banding together they stood a fighting chance. Some of the more conservative, more highly paid, more promanagement screenwriters took some convincing to join the SWG, but in the end the 1936 vote to amalgamate the unions was unanimous. Parker, Dudley Nichols, and some of the other leftists resigned from the SWG board to make room for newly elected members that included James Kevin McGuiness and Morrie Ryskind, both of whom had originally been opposed to the guild.

But only days later, the illusion of unity crumbled when sixty members announced that they were defecting to form their own union, Screen Playwrights. The new group declared their opposition to the idea of a closed shop and denounced SWG as a radical outfit controlled by communists. Within a mere week, more than one hundred members would leave for Screen Playwrights, baited by studio offers of lucrative long-term contracts. Pro-studio screenwriters, working in collusion with producers, had pulled off a ruse of being union sympathizers and had undermined the SWG. By the summer of 1936, the SWG had lost almost all of its members, with the exception of a fervent core of writers, including Parker and West (Meade 277; Martin 275). For fear of studio reprisals, meetings were held in secret.

In April 1937 the SWG received new life when the Supreme Court declared the Wagner Act constitutional, which meant that collective bargaining was necessary and that house unions, such as the Screen Playwrights, were forbidden. The newly reorganized SWG had its first open meeting June 11, 1937, and more than four hundred writers attended. Nichols was elected the new president. Yet the war between the right-wing Screen Playwrights and the left-wing SWG continued. The Screen Playwrights were now claiming that writers were artists, not workers, and therefore not eligible to unionize under the Wagner Act. To those writers who felt that they had been invited to Hollywood because of their individual creativity only to be punished for it within the studio system, this unfruitful line of reasoning must have seemed like the height of irony. The Screen Playwrights' argument ignored the fact that artists have control over the final product, whereas contracted workers—such as screenwriters—seldom do.

Even so, Hollywood provided Fitzgerald, West, Parker, and Schulberg with a living in 1937; in turn they provided Hollywood with scripts for the assembly line, some of which proved to be the blueprints for good films.

Hollywood allowed these authors to keep working on their fiction, enhanced their support of each other, and gave them ideas to write about and new ways to write about them. In short the American movie industry allowed them to continue being professional writers, despite the fact that it refused to recognize the SWG as a professional organization.

The Prince and the Producer: Schulberg and "What Makes Sammy Run?"

In *What Happens Next: A History of American Screenwriting*, Marc Norman parses two phrases from studio-era contracts that appeared in no other Hollywood artist's agreement of the time. "The first was: 'the studio, hereinafter referred to as the author.' . . . A screenwriter's output under a studio contract—here's the second phrase—was a 'work for hire,' meaning piecework, performed for a salary, the same as electricians and stage carpenters. A Hollywood writer's creations no more belonged to him or her than the Renaissance set standing on Stage 10 belonged to the men who hammered it together. With screenwriters squeezed between the jaws of those two phrases, the moguls could sleep easily; screenwriters not only did not own what they wrote but, strictly speaking, they did not even write it" (133).

One of the key issues the SWG wanted control over was the awarding of writing credits. Although by all accounts Budd Schulberg made significant contributions to *A Star Is Born* (Ames 28; Fine 110; Schatz 184; Thomson 218), he received no screen credit from producer David O. Selznick for his participation. Once his draft was submitted, he was quickly shuffled to another Selznick project, the 1937 comedy *Nothing Sacred* (Beck 7). His name does not appear on that film either. Another screenwriter might have thrown a fit, but it did not worry Schulberg much.

Because he was born into the movies, Schulberg seems to have understood atavistically some of the particulars about film writing that took other authors years to realize. At seventeen he had worked as a publicist at Paramount, churning out semifictional narratives about the early lives of the stars. After graduating from Dartmouth in 1936, he had taken a job with Selznick, a family friend. After a short time as a reader of scripts, he had been promoted to junior screenwriter and assigned to *A Star Is Born*. But he never expected any creative control.

Film was a visual medium, and it was a producer's medium. Working hard on scripts was admirable, but becoming cathected to them and crying over the films made from them was unwise. More screen credits meant more money, but they never meant that the movies belonged to you. In the final analysis, the corporate screenwriter under the Hollywood studio system was more of an adviser than a creator. Unlike the poet or novelist or dramatist, the screenwriter usually did not start typing because he had something to say. He usually started typing because a book or play needed to be adapted for the silver screen or because the bosses wanted to copy a recent successful film. The front office hired screenwriters to provide creative options; it did not hire them to make creative decisions. Schulberg grew up knowing that the screenwriter was more of a craftsman than an artist, more of a carpenter than an architect. Scripts were not written in Hollywood; they were assembled. With so many writers behind each film, Schulberg once said, "it was like laying linoleum, different people working on different little squares" (qtd. in Fine 117–18).

Schulberg was given twenty-five dollars a week to add his patches to the *A Star Is Born* quilt. Pleased with his work on the film, Selznick bumped him up to fifty dollars a week. By paying him a junior writer's salary and making him pay his dues, Selznick thought he was grooming his young employee to be a producer. Selznick had been B. P. Schulberg's assistant at Paramount, and he assumed the dynasty would continue with the young Schulberg working for him, and his own son eventually working for Schulberg.

But in 1937 Schulberg's primary interest was not the movies. Like Fitzgerald, West, and Parker, he wanted to publish fiction. When Schulberg reminded Selznick of this, his disappointed boss responded by saying: "I know. . . . But I felt that if I kept you with me long enough sooner or later your producer's blood would begin to assert itself" (qtd. in Fine 111). Following the "write what you know" creed, the producer's son Budd Schulberg would write a case study about the film industry, a world he knew more intimately than Fitzgerald or West, who were working on their own Hollywood fiction, ever could.

Sold to *Liberty* magazine in the summer of 1937, "What Makes Sammy Run?"—Schulberg's first professional publication—provides a rich opportunity for examining concepts of authorship in Hollywood, a theme Schulberg returned to again and again in his writing. Much of the scholarly activity surrounding film authorship has focused on authorship as it relates to control of a film's style and meaning. But authorship is more than a particular function; it can also be an imprimatur or branding strategy, one of the many factors that goes into creating a commodity. Humanism is not the only *-ism* that embraces the concept of authorship—capitalism does too. Designating authors allows for categorization, brand recognition, and (hopefully) profit. Sometimes a signature is not in a distinctive camera angle; it is in a name or number. All Elvis movies are Elvis movies; 007

can stay around forty forever; Jason can put on his hockey mask to die XXV times; and for years Alfred Hitchcock, the impresario who the critic Peter Wollen once called "at least as important an artist as, say, Scott Fitzgerald" (160), presented televised thrillers he neither wrote nor directed. In these instances authorship is not a function of origin; it is a function of valorization.

By releasing the work of others under his own name, Schulberg's Sammy Glick is attempting to increase the value of the Sammy Glick brand name. The antihero of "What Makes Sammy Run?" is a writer-producer who produces almost no writing. His radio columns are plagiarized from Somerset Maugham; he is invited to Hollywood on the merits of another man's script; and he increases his cultural and economic capital as a screenwriter by slightly altering the details of a recent movie. Instead of being ashamed, Sammy brags about it: "I used entirely the same construction as *Five Star Final,* scene for scene, only I changed the characters, and I made it funny" ("What Makes" 298). Although the producer Jerry Wald is said to be the prototype for the Sammy character, this type of appropriation is close to what Schulberg's boss Selznick was doing with *A Star Is Born*—taking the construction of one of his earlier films, *What Price Hollywood?* (1932), inserting a love plot for the characters, and, with the help of Dorothy Parker, making it funny.

Sammy demonstrates that creative ownership in the film industry can be achieved through means other than artistry. Glick is a mediocre writer but a genius at marketing himself. By end of the story, every movie he works on instantly becomes a Sammy Glick movie. As he leapfrogs from New York copyboy to radio columnist to screenwriter to Hollywood producer, his determination overrides his lack of originality. Who needs talent when you have tenacity? Sammy's star is on the rise, and his friend-enemy, a genteel playwright named Al, hitches a ride and serves as his biographer. Al's last name, appropriately, is Manners. When his drama column loses space to Sammy's radio column, a blatant metaphor of art being swallowed up by mass culture, razor-sharp sarcasm is the only weapon he uses in retaliation. But his irony is no match for Sammy's iron will.

In the novel Al will go through a complex moral struggle regarding artistic integrity once he is in Hollywood, but at the end of the short story he has quickly capitulated to Sammy's worldview. He realizes that the future of film authorship is Sammy Glick: "My agent tells me I may go to work for him next week, and I'd still rather have my name on a Sammy Glick production than any picture in town" (299).

Fitzgerald in Hollywood, 1937. Photograph by Carl Van Vechten,
courtesy of the Library of Congress

But if it is a "Sammy Glick production," it has already been branded
with someone else's mark of ownership—Sammy Glick's. Sammy, and
Sammy alone, will decide who gets screen credit. Couple this with the fact
that he is an admitted plagiarist, and Al's chances for seeing his name
onscreen look slim indeed. The story ends with this glimpse of the once-
proud Manners as a dried-up and corrupted screenwriter. The writer as
gentleman amateur, more interested in seeing the plays than writing about
them, has devolved into a credit-hungry whore. With this story Schulberg,
a Hollywood favorite son, begins his career-long examination of movie
industry's effect on the American writer.

Fighting Over *Three Comrades:* F. Scott Fitzgerald

Like the fictional Al Manners and the real Budd Schulberg, in the late 1930s F. Scott Fitzgerald was an Ivy League–educated screenwriter with a paucity of film credits. In 1937, deeply in debt, he returned to Hollywood with a six-month MGM contract at $1,000 a week with an option of a raise to $1,250 the following year, a salary that again placed him among the highest-paid screenwriters in Hollywood (Hamilton 145; *Correspondence* 475). It was not as much as Parker was making ($1,750–$2,500), but it was a lot more than West's ($350) and Schulberg's ($50) established salaries, and it was a remarkable sum considering the fact that he still had zero film writing credits after years and years of attempts.

In 1937, after a lackluster polish on a script titled *A Yank at Oxford,* he began working on an adaptation of Erich Maria Remarque's novel *Three Comrades,* a love story set after World War I and revolving around the lives of three German soldiers all in love with the same woman. The film would be responsible for Fitzgerald's first—and only—screen credit. As preproduction was beginning, he wrote Scottie of his plan to "keep my hand on the wheel from the start—find out the key man among the bosses and the most malleable among the collaborators—then fight the rest tooth and nail until, in fact or in effect, I'm alone on the picture. That's the only way I can do my best work" (*Letters of FSF* 117). With his naturalistic talk of "tooth and nail," Fitzgerald sounds a bit like Sammy Glick, ready to engage in a Darwinian struggle for supremacy. He also displays a recognition of Hortense Powdermaker's anthropological observation that creative groups in Hollywood—writers, directors, actors, editors, cinematographers, producers—were dependent on each other, but that they were simultaneously engaged in a constant struggle for control and dominance (29–30).

Still for every piece of information Fitzgerald picked up about Hollywood codes, there were other messages he simply kept missing. Behind the wised-up language, he continues to cling to the notion that a single writer, and only a writer, can author a motion picture. Fitzgerald needed the bump in his salary working solo on a picture could offer. In 1937 his debts exceeded forty thousand dollars, and his agent Ober had been unable to place his stories for more than a year (Bryer 106). But there was still another reason he wanted to be "alone on the picture." Unlike West, Schulberg, and Parker, who accepted the collaborative system—though certainly not its unfair assignment of credits and its labor practices—Fitzgerald hated working with others, especially those he considered his literary inferiors.

Submitting his draft of the *Three Comrades* screenplay to producer Joseph Mankiewicz, he felt confident that he would receive sole writing credit and that the script would not need any more "cooks" (*Correspondence* 478). But a few days later, Mankiewicz assigned Ted Paramore to assist Fitzgerald in revising it. Fitzgerald had satirized Paramore, whom he had known in New York, in *The Beautiful and Damned*, where he appears as the prig "Fred E. Paramore." Yet in 1921 Fitzgerald had written to Wilson, "I like Ted immensely. He is a little too much the successful Eli to live comfortably in his mind's bed chamber, but I like him immensely" (*Crack-Up* 256).

Fitzgerald thought Paramore would be working beneath him to help with technical language and form; Paramore wanted to make extensive content revisions. Fitzgerald grew furious that the Hollywood hack dared to think himself his creative equal. Claiming possession of superior taste and judgment—the gold bullion of highbrow cultural capital—the famous author then fired off an angry letter to his collaborator: "I prefer to keep responsibility for the script as a whole. . . . when you blandly informed me yesterday that you were going to write the whole thing over yourself, kindly including my best scenes, I knew we had to have this out. . . . If you were called on this job in the capacity of complete rewriter then I'm getting deaf. . . . I did not write four out of four best sellers or a hundred and fifty top-priced short stories out of the mind of a temperamental child without taste or judgment" (*Letters of FSF* 559).

Most screenwriters learned quickly that there is no such thing as "the script as a whole." Even if one person is responsible for making the entire component, it is still only a part crafted to make the larger machine run more smoothly. The screenplay is not meant to exist on its own, not even to the extent that a dramatic work for the theater, by Samuel Beckett, for instance, might come alive on the page. The mediocre businessman Shakespeare may not have realized that he was the great playwright Shakespeare, but to this day there is still no *Hamlet* of screenplays. The Hollywood script is a written invitation to make art, not a freestanding literary artwork in its own right. A screenplay only achieves fruition through image, dialogue, sound, music, and graphics. A drama text can be repeatedly performed and restaged and reimagined; but once filmed, a screenplay becomes fixed.

The producer Mankiewicz—not the screenwriter Fitzgerald—would ultimately bear the "responsibility for the script as a whole." Powdermaker writes: "Although movies are made by many people in the setting of a big industry, certain individuals have power to strongly influence them, while others are relatively powerless" (3). The studio system was organized as a hierarchy, not as a collaborative. MGM was not a kibbutz. Everyone did not have equal say in making decisions; everyone did not have common goals. MGM paid their writers a lot of money to do it the producer's way. After the Fitzgerald/Paramore draft of the *Three Comrades* script was submitted, the producer skimmed off the cream and rewrote the screenplay himself. In his guiding hands, power translated into something resembling authorship.

When Fitzgerald read this revision of the revision of his adaptation, he sent Mankiewicz a letter even angrier than the one he'd written to Paramore: "I gave you a drawing and you simply took a box of chalk and touched it up. . . . I guess all these years I've been kidding myself about being a good writer. . . . For nineteen years, with two out for sickness, I've written best-selling entertainment, and my dialogue is supposedly right up at the top. But I learn from your script that you've suddenly decided that it isn't good dialogue and you can take a few hours off and do much better" (*Letters of FSF* 563).

Again Fitzgerald mentions his writing credentials, and again he proclaims his superior taste and judgment. He always believed that if he could write a good book, he could write a good movie. But as we have seen in earlier chapters, the different media call on different sets of writing skills and require different expectations from the writer. Whereas fiction is written for the self and an ideal public, the studio system tried to convince authors that screenplays are written for producers. Fitzgerald was not writing *Three Comrades* for the popular audience that consumes "best-selling entertainment"; he was writing for the consumption of Joseph Mankiewicz. This irked Fitzgerald to no end. In his copy of the final shooting script, he crossed out "OKed by Joseph Mankiewicz" and replaced it with "Scrawled Over by Joseph Mankiewicz" (*FSF: A Life in Letters* 343–44).

As for Fitzgerald's claims of superior judgment, he should have realized that fiction is judged largely on the final product, while screenplays are judged largely on completion time. Slow writers were bad writers. Schulberg could polish a script quickly. Parker could rattle off dialogue. West was a bit pokier, but the stakes were lower at the places he worked, as was the quality of the films. By all accounts Fitzgerald was a slow worker, and MGM producers were seldom satisfied with the work he submitted. It took him too long to write his scripts, and to make matters worse, the work he submitted did not move the narrative along quickly enough. The lyricism of his prose compensates for lackluster plotting in his novels, but Fitzgerald's screenplays cannot overcome this weakness.

A script's main requirement is pace: obviously a movie needs to move. There must be little or no character background, and absolutely no digression. Story is much more important than character. A look at Fitzgerald's version of the *Three Comrades* script, published as part of Southern Illinois University Press's Screenplay Library, shows that some of the scenes Fitzgerald pleaded with Mankiewicz to restore would have weighed the picture down. For example his version included lengthy conversations between characters that used dialogue to convey information about setting and theme that the camera was already going to be taking care of. Fitzgerald's dialogue also sounds stilted when read aloud. The novelist had written for the page, not for the screen. Strong film dialogue sticks close to the patterns of real speech—with all its imperfect interruptions, truncations, and pauses.

In his book on Fitzgerald's screen writing, Wheeler Winston Dixon correctly observes of Fitzgerald's *Three Comrades* script: "[He] relies all too heavily on words to convey his meaning. . . . he sought to interweave two stories into one: the emotional relationship of the three comrades, and a near documentary depiction of social conditions in Germany during the Depression" (58). Some other segments that Fitzgerald wanted onscreen are comically bad. Here is one character, Bobby, calling another, Pat, for a date:

54: A SWITCHBOARD
with a white angel sitting at it.
ANGEL (sweetly): One moment, please—I'll connect you with heaven.
CUT TO:
55: THE PEARLY GATES
St. Peter, the caretaker, sitting beside another switchboard.
ST. PETER (cackling): I think she's in.
CUT TO:
56: BOBBY'S FACE
still ecstatic, changing to human embarrassment as Pat's voice says:
PAT: Hello.
BOBBY: Hello.
CUT TO:
57: A SATYR, who has replaced the angel at the switchboard—
pulling out the plug with a sardonic expression. (*"Three Comrades":*
The Screenplay 44)

After reading the scene, MGM executive Eddie Mannix screamed: "How the hell do you photograph *that?*" (Latham 135–36). In addition to being unfilmable, Fitzgerald's proposed switchboard episode would have been completely out of whack with the rest of *Three Comrades*—after all the story takes place in Nazi Germany, and Pat is wasting away from tuberculosis. Because Fitzgerald's attitude was that he was writing *for* the movies instead of *to* them, he lapsed into sappiness. Writing down to his material led him into bad writing, and into bad relationships with his collaborators. On *Three Comrades* Mankiewicz had curtly exercised his authority, but he had also made the correct, movie-specific creative decisions.

Making a Living on Poverty Row: Nathanael West

A stagnant salary and an excess of professional pride were two reasons Fitzgerald disliked being paired with others, but another benefit of earning a solo credit was that it often allowed you the chance to move on to writing originals for the screen. Rather than adapting someone else's novel or play, Fitzgerald wanted to chase the ghost of authoring his own films. But MGM, where Fitzgerald worked, had lots of money to buy properties, so they had little desire for originals.

On the other hand, Republic Pictures, where Nathanael West worked, could not afford to buy many properties. A large number of stories originated in-house. In 1937 West pitched original stories so he could increase his screen credits, which would then increase his weekly salary. Unlike Fitzgerald he was not interested in mastering the craft of screen writing or in seeing his film vision realized. There is no room for emotional engagement in West's novels, but movies thrive on it. His novels speak out against technology, but film embraces it. Friend and fellow Republic Pictures screenwriter Wells Root comments on West's detachment from his scripts: "I think he figured in respect to producers and directors that movies were their business, not his. He was a sort of architectural assistant, working on plans for a house" (qtd. in Light 143).

In 1990 Ian Hamilton called West's Republic films "extremely difficult—if not impossible—to view" (163). Presumably he was talking about their scarcity, not their quality. But since the rise of the Internet, video copies of these movies are now widely available. I was also able to view several of West's screenplays at the New York State Archives in Albany, which houses the largest collection of film scripts in the world.

One of the movies West worked on in 1937, *Born to Be Wild*, the story of two men driving a truck filled with dynamite, was conceived, treated, and scripted by West alone. The screenplay is fast-moving and suspenseful, with the tension occasionally broken by the wiseguy banter between the drivers. It is well structured and contains believable dialogue—two traits Fitzgerald's *Three Comrades* script lacked. The film version, though clearly shot on a shoestring, contains an enjoyable performance from Ward Bond as the chattier of the two truckers. *Born to Be Wild* also seems to have begat Henri-Georges Clouzot's 1953 film classic *The Wages of Fear* and is a distant cousin to the History Channel series *Ice Road Truckers*.

Working on the fringes of the American film industry, West was even able to dose some of his Republic films with his own leftist political agenda, especially 1936's *The President's Mystery* (1936) and *It Could Happen to You* (1937). To make them overlook the low pay, Republic Pictures offered its writers the type of worker-friendly contracts the SWG was pushing for. Sharing the studio lot with West were die-hard unionists such as Horace McCoy and Lester Cole. But the boss at Republic, Herb Yates, did not like lefties. Jay Martin writes of the West-scripted, pro-Roosevelt, pro-union *The President's Mystery:* "When Yates viewed his most recent film in New York in early September, he was outraged. A supporter of Alf Landon, he declared that the picture—made for $105,000, the most expensive Republic Picture until that time—had cost less than he had bet on Landon, and he was determined not to release it. Nevertheless, economics prevailed" (278). There is not much mystery in *The President's Mystery:* corporate capitalist fishmongers want to shut down a rural cannery collective; fifty-three long minutes later they are foiled—as we expected. It serves to remind us that movies, especially low-budgeted ones, usually get greenlighted not because there is something unique about them, but because there is something familiar about them.

The following year, much to Yates's consternation, his company put out *It Can Happen to You,* a film even more overtly political. A card included with a videotape version of the film describes it as the story of "an immigrant's son who wants to buy a citizenship school for foreigners, but finds himself involved with the wrong crowd." This "wrong crowd" includes a blackmailing Nietzschean fascist called Professor Schwab, who "dreams of the time when his political philosophy will be the rule in America" (Video Yesteryear Recording). After West's treatment was accepted, he worked on the final script with Samuel Ornitz, later famous for being one of the Hollywood Ten. On the page on and on the screen, the film's evil intellectual is very evil, and the earnest hero is very earnest. The inevitable defeat of the Nazi menace in the third act is of historically prescient interest. But like most Republic films, *The Quiet Man* (1952) being a notable exception, the sets look cheap, the acting is wooden, and every scene looks like it was shot with only one setup and in only one take.

Republic Pictures made movies for rural theaters that could not afford the big-city prices charged by the major studios. Because West was involved with the Screen Writers Guild's battle for recognition, a place such as MGM or Paramount would not touch him, especially since he lacked the literary reputation of someone like fellow SWGer Dorothy Parker (or the insider clout of young Communist Budd Schulberg) that might have caused the major studios to look the other way at his political activities. So it was either a "Poverty Row" studio for West or nothing. On the positive side, working at Republic was not without its advantages. The company made so many films, and made them so hastily, that West could not help but get a crash course in the praxis and craft of screen writing. During 1937 he worked on at least nine films, probably closer to a dozen.

If there is little evidence that West took pride in the finished films, he felt no disappointment in them, either. Above all else he liked the money screen writing afforded him—it was allowing him to finish a draft of *The Day of the Locust* and begin work on a play titled "Gentlemen, the War!" He did not mind daily life at the studio too much, either. A die-hard pessimist and misanthrope, West was also one of the most gregarious people in Hollywood. He thought writing bad movies was funny, and he liked visiting his coworkers in their offices and feeding them lines for their scripts (Dardis 154, 182). After hours, in the social club atmosphere of the back room of Stanley Rose's bookshop, West liked bellyaching with writers such as Parker and Schulberg about draconian studio management (*Four Seasons* 147–53). In the Los Angeles literary community, he found the approbation and support of his peers, if not the commercial and critical success he desired.

Although West cared little for screen writing, he cared a great deal about screenwriters. Most screenwriters at any given time were out of work, and those who were employed were often a whim away from being let go without credit or compensation. At many studios it was common practice to fire someone to avoid paying him a bonus or a holiday, then turn around and rehire him a day or two later. West, like most of the other members of the Screen Writers Guild, was not a card-carrying Communist, but he saw the need to foster an organization that would aid writers with the economic and creative struggles they were facing. On the other hand, as Jay Martin writes, "His sympathies, basically, were with people rather than programs. . . . He always remained interested in the guild's goals— and intensely committed to the dignity and freedom of the writer—but he was bored by its rhetoric and gesticulations" (344, 348). West lacked the political earnestness of Schulberg, the intensity of Parker, and the missionary zeal of them both.

At the Academy Awards in February 1936, when Dudley Nichols won best screenplay for *The Informer*, he turned down the award. In a letter to the academy, he wrote: "To accept it would be to turn my back on nearly a thousand members of the Writers Guild, to desert those fellow-writers who ventured everything in the long-drawn-out fight for a genuine writers organization, to go back on convictions honestly arrived at, and to invalidate three years work in the Guild, which I should like to look back upon with self-respect" (qtd. in Schwartz 51). Nichols, a founding member of the SWG, happened to be one of the highest-paid writers in Hollywood.

Writers such as Nichols, Schulberg, and Parker all rocked the Hollywood boat when they could have easily just gone along for the ride. Schulberg's bloodline and Parker's fame assured them both of a comfortable living in Hollywood, yet they, like Nichols, chose to use their power to aid the less fortunate. Literary histories tend to paint the 1930s as "the Red Decade," and it is easy to assume mistakenly that most artists of the period leaned to the left. But the Popular Front was not really all that popular. In truth, as historians such as Barbara Foley and Richard Pells have noted, the majority of American writers between the wars—like the majority of the American people between the wars—were a conservative bunch, more interested in baseball scores than how many Loyalists were being killed in Spain.

In Hollywood, where stratification was the norm, the organizations of the Popular Front and their common mission of social justice served to relax boundaries between rich and poor and between highbrows and lowbrows. But some well-intentioned cultural missteps were made. When screenwriter Donald Ogden Stewart was asked to contribute magazines to a Communist Party youth center, he loaded his car with copies of *Vogue* and *Country Life*. Well-off writers who were politically active, such as Stewart, Schulberg, and Parker, were often accused of being poseurs, the foreparents of the slumming phenomenon Tom Wolfe coined "radical chic."

In 1937, to the horror of his father's friends in Hollywood, Schulberg officially joined the Communist Party (Beck 7), a fashionable organization to which fellow traveler Parker is widely thought to have already belonged (though an FBI investigation on her could not make it stick). Despite membership and meetings being a closely guarded secret, the Hollywood Communist Party threw drunken bashes and offered an attractive range of dating opportunities (Schwartz 86, 92). Eventually Schulberg would get tired of receiving party assignments and bristle at how doctrinaire the leaders could be over creative content, but his attraction to worker's issues was more than just a spoiled rich boy's rebellion. He and Parker were more than swimming-pool Reds; they were socially committed professionals. They were not radical out of guilt; they were radical out of a sense of justice and equality.

It is important to remember that despite its ultimate goal of overthrowing the American government, some of the more noble goals of the Hollywood Communist Party were to bolster unions, to aid in voter turnout for local political campaigns, and to fight fascism. Parker was serious about achieving these latter goals, yet after joining the party her reputation as a "amateur revolutionary" (Meade 255) clung to her more than ever. Nancy Schwartz writes, "All of her friends found it amusing to imagine the willful Dottie subjecting herself to Communist Party discipline. The news media was not only amused but irked by the politicization of the former Round Table member" (83).

Parker, who was old enough to be a member of the Lost Generation, had found a sense of purpose in California. Her work on behalf of the Screen Writers Guild shows that she was not "slumming" in Los Angeles and just passing through; she was trying to be a productive Hollywood citizen and a socially committed author. When Congressman Martin Dies, chairman of the House Un-American Activities Committee (HUAC), began coming to town to root out Communists in the late 1930s, Parker publicly denounced him, writing in an open letter in *Directions* magazine that he wanted to "destroy the Hollywood progressive organizations—because you've got to control this medium if you want to bring fascism to this country. . . . we're grateful to Hollywood for our jobs and we're grateful for the opportunity it gives us to speak for American democracy" (5). In addition to Parker's SWG activities, she was a founding member of the Hollywood Anti-Nazi League and a member of the League of American Writers (LAW), a group dedicated to organizing classes for writers and offering aid to European authors escaping fascism.

In 1936 the LAW had helped sponsor the Western Writers Congress in San Francisco, at which Parker, Schulberg, and West all gave speeches. The author John Fante reported to H. L. Mencken that Parker had "breezed into the hall wearing a Hollywood fur coat that must have easily cost two grand, and promptly the poor red women sighed adoringly" (Moreau 106). But according to one of these "poor red women," the poet Ruth Lechlitner, "Through the League [of American Writers] there developed a

Parker pondering scripts. Photofest

genuine feeling for fellowship among both established and beginning writers. . . . For the young writer especially, the League Meetings were a source of hope and encouragement" (qtd. in Denning 225). Viewing writing as both a marketable skill and an agent for change, the league offered courses in genre fiction, script writing, and journalism. *Writers Teach Writing,* a pamphlet put out by the LAW, reflects this approach to writing as a craft and a profession.

Although Parker did not contribute to this publication, there is evidence that she took the screen-writing work itself more seriously than her constant wisecracks might have indicated. In 1937, the same year she was elected to the newly revitalized Screen Writers Guild's executive council, she claimed in *Screen Guilds Magazine:* "Through the sweat and tears I shed over my first script, I saw a great truth—one of those eternal, universal truths that serve to make you feel much worse than when you started. And that is that no writer, whether he writes from love or for money, can condescend to what he writes. You can't stoop to what you set down on paper; I don't know why you can't, but you can't. No matter what form it takes, and no matter what the result, and no matter how caustically comic you are about it afterward, what you did was your best. And to do your best is always hard going" (qtd. in McGilligan 7).

Her remarks remind us of fellow screenwriter Ben Hecht's famous assertion that "it's just as hard to make a toilet seat as a castle window" (*Child of the Century* 194). But it is important to note that the "sweat and tears" Parker sheds are over her scripts, not over the films made from her scripts. As we have seen, it is a distinction her friend Fitzgerald was having a hard time making.

Just as a new recruit who is opposed to war can sometimes take great pride in becoming the best soldier in the company, Parker was dismissive of the film industry and those who ran it, but she needed to give the work itself its due respect. Like other writers who first made their bones in another medium, she quickly came to the realization that screen writing was not easier or less creatively taxing than playwriting or novel writing or poetry writing. It was not, as some said, a "soft racket." Screen writing involved labor (sweat) and a measure of personal involvement in that labor (tears). Parker claimed she did not know why she could not "stoop" to her writing assignments, but the answer is clear: She took pride in being a professional writer. She wanted to work hard and do well at the things she could do well. Like a good craftsperson, like the LAW contributors to *Writers Teach Writing,* she found herself able to make an object, see that it worked, and turn her attention to the next object. As she was shuffled from script to script, Parker tried to produce a quality product. A strong sense of professionalism often trumped her eastern literary condescension. How her part fit into the whole, or whether it would be used, did not concern her. For both Schulberg and Parker, the satisfaction of a job well done was often its own reward. Their work on *A Star Is Born* is one such example.

How the Script for *A Star Is Born* Got Made

A close look at the production history and content of *A Star Is Born* casts some illuminating light on studio-system labor, Hollywood artistry, and movie authorship. The film begins and ends with close-up shots of a script titled *A Star Is Born*. In the opening scene a masculine hand reaches into the frame and marks the document with a "FINAL SHOOTING SCRIPT" stamp. This self-reflexive gesture acknowledges that movies are written, not just acted and directed. The word FINAL reveals that a Hollywood script goes through several drafts. The entire phrase also implies, and correctly so, that once the movie starts filming the writer's job is finished, but that the screenplay is still subject to change before shooting wraps up.

But the cinematic self-consciousness and lifting of the scrim only extend so far. Like all films about film, *A Star Is Born* reveals parts of the movie-making process while keeping others secret. The content of the film demystifies, but the style remystifies. We see the actress Esther Blodgett (Janet Gaynor) being primped by makeup artists before stepping in front of the cameras, but we do not see the actors who play the makeup artists in the makeup chair themselves, and we do not see the cameras that film Gaynor's character as she prepares to step in front of the cameras. Along the same lines, the screenplay pictured onscreen does not begin or end with a written direction to "show script." No author is credited on its title page. The opening credits to the movie itself, however, announce it as a "Selznick International" production. Just as Joseph Mankiewicz had the final stamp of approval on the *Three Comrades* script, only David O. Selznick, producer of *A Star Is Born,* possessed the authority to label the film's script as final.

Under Selznick's iron-fisted supervision, more than a half-dozen writers, among them Parker and Schulberg, worked on the screenplay. Parker even received an Academy Award nomination for the script. The movie's director was auteur William Wellman, who won the Oscar for the film's original story. If Wellman both originated the movie and directed it, he would seem to have the strongest claim to creative ownership. Yet in the final analysis, Selznick is the closest thing the film has to an author. When Wellman was handed the Academy Award, he gave it to Selznick to hold, telling the producer he deserved it more. Selznick pretended to be shocked and flattered, but down deep he agreed. He never gave the statue back.

Authored texts not only have origins of physical production; they also have origins of artistic intention. Selznick managed *A Star Is Born* from

David O. Selznick. Photofest

inception to completion, bringing the right people together and making all the major decisions on the film's content and style. In addition to overseeing workers and budgets and deadlines, a producer's traditional roles, Selznick fancied himself a writer who did not need a typewriter. Like Sam Goldwyn, Darryl Zanuck, and Irving Thalberg—the managerial/artistic double threats he modeled himself after—he wanted to provide the guiding vision behind the films he independently produced. Selznick's true genius, like Sammy Glick's, resided in brand management. He controlled not only the marketable product, but also creative authority over the films themselves.

Jack Stillinger, among many other critics, believes that "as a rule, the authorship of films is so complicated and diffuse as to be, for all practical purposes, unassignable" (174). Because of Hollywood's collaborative work practices, he argues, film authorship is not a richly complex concept; it is a meaningless one. But as with the Fitzgerald/Mankiewicz friction, authorship-type issues that appear to be about creative vision are actually matters of power and control. In assessing Hollywood authorial claims, it is usually more fruitful to look at memos, correspondence, and other printed material than it is to look for "signatures" in the frames and scenes of the motion pictures themselves.

Selznick believed *A Star Is Born* was his film, writing in a 1973 letter: "I refused to take credit for it as a matter of policy. . . . The actual original idea, the story line, and the vast majority of the story ideas of the scenes themselves are my own" (Behlmer, *Memo from DOS* 106). Wellman countered Selznick's claim by saying: "I gave David 'A Star Is Born.' . . . Now in his memoirs he said he wrote it. He did like hell! He had a couple of guys come in here and they rewrote it and I rewrote it right back to the way it was, so it finished up just as it was" (Schickel 218). However, as the opening shot of the film itself makes plain, the script that appears on the page is never the script of what appears on the screen. It is a truth universally acknowledged in Hollywood that any film script is subject to revision at any time before the cameras begin to roll, and usually even after. Characters and scenes can change; the idea usually stays the same. Both Wellman and Selznick claimed credit for the idea of *A Star Is Born,* but the narrative geometry of a woman entertainer on her way up and a man on his way down really was not original. It is the plot of Theodore Dreiser's *Sister Carrie,* as well as several other naturalistic novels, and the films *The Blue Angel* (1930) and Hollywood tragedies such as *Her Face Value* (1921), *The Part Time Wife* (1925), *Excess Baggage* (1928), *Big Time* (1929), and Selznick's own *What Price Hollywood?*—not to mention the rocky Hollywood marriage of Al Jolson and Ruby Keeler—chart exactly the same axis.

In still another memo, Selznick claims that the Hollywood community itself—especially the plots of decline that befell actors John Barrymore, John Gilbert, and John Bowers—provided all the raw material the writers of *A Star Is Born* needed. He writes of the film's genesis: "We started without anything more than a vague idea of where we were going, and it was really an easy script to write. We had two sets of writers on it, curiously, and Dorothy Parker and her husband, Alan Campbell, did the final dialogue and some amendments in the scenes. But I can say this, that 95% of the dialogue in that picture was actually straight out of life" (Behlmer, *Memo from DOS* 96).

Actually three different sets of writers (Wellman/Carson, Parker/Campbell, and the uncredited team of Schulberg/Lardner), not two, worked on

A Star Is Born. Still another writer, Roland Brown, worked on the script for a few days after Parker and before Schulberg (Kinney 34). But to hear Selznick tell it, all the writers really needed to do anyway was catch some of the anecdotes floating around Hollywood and pin them onto the screenplay.

Statements such as Selznick's take the writer out the creative equation, making him or her a collector of material rather than a creator of it. It is almost as misleading as saying that 100 percent of the words used in the screenplay were straight out of the dictionary; they just needed to be put in the right order. Behind Selznick's hunch that writing is more transcription than inspiration, we can hear the traditional Hollywood belief that someday a system would be figured out to do away with writers entirely. The cliché "time is money" was a perfect fit for the Hollywood studio system, where the assembly-line mode of production fostered an atmosphere of constant crisis. Shooting could not start until the writers were finished, so the writers could never be finished fast enough. Part of what rankled screenwriters about those in the front office was that so many of the executives believed that they could do the writer's job faster and better than the writer could. Designing costumes and building sets and composing the film score were jobs for specialists, but the writer's specialization was not seen as being very special. If a movie was a hit, the producer would take the credit. If it bombed, usually the script was blamed. *A Star Is Born* was a hit, and Selznick took most of the credit.

Perhaps he deserved to. As can be expected, biographers writing on Parker, Selznick, and Schulberg want to make a claim for their subjects as vital to the finished film. The movie's famous curtain line, "This is Mrs. Norman Maine!" has been attributed to everyone who worked on the script. Tom Schatz's *The Genius of the System* is more objective than these accounts, though it relies heavily on Selznick's own notes. According to Schatz, Wellman and Carson's version of the script was too melodramatic, so Selznick started looking for another team to add more comedy. At the time Parker and Campbell were under contract to Sam Goldwyn, but Parker's cynicism bothered Goldwyn. The producer jumped at the chance when Selznick asked to borrow her, and Parker and Campbell were brought in at $1,750 a week. The move appears to have worked. The film scholar Rudy Behlmer has found evidence that Parker/Campbell provided much of the venom in press agent Libby's tirades against Norman (98). After Maine drowns, Libby says of the alcoholic has-been: "It was the first drink of water he's had in twenty years, and he had to get it by accident." And when a delivery boy calls Maine "Mr. Lester," it is easy to hear Campbell's voice protesting years of being called Mr. Parker. After Campbell and Parker submitted their draft, Selznick shuffled them onto *Nothing Sacred* "to add women's dialogue and bright repartee" (Kinney 33). Selznick's scripts, like many other producers', were not so much team written as they were team rewritten.

Selznick then brought in Schulberg and Ring Lardner—at a bargain-basement twenty-five dollars a week apiece—to tighten up *A Star Is Born*. Parker's strength was dialogue. Schulberg excelled at plot and structure. According to Schatz, Schulberg took out a scene that had Norman driving drunk and killing a motorist. The junior writer convinced Selznick that such a plot point would steer the film toward being a "social problem" picture (184). All of Schulberg's suggestions were not implemented, however. He also felt that the opening scene, set in the rural Midwest, caused the movie to get off to a slow start. But Selznick kept it in, and he was right to do so. Christopher Ames posits in *Movies about the Movies* that *A Star Is Born*'s beginning establishes Hollywood as the last frontier, a homeland El Dorado, the epicenter of the American dream. He writes: "These scenes in the Dakota wilds not only establish Esther's naïveté and the long reach of Hollywood, but also introduce the resonant metaphor of moviemakers as pioneers" (28).

Selznick had a vision of what the movie could be and should be. Here is Schulberg describing how the final shooting script was put together: "I'll be damned if I didn't see it with my own eyes: David Selznick with a scissors taking the three screenplays, cutting them apart, literally cutting out two lines here and five lines there, making his own David Selznick screenplay, and the goddamn thing was one of the best Hollywood movies of all time" ("Two Conversations" 132–33).

Throughout every stage of production, Selznick maintained control over the film's style and meaning. Even after *A Star Is Born* was edited and ready for release, he kept working on it. After a test screening, he decided to go back and tighten up Norman's suicide walk into the ocean (Schatz 186), one of the film's most memorable images. With this amount of producer input, it is no wonder that the movie executive in Selznick's film, Oliver Niles (Adolph Menjou), comes off as kind, fair, and erudite.

In keeping with Selznick's debate with Schulberg over whether or not producer's blood is thicker than typewriter ink, the avuncular Niles is the polar opposite of Schulberg's rapacious Sammy Glick—save for one respect. Both characters possess goof-proof instincts about what the public wants.

Niles signs Esther on the basis of nothing. As Ames points out, in the 1950s remake Judy Garland's character sings and dances; she is already

Janet Gaynor, Fredric March, and Adolphe Menjou in *A Star Is Born*. Photofest

in show business when she is discovered and has evident talent (53). But in the 1937 version, the producer signs Esther because "I like you, and I have a feeling the public will too." No major American industry knew less about itself and its customers than the film industry, and producers often projected their own tastes onto the public. Still, despite their best efforts, the studios never discovered the star-making formula. The 1937 *A Star Is Born* tells us nothing about what it takes to be a star. In line with the demystify/remystify sleight of hand that characterizes the movie about movies, we see that inside of the star Vicki Lester lives Esther Blodgett, but we never see that inside of Esther lives the star Vicki.

Films made in Hollywood about creative people seldom reveal anything about creativity. Actors and writers, with their innate talents and skills, were often a mystery to producers. Luck and hunches were things those in the front office understood. Crossing his fingers, the producer in *A Star Is Born* sticks a powdered wig on Vicki's head, casts her in a costume drama, and watches the audience transform her into a celebrated actress. Aside from comically bad impressions of Greta Garbo, Katharine Hepburn, and Mae West—herself by 1937 already a comically bad impression of herself—we never see Vicki acting for more than a few seconds.

Janet Gaynor is a fine actress. It is not her fault we cannot figure out what makes Vicki a star. Even if the studios knew the fame equation, they still would not let on.

Explaining stardom would decrease its wattage. Because Hollywood film must always have it both ways, *A Star Is Born* is a warning tale about Hollywood that winds up glamorizing the very dreams it calls into question. Vicki's desire to mimic her favorite stars mirrors the audience's own mimetic desire. On one hand the film cautions women not to leave the farm for the footlights, but the deeper message is that maybe you, dear viewer, have that certain something the camera will love. On a certain level, *A Star Is Born* is sobering: stars are born, not made; for every star that is born, one dies. Vicki's star is on the rise; Norman's is on the wane. When she first gets to Hollywood, Esther is shown a room where a half-dozen switchboard operators are being overwhelmed by calls from aspiring starlets. Unlike the switchboard scene Fitzgerald wrote for *Three Comrades,* this episode is right in sync with the tone and style of the film. The receptionist tells the ingénue that her chances of making it are "one in a hundred thousand." A saucer-eyed Esther replies innocently: "But what if I'm that one?" *A Star Is Born* serves to demonstrate that almost anyone can be a star, but providence has already decided which ones are. Only a movie producer, that oracle of Hollywood, can divine if you have been kissed by an angel or not.

The film's representation of the path to stardom bears out sociologist Leo Lowenthal's observation that popular magazine biographies of famous people almost always depicted their subjects as the passive recipients of amazingly good fortune. Fame pushed itself on the famous, and these celebrities bent to fame's will. Rising in the world is a matter of going along for the ride. No work is necessary to become famous. You have either already got it or you do not. It will either be handed to you or it will not. If Selznick's *A Star Is Born* script can write itself, maybe it is no wonder that its heroine can become a successful actress without acting. In the absence of training and talent, Vicki's natural charisma carries her over. Movie producer Sammy Glick uses pluck and nastiness to claw his way up cinema's corporate ladder, but Vicki floats to the top through a sweet bubbly mixture of luck and industry kindness.

A Star Is Born is more forgiving of Hollywood than is "What Makes Sammy Run?," even in the scenes Schulberg is said to have written. Sammy uses Max Weber's terrible trio—charisma, bureaucracy, and force—to cement his power and feed his megalomania, but whatever power Vicki's stardom grants her, it never goes to her head. She begins the film a timid rube and ends it as a strong survivor. Sammy runs away from his family and a life of urban poverty; Vicki wants to run back to a life of rural simplicity. After a pep talk by her beloved grandmother, she decides to stay in Hollywood. Proudly declaring herself Mrs. Norman Maine, the widowed Vicki places her husband before her career, and her adoring public—the same public who abandoned Norman—now wants her even more for it. If there is a villain in the film, it is the fickle audience. A fan at her husband's funeral tells her, "Don't worry about it, honey. He wasn't much," but Vicki as the grieving widow is her most popular role ever. The crowd rips off her veil, an attempt to reveal the ordinary woman beneath the Hollywood persona, but the veil is not hiding anything: Vicki Lester, Esther Blodgett, and Mrs. Norman Maine are all exactly the same person.

At the conclusion of the film, Grandma Lettie stands at a microphone and tells the radio audience how happy she is to finally be in Hollywood after all these years. If Norman's decline showed the perils of stardom and the movie capital, Grandma Lettie makes sure filmgoers leave the theater back in love with the movies. Her onscreen address to the radio audience is actually targeted to those in the film audience. She says: "Maybe some of you people listening in dream about coming to Hollywood, and maybe some of you get pretty discouraged. Well, when you do, just think about me. It took me over seventy, um, sixty years to get here, but here I am and here I mean to stay."

Selznick biographer David Thomson believes that Schulberg came up with this finale, as does Schulberg's biographer Nicholas Beck, but the truth will never be known. What is certain, however, is that screenwriters Parker and Schulberg never felt especially attached to the picture, despite the fact that their contributions were clearly significant. As we have already noted, Schulberg was sticking around in his hometown and observing Selznick in order to soak up material for his true love, Hollywood fiction. Parker was proud of her work on A Star Is Born when the film came out, but according to biographer Marion Meade, she disowned it in later years when it started becoming a classic (263). She wanted to be remembered as a poet or fiction writer, not as the Academy Award–nominated screenwriter of A Star Is Born.

5

The Big Canvas(es)

LESSONS TO
BE TAUGHT
IN 1938–1939

When Gertrude Stein spoke of a "lost generation," we took
it to ourselves and considered it the prettiest compliment we
had. I think the trouble with us was that we stayed young too
long. We remained in the smarty-pants stage—and that is not
one of the more attractive ages. We were little individuals; and
when we finally came to and got out it was quite a surprise to
find a whole world of human beings all around us.

Dorothy Parker, "Sophisticated
Poetry—and the Hell with It"

Intellectual labour carried out collectively, within technically
and socially differentiated production units, can no longer surround itself with the charismatic aura attaching to traditional
independent production. The traditional cultural producer was
a master of his means of production and invested only his cultural capital, which was likely perceived as a gift of grace.

Pierre Bourdieu, *The Field*
of Cultural Production

ଛୢ

The twilight of a decade is a natural time for people to take stock of their
lives. With the 1930s coming to an end, F. Scott Fitzgerald, Nathanael
West, and Dorothy Parker were reflecting on where they had come from
artistically and where they were headed professionally. Did they still have
something to say as literary writers, and would the market allow them to

keep saying it? Fitzgerald's debts were rising, and his film career was rapidly losing whatever momentum the small push from the credit on *Three Comrades* had given it. Parker was gathering a book of her short stories, *Here Lies,* but her screen-writing career was slowing down. West was racking up movie credits, but fame as a novelist was the elusive target he had spent the 1930s shooting for. A canvass of their own careers was leaving all three authors frustrated. But Hollywood was not the cause of this frustration. Writing for the movies had not only provided these writers with money and the occasional shelter of moral support from their comrades but also offered them material for their art.

After years of work, West was preparing to publish *The Day of the Locust,* his most ambitious book to date. His entire corpus had been concerned with dreaming and escape: *The Dream Life of Balso Snell* depicted the dream of a poet who wishes to escape into literature; *Miss Lonelyhearts* explored an escape into religion; *A Cool Million* examined the American dream; and *Day of the Locust* would focus on the escape into celluloid. If the Hollywood studio system was truly the dream factory, then West had finally traced back his major theme to its source.

While West was concentrating on Hollywood's outsiders, those who bought fantasy, other novelists were examining Hollywood's insiders, those who manufactured fantasy. Fitzgerald was beginning a book about the inner machinery of the film industry, and producer Sammy Glick, the antihero of several Schulberg short stories, was getting his own novel. The 1939 screen-writing collaboration between Fitzgerald and Schulberg would eventually find its way into both of these literary works.

In his Fitzgerald biography, Andrew Turnbull calls young Schulberg "an ambitious junior scriptwriter hungry for credits that would push him up the Hollywood ladder" (297). But Schulberg was not Sammy Glick—at least not yet. He still held out hope for a American cinema of art made by the people for the people. In a July 2, 1939, article for the *New York Times* titled "Hollywood's Second Generation," Schulberg reports on a film industry in its golden age in terms of quality products, and he anticipates an increased recognition of the screenwriter's role in the filmmaking process: "As the screen writer wins greater dignity, the Guild will become more and more of a constructive force. And since the advent of sound and the gradual raising of artistic standards, the need of good stories and outstanding writing becomes more vital."

Schulberg's optimism was understandable. A partial list of the most popular movies of 1939 could double as a partial list of the greatest films of all time: *Beau Geste, Dark Victory, Drums along the Mohawk, Gone with the Wind, Goodbye Mr. Chips, Gunga Din, The Hunchback of Notre Dame, Love Affair, Mr. Smith Goes to Washington, Ninotchka, Of Mice and Men, Stagecoach, The Wizard of Oz, The Women*. New York's Museum of Modern Art had recently opened a film library collection, a high cultural acknowledgment that motion pictures were now being recognized as a serious art form. More than fifty million Americans filled 15,115 theaters every week to watch four hundred new films a year (Rosten 3–4, 378–79). Hollywood was turning out mass entertainment of the highest quality, and American authors could not help but notice.

Schulberg wrote that one such author, Fitzgerald, "believed in film as an ideal art form for reaching out to millions who might have never read a serious novel" (*Four Seasons* 98). There is also some evidence that Fitzgerald was becoming more empathetic to Hollywood labor issues toward the end of the decade. According to screenwriter Harry Rapf, in the late 1930s Fitzgerald told Schulberg he thought of himself as a communist (Beck 8), and Matthew Bruccoli writes that with it becoming increasingly clear that his immediate financial future rested in Hollywood, Fitzgerald— under Schulberg's influence—had become more interested in the Screen Writers Guild (*Some Sort* 453). But make no mistake: Fitzgerald's letters of 1938–39, especially those addressed to Perkins, clearly demonstrate that he saw himself as a novelist above all else: "I long to make some picture money and get back to the novel" (*Correspondence* 537), he wrote to his longtime editor.

Preaching at People in Some Acceptable Form

Like Fitzgerald, West had never made a secret of the fact that he was hanging around the movie industry primarily to support his thirst for book writing. Although he was gaining more prestigious jobs, leaving Republic Studios for stints at "major minors" such as RKO and Universal and gaining a solo screen credit on the A movie *I Stole a Million*, literary success was still West's goal. Random House, his largest and wealthiest publisher to date, was putting out *The Day of the Locust*, and West mentioned to his editor, Bennett Cerf, that he might need "blurbs from important people" such as Parker and Dashiell Hammett (*Novels* 784).

West also sent Fitzgerald the novel's galleys, hoping for his endorsement. The letter the younger writer enclosed provides a clear view into his ideas regarding the friction between writing as a vocation (the work he is called to do) and writing as a profession (the work he can market and sell).

Thanking Fitzgerald for mentioning him in the 1934 preface to *The Great Gatsby*, West explains the source of his difficulty in reaching an audience:

> Somehow or other I seem to have slipped in between all the "schools." My books meet no need except my own, their circulation is practically private and I'm lucky to be published. And yet, I only have a desire to remedy all that BEFORE sitting down to write, once begun I do it my way. I forget the broad sweep, the big canvas, the shot-gun adjectives, the important people, the significant ideas, the lessons to be taught, the epic Thomas Wolfe, the realistic James Farrell—and go on making what one critic called "private and unfunny jokes." Your preface made me feel that they weren't completely private and maybe not even entirely jokes. (*Novels* 791–92)

There was a disconnect between West's politics and his writing practice, making it difficult for his contemporaries to categorize him. In 1939, the year this letter was written, he, like Schulberg, had accepted increased responsibilities within the SWG by serving as an elected member of its board, and he was willing to lend his signature to progressive causes, such as the antifascist and prolabor Motion Picture Guild, which hoped to make socially conscious films outside of the Hollywood system (Schwartz 322). Throughout the 1930s, however, West had been unable—or perhaps unwilling—to use his books to tout his politics or to deliver a sermonic message that would enact change. In a similar letter sent to Jack Conroy, author of the classic proletarian novel *The Disinherited* and editor of the magazine *Anvil: Stories for Workers*, he argues that if he were to use *The Day of the Locust* to depict Hollywood's "sincere, honest people" and their "great progressive fight," it would clash with his satirical aims, and "the whole fabric of the peculiar half-world . . . would be badly torn by them" (qtd. in Martin 337).

Conroy, who had grown up in a mining camp, was opposed to the sort of late modernist literature his friend West wrote and even more contemptuous of the training he had received to write it, as evidenced by his snide address to the American Writers Congress a few years earlier: "The troubles of a worker who is attempting to mirror the life around him are many and varied. In the first place, very few worker-writers have ever graduated from college, and still fewer of them have been able to spend a year or so in the Paris Latin Quarter where it is possible to learn the writing of proletarian literature in the technical manner of Marcel Proust and James Joyce" (83). Conroy had spent time in the Federal Writers' Project in the Midwest collecting railroad folklore and trying to record the voice of the people, but West had always kept himself at a distance from the sentimentality, folksiness, and social realism of the Popular Front and its celebration of the common man.

Most writing about honest people struck West as dishonest. He told Malcolm Cowley he was constitutionally unable to believe in the feel-good platitudes of Ma Joad in John Steinbeck's *The Grapes of Wrath* (1939): "I want to believe in her and yet inside myself I honestly can't. When not writing a novel—say at a meeting of a committee we have out here to help the migratory worker—I do believe it and try to act on that belief. But at the typewriter by myself I can't" (*Novels* 795). Unlike Steinbeck's books or Conroy's, West's novels had no slogans for the people, and they were therefore of little value to exponents of proletarian literature. His books read like cautionary tales and have the air of jeremiads, but they do not specify what exactly we should be looking out for. West senses that something has broken down in American life, but he does not tell us how to fix it. Other avenues to critical appreciation from his peers were closed to him as well. His writing lacked the beauty, the scope, and the foregrounding of significant ideas that the 1930s highbrow press might have responded to, and his books were too dirty for libraries. Although admired by his fellow writers, he belonged to no marketable "school" or movement. West was the most respected and famous ignored and disrespected writer in Los Angeles.

There are, of course, "significant ideas" in West's books. But just as Fitzgerald had fallen out of critical favor in the 1930s, it would take several decades for West's "half-world" to be appreciated—yet even now "the schoolmasters of ever after" are not quite sure what to do with him. *A Cool Million,* like the high school reading list staple *The Great Gatsby,* depicts a quixotic campaign to collect on the promises of the American success myth. But lacking Fitzgerald's lyrical gift for giving his short novels the feel of a big canvas, West's black humor does not always make his "lessons to be taught" as clear as Fitzgerald's style might. A darkly comic nihilist in his life and his art, a teller of the type of "private and unfunny jokes" that would be better appreciated after the coming of 1960s writers such as John Hawkes and Thomas Pynchon, West was much less preachy than Fitzgerald, the man he was writing to for help.

As Fitzgerald got older, he got more pedantic and more worried about his artistic legacy. He was always generous with writing advice to colleagues, and he was thoughtful enough to send books to friends on a regular basis, but as Schulberg would realize during their screen-writing trip and John O' Hara would discover at around the same time, the flip side of Fitzgerald's largesse was often his desire to collect intellectual disciples. Sheilah Graham's *College of One* tells the story of her 1938–39 journey through the great works of literature, a tour Fitzgerald carefully mapped out for her and firmly guided. By the end of the journey, he had basically molded the politically conservative Graham into the sort of liberal humanist reader who would enjoy reading him. Was it such a stretch that if a Hollywood gossip columnist could be taught to appreciate the finer things under his tutelage, maybe Hollywood producers would eventually come around and start listening to him?

Fitzgerald had landed yet another literary acolyte. His college-age daughter, Scottie, had decided to become a writer, and his letters to her during this time are full of dogmatic advice and assessments of his own career trajectory. As a way of keeping her from dropping out of Vassar, of reminding her of the sacrifices he was making for her education, he told her his screen-writing work was "the last tired effort of a man who once did something finer and better" (*Letters of FSF* 33). It was not film writing that was wearing him out; it was writing under the gun for Hollywood producers. Still, if he could not achieve popular success with his film work, Fitzgerald implies, perhaps his "finer and better" work, the novels, would be his lasting legacy. In another letter to Scottie, written in 1939, he appears to chalk up his inability to hold onto popular success as an artistic decision. His failures are principled, noble refusals to pander to the audience: "I guess I am too much a moralist at heart and really want to preach at people in some acceptable form rather than to entertain them" (*Letters of FSF* 63). Fitzgerald had done his share of both during his career, but West, like Miss Lonelyhearts, was neither minister nor minstrel.

In the late 1930s, West was struggling without success to build a fiction-writing career that could support him. Parker and Fitzgerald were helping him to keep hammering away by promising him their endorsement of his book. Parker's blurb for *The Day of the Locust* read: "It's brilliant, savage, and arresting—a truly good novel." Fitzgerald's comments came too late to be used to promote the book. He called it a work with "scenes of extraordinary power" that "puts Gorky's 'The Lower Depths' in the class with the 'Tale of Benjamin Bunny.'" But despite lending their support and fame to a struggling writer, Parker and Fitzgerald were experiencing vocational problems of their own. West had spent the 1930s hoping to gain a literary foothold; they had spent the decade in constant fear that they were slipping.

In 1939 Viking published *Here Lies,* a book of Parker's collected stories marked by a funereal title that could not help but remind her that she had produced very little fiction recently. If she was working on fewer scripts as the 1930s were coming to an end, she was composing even fewer short stories. Despite the dearth of new fiction flowing from her pencil, she wanted to bolster her reputation as a fiction writer, and a book of collected stories seemed like a good way to do so. Only three of the stories contained in *Here Lies* were new—the Hemingwayesque "Soldiers of the Republic," "The Custard Heart," and "Clothe the Naked," a weepie about a poor, blind, black child. In these stories Parker is moving toward dealing with progressive issues and stepping away from the witty interior monologues she was known for. But none of these pieces is of the same rank as "Big Blonde" or "Horsie." Without a coat of humor to help it go down, the sentimentality in Parker's stories is unpleasant to swallow.

As "Clothe the Naked" demonstrates, Parker's fire for civil rights was burning hot, but her interest in labor issues may have been cooling a bit. The major battle over which organization would speak on behalf of screenwriters, the worker-friendly SWG or the producer-supported Screen Playwrights, had ended in 1938 with the National Labor Relations Board having recognized the SWG as the official union voice of writers in Hollywood. The NLRB had ordered producers to sit down with union representatives immediately, but the studios had responded with more litigation.

During the lengthy struggle for SWG recognition, few union members had worked harder than Parker. At her own professional risk, she had campaigned for equity and collective bargaining, a minimum wage scale, a minimum employment period, advance notice prior to dismissal, fair distribution of screen credit, and protection of rights for future work done in the emerging medium of television. She had been the very picture of a successful, socially committed screenwriter. She had even put her politics onscreen. Parker had helped finance a documentary on the Loyalist cause titled *The Spanish Earth.* It was an issue she felt passionate about, as did many other screenwriters, perhaps because the Spanish Civil War, which pitted workers against tyrants, seemed to mirror their own struggle in Hollywood. Reporting for the *New Masses* in 1939 about her trip to Spain, Parker wrote: "There I was, then, wild with the knowledge of injustice and brutality and misrepresentation, . . . At that same time I saw many rich people and, in this I am not unique, they did much in my life to send me back to the masses, to make me proud of being a worker, too"

(*Portable* 462–63). Perhaps here Parker is playing a bit of a role. But there can be no doubt that she is correct in calling herself a worker. Her work was writing, and that work was very real.

Parker still continued to experience phantom slumming fears. When a *Pacific Weekly* reporter writing a 1939 article titled "Are Film Writers Workers?" on the NLRB hearings asked her about her work in the movie industry, she told him, "I want nothing from Hollywood but money, and anyone who tells you he is here for anything else or tries to make beautiful words out of it lies in his teeth" (371). This hardly sounds like the artist who had eloquently described her kinship with Spanish laborers and the screenwriter who had made beautiful words out of her inability to condescend to what she puts down on paper. Even if we make allowances for Parker's difficulty in holding back a caustic zinger, her response still seems like a failure to get the message of the Screen Writers Guild—that writers *are* workers—to a wider audience. On the other hand, if all she truly wanted from Hollywood was money—not fair labor conditions for her coworkers, the satisfaction of a job well done, membership in a writing community, or even an Academy Award for best original screenplay— she had earned plenty of cash in the recent past. After West's sister Laura, the screenwriter wife of S. J. Perelman, had gotten pregnant in 1938, Parker and Campbell had taken over her lucrative MGM contract, with Zeppo Marx serving as her agent (Meade 287).

After working on several scripts for MGM, among them *Sweethearts* (1938), a hit starring the bankable duo of Nelson Eddy and Jeanette Mac-Donald, the writing team had contributed to the less successful *Trade Winds* at United Artists, a movie featuring their friend Fredric March. This had marked the end of the most productive period of Parker's screen-writing life (1933–38). In 1939, the year she made her comments to *Pacific Weekly* and wrote the *New Masses* article, Parker did no movie work at all. This, coupled with the publication of *Here Lies*, could account for the increased acidity in her feelings for screen writing in general and Holly-wood studios in particular.

On the other hand, since the 1920s virtually everything Parker ever said needed to be taken with a grain of salt (or arsenic). She still paid SWG dues in 1939, and perhaps her checkbook belied her harsh words. Stuart Silver-stein's introduction to *Not Much Fun: The Lost Poems of Dorothy Parker* argues that Parker forged a hard armor to cover her bleeding heart, leaving out sappy love poems from her collections in favor of tough, cynical verse and crafting a world-weary persona (34). But it is also clear that she had a tendency to wear her heart garishly on her sleeve if she felt the occasion called for it. Silverstein goes on to criticize Parker's politics, especially her failure to denounce Stalin after the August 24, 1939, nonaggression pact with Nazi Germany, an issue that caused bosom friend Robert Benchley to stop speaking to her. Silverstein writes: "Even if Dorothy's intent *was* pure, which is doubtful, she still condoned, and outspokenly supported, and even helped finance the monstrous policies of a hostile and genocidal regime. Determining whether she was a rogue or merely a fool is a melancholy task" (49). From a twenty-first-century vantage point, Parker's long embrace of Communism appears dangerously naive. But there can be no doubt that she had a soft spot and an open wallet for humanity and humanistic causes, despite not looking deeply enough into each of the multiple organizations to which she was contributing her time, money, and name.

A few years earlier, she had written in the *New Masses* that she had no group affiliation except for "that not especially brave little band that hid its nakedness of heart and mind under the out-of-date garment of a sense of humor" (qtd. in Meade 273). This retrospective, self-deprecatory turn is echoed in Parker's 1939 address to the crowd at the third League of American Writers conference. In the address, titled "Sophisticated Poetry— and the Hell With It," she turns her back on her early work and early fame in a monologue worthy of MGM by way of Malcolm Cowley. You can almost hear the violins behind her words: "I think the best thing now about writers is that they grow up sooner. They know you cannot find yourself until you find your fellow men—they know there is no longer I; there is we" (*Portable* 560).

With a collection of old stories dressed up and waked as *Here Lies,* a dip in her interest in the SWG, diminishing film work, a discrediting of the writing that had made her famous, and discussion of a new generation of superior writers, it looked like Parker was ready to deliver the eulogy on her career.

The Comeback: F. Scott Fitzgerald and "The Lost Decade"

If Parker was publicly behaving like a has-been, Fitzgerald was having an even stickier public-relations problem. In *Beloved Infidel* Graham tells the story of Fitzgerald making a surprise visit to a school production of a play based on "A Diamond as Big as the Ritz." The students truly are surprised—to find him alive. It was a common mistake in the late 1930s. Budd Schulberg talks of being stunned when Walter Wanger, a producer with United Artists, told him that he was being paired with Fitzgerald to write *Winter Carnival,* a romantic comedy set at an Ivy League college. Schulberg thought Fitzgerald was dead (Beck 25).

The tale of the Fitzgerald/Schulberg meeting and the disastrous screen-writing trip to Dartmouth that followed it is one that has been retold time and again—especially by Schulberg. Its outline is as follows: Fitzgerald got drunk on the plane, stayed drunk in New Hampshire despite Schulberg's attempts to babysit him, caught a huge cold, acted like a fool at a meeting with faculty and students that Wanger had arranged for the purpose of showing him off, got himself and Schulberg fired when it was revealed that no work on the script had been done, and wound up attached to an IV in the hospital. It is a well-known fact that this story forms the basis for *The Disenchanted*, Schulberg's 1950 novel that looks back at the 1930s. Fitzgerald gets poured into the character of Manley Halliday, a drunken novelist whose best days are long behind him. What is less well known, however, is that the anecdote finds its way into "The Lost Decade," a powerful Fitzgerald story published in *Esquire* in 1939 that is a tale of renewal rather than decay.

The February debacle at Dartmouth that would inspire Schulberg's novel and Fitzgerald's short story had come on the heels of a bad start of the year for Fitzgerald. Despite the fact that he was becoming more comfortable with components of film grammar such as *montage, dissolves,* and *wipes,* Fitzgerald still was not a skilled screenwriter, nor was he a happy one. He lacked West's ability to detach himself from the script, and he possessed neither Schulberg's knack for structure nor Parker's ear for spoken dialogue. Yet of the four, Fitzgerald was the one who most wanted to put a distinctive mark on the movies he worked on. "Madame Curie," a script for Greta Garbo he thought was the prestige project that would finally rocket him into the front ranks of Hollywood screenwriters, had gone shelved when MGM canceled it a few days into 1939. The studio had then loaned him to David Selznick for three days to work on *Gone with the Wind*. Reports vary on the success of this collaboration.

Fitzgerald had been charged with the primary responsibility of working on characterization for Aunt Pittypat, and Selznick had also wanted him to do a general polish of the script, but many sources report that in the end he had very little impact on the finished film. He had gotten along fine with Selznick, but he had felt constrained. He grumbled to Maxwell Perkins that the producer had forbidden him to use any words in the screenplay that did not appear in the source novel (*Letters of FSF* 284), a story backed up by Gavin Lambert's *GWTW: The Making of "Gone with the Wind."* If Fitzgerald wanted to use a noun or adjective, he had to thumb through Mitchell in search of it.

Selznick had also made him use marginal notes to justify each tiny change he made in the script. Referring to a copy housed at Princeton, Aaron Latham points to a scene where Scarlett wraps a yellow sash around Ashley and the soldier remarks, "It looks like gold." Latham notes that Fitzgerald had crossed out the line and had reminded Selznick: "This is Technicolor" (213). Whereas Lambert credits Fitzgerald with tightening the script and making it less talky (71–72), it comes as no surprise that Selznick—the self-proclaimed author of *A Star Is Born*—swears that Fitzgerald had no effect on the film whatsoever (Behlmer, *Memo from DOS* 444).

Returning to MGM after *Gone with the Wind*, Fitzgerald had been informed that the studio was letting him go. His salary of $1,250 a week was far too high to have him just sitting around. During his eighteen months at MGM, he had made $85,000 (Bruccoli, *Some Sort* 451), but he was still deeply in debt. In a fight that had been brewing for years, Harold Ober, his agent, had refused to lend him any more money, and this argument would result in the two parting company before the end of the year. In 1938 Fitzgerald had written "Financing Finnegan," a humorous story about a bullying, Hemingwayesque author—half genius and half con man—who cannot repay the money his agent and publisher have invested in him. By 1939 the joke was less funny. At the time of the Dartmouth trip, Fitzgerald had been a free-agent screenwriter on the verge of having no literary agent. Without Ober to broker deals for him, he now needed Hollywood more than ever. As he wrote to Scottie: "Sorry you got the impression I'm quitting the movies—they are always there" (*Letters of FSF* 48).

But while Fitzgerald may have been down, he was far from out. He had some serious writing left in him yet, as "The Lost Decade" demonstrates. In Schulberg's *The Disenchanted,* pathological drinking thwarts the literary comeback of Manley Halliday, the Fitzgerald stand-in. But the successful "comeback" from alcoholism depicted in Fitzgerald's own "The Lost Decade" is even more profound than an artistic or professional one. The story has often been misread as the tale of a famous architect's creative and spiritual bankruptcy after emerging from a decade of drunkenness. Sergio Perosa writes: "There seems to be no possible escape or redemption for him: lost in the struggle for life, he has exhausted all possibilities of resistance. His existential predicament has reduced him to the state of a straw man" (145). But Louis Trimble is not only free of the bottle; he has also been freed from his stunted imagination and clouded perceptions. After a horrible cognitive crash, he finds his creative genius has been rebooted.

Whereas Halliday takes a masochistic delight in constantly torturing himself with self-analysis of his past failures, Trimble faces the future head-on and is ready to soak up the New York City around him.

The Depression is over, the 1939 World's Fair is in town, and Trimble's alcoholic haze has been lifted. The story begins with him visiting a news-weekly, which seems to suggest that he is still newsworthy. His babysitter for the afternoon is Orrison Brown, a young college graduate who thinks the name "Louis Trimble" belongs to the past. Sharing Schulberg's scalp and resume, Brown is "a curly-haired man who a year before had edited the Dartmouth Jack-O-Lantern" (*Short Stories* 470). Rather than revisit such old haunts as 21, Trimble wants to have lunch "where there are young people to look at"; rather than look at the buildings he designed, the architect wants to study "the back of people's heads . . . their necks—how their heads are joined to their bodies. I'd like to hear what those two little girls are saying to their father. Not exactly what they're saying but whether the words float or submerge, how their mouths shut when they've finished speaking." The artist wants to observe things as if it were the first time. He wants to "see how people walk and what their clothes and shoes and hats are made of. And their eyes and hands" (471–72). This character—not to mention this prose—is a far cry from Schulberg's Halliday, a "disillusioned amanuensis of a dying order."

Just as Halliday makes his screen-writing partner, Shep, rethink his proletariat literary manifesto, Trimble causes Orrison to become hyper-aware of his surroundings. At the end of the story, the young writer feels "the texture of his own coat" and reaches out to press "his thumb against the granite of the building by his side" (473). Shep and Orrison are very much alike, but Trimble is miles away from Manley Halliday. One is a ghostly presence who dies; the other is a vital artist reborn. One holds on to romanticized memories of the past; the other embraces the tangible reality of the present. If Halliday contains Schulberg's reconstructed memories of a broken-down and distorted Fitzgerald, Trimble projects Fitzgerald's slightly idealized vision of his future self. Aside from a name that suggests the DTs, we do not really sense Trimble's struggle not to get drunk: "There was nothing about him that suggested or ever had suggested drink" (473). Trimble emerges from a decade of abusing himself with alcohol as if he has just woken up from a witch's spell—a little dazed but no worse for the wear. The architect of the 1920s, like the architect of *The Great Gatsby*, is ready to start designing new projects again. Having come back from the other side, his past failures will only sweeten the new successes to come.

Saying that "The Lost Decade" catches Fitzgerald painting a rosy self-portrait does not take away from its achievement. Although the story consists of a single episode and its brevity puts it in danger of being written off as a mere sketch, the piece is fully realized, emotionally honest, and resonant. The dialogue is sharp, and the descriptive paragraphs are succinct. Morris Dickstein writes: "It may not be the lyrical, romantic Fitzgerald of the 1920s who most claims our attention today, but the shattered disillusioned Fitzgerald of the 1930s. . . . he was the source of the myths that circulated around him, but unlike Hemingway, he saved the myths that surrounded him for his own work, not simply for the gossip columns. This points to the great difference between a writer who breaks down and cannot work and one who uses his frustrations and disappointments as new material" (82). "The Lost Decade" demonstrates in both style and theme that although the year had seen Fitzgerald lose his agent, his MGM contract, and a share of his confidence, he had retained his talent and his hope for the future.

Bad Models in a Bad School: Nathanael West and *The Day of the Locust*

Another writer undiscouraged at decade's end, despite numerous obstacles, was Nathanael West. Although West is a far less blatantly autobiographical writer than Fitzgerald, or even Schulberg of *The Disenchanted*, in an early draft of *The Day of the Locust* the story is told from the narrative point of view of the screenwriter Claude Estee. However, just as "The Lost Decade's" Trimble is an architect rather than an author, having a screenwriter as the focalizer might have been too obvious a choice for West. In revision Claude was demoted to the chorus, and the book was rewritten in the third person, with set designer Tod Hackett taking on top billing. Although the change was made partially because the novelist did not want his main character to be too closely identified with him, autobiographical traces remain.

Both West and Tod received Ivy League educations. When Tod is recruited out of the Yale School of Fine Arts by Hollywood, his friends worry that he is selling out and will never paint again—echoes of Edmund Wilson and James T. Farrell warning West that prostituting in the movie business would dry up his creative juices. Yet just as West viewed Hollywood as a means to an end, a place to potboil while he soaked up material for his "real" writing, Tod does not mind hacking at National Films if it continues to provide him with inspiration for his masterwork. Both create dreams during the day and puncture them at night. Both draw upon their observations of Hollywood artifice to produce their art. Both see Los Angeles as a site of constant struggle where cultural currents converge and clash.

Where the architect Trimble draws strength from the sights and sounds of the streets of New York as the city itself really is, Tod the painter bathes himself in Los Angeles's atmosphere of simulacra. For him, as for West, mimetic realism just will not cut it: "He would never again do a fat red barn, old stone wall or sturdy Nantucket fisherman" (*Novels* 242). The action begins with Tod at his office window, watching a mob of extras dressed in nineteenth-century military uniforms being chased by an assistant director wearing a polo shirt. Geography, history, and native culture are all malleable in Hollywood. The Gingos are an Eskimo family brought to Los Angeles to appear in a *Nanook of the North*–like documentary. When the movie wraps up, they stay in Hollywood, wearing their native garb and surviving on the fish they hunt in Jewish delis. A wrinkled Native American wearing a signboard advertising "Genuine Relics from the Old West" speaks in the shtick of the vaudeville team Weber and Fields.

West's version of modernism, like the movie camera, breaks the world into fragments. Narrative, time, and place are blurred and juxtaposed. Egyptian temples in Los Angeles are next door to Swiss chalets. Transplanted Midwest bookkeeper Homer Simpson's house is decorated in a mishmash of styles and periods. He has two rooms that are furnished and decorated identically. If things are identical, then there cannot be an original. West illustrates the point that technology allows things to be mass produced, stamping out copies that cannot be distinguished from their source. Mass-produced hinges on Homer's doors are made to look like they are handcrafted, just as the projector makes the artificial look real.

Throughout the novel, especially in those scenes that concentrate on Tod, the natural is described in terms of sets and costumes. The moon is "a bone button"; flower petals are "wrinkled like crepe"; leaves are "heavy with talcumlike dust"; and birds scatter "into a thousand glittering particles like metal confetti." The supermarket, like the studios a purveyor of consumer goods, bathes its products in artificial light to make the natural appear more real, the oranges more orange. The California hills outlined in violet piping (243) match the violet piping on the chairs in Mrs. Jenning's screening room (258). The clothes the faceless masses wear are just costumes: ladies who have never been at sea wear sailing outfits, and people who have never been on a court wear tennis clothes.

Faye Greener has been created by Hollywood. By reading fan magazines, studying the trade papers, listening to gossip on the studio lots, and going to the pictures, Faye is trying to discover the formula for becoming a star. The words she speaks on film are delivered badly, and her offscreen "lines" are said unconvincingly, but the content of what she says does not really matter to the men she comes in contact with during the novel. This audience is too captivated by her beauty to listen, anyway. In Parker's "Glory in the Daytime," we meet a great thespian whose age becomes pathetically transparent once she leaves the footlights. In West's "The Sun, the Lady, and the Gas Station," we see an actress whose face melts in daylight. But Faye's beauty is natural; it is structural, "like a tree's" (319). She is a bad film actress whose only starring role is in her everyday life. West's narrator writes of Faye's male spectators: "None of them really heard her. They were all too busy watching her smile, laugh, shiver, whisper, grow indignant, cross and uncross her legs, stick out her tongue, widen and narrow her eyes, toss her head so that her platinum hair splashed against the red plush of the chair back. The strange thing about her gestures and expressions was that they did not really illustrate what she was saying. They were almost pure. It was as though her body recognized how foolish her words were and tried to excite her hearers into being uncritical" (357).

The book's narrative gaze acts like the camera to break the female body into parts: legs, tongue, eyes, and so forth. The distance between Faye's objectified body and her words, the gap between the signifier and the signified, seems to be the location of her artifice. But her body acts to blur the line between the real and the artificial by protecting her words. Sometimes her body makes "automatic" seductive gestures, at other times she uses a smile or caress as a "reward" (355). Even Tod and Claude, studio employees well acquainted with the production of artifice, cannot help falling for her.

When she meets Claude at a postcockfight party, the actress assumes "her favorite role" of being "very much the lady." No one is convinced by her act, if that is what it can be called, yet they make fools of themselves to get her attention. The men laugh at Faye's "voice stiff with hauteur" (354), yet when Claude speaks to her, "everyone was aware of the begging note in his voice, but no one smiled. They did not blame him. It was almost impossible to keep that note out when talking to her. Men used it just to say good morning" (356). As a person she is a joke to them, but as an object she is irresistible. Her body "excites her hearers into being uncritical" and makes them lose control over the timbre of their own words.

Tod desires both to desire Faye and to distance himself aesthetically, even anthropologically, from that desire. In an early attempt to analyze his feelings for her, to wake himself from the spell she has over him, Tod convinces himself that Faye's affectations are "so completely artificial" that he finds them "charming" (292). It is precisely her artifice that draws him to her, as if by magic. Although Tod prides himself on being immune to the lure of artifice—after all, his job is to create it—he is caught up in a frantic yearning to possess Faye as an object. Angry with her rejection of him, the artist tries to cast a mojo of his own. He rolls up the sketches he has made of her, binds them with a string, and locks them in a trunk. He believes, like a "witch doctor" (337), that if he can control the image, control the fetish object, he can control the person.

Tod makes repeated attempts to take Faye by force. Like the "cheated" he has come to Hollywood to paint, he erupts with sexual violence born out of frustration. As the novel ends, he loses the ability to distinguish between the real and the artificial. He escapes the riot by imagining he is working on his art and mistakes a police siren for his own voice: "He felt his lips with his hands. They were clamped tight. He knew then it was the siren. For some reason this made him laugh and he began to imitate the siren as loud as he could" (389). Copying the artificial, confused about what is the original, Tod is captured by the very phenomenon that he has been studying. The ethnographer has gone native and gone mad.

Of the major characters, only Faye Greener, the Carrie Meeber of the movies, makes it through the book relatively unmarred. She has built a shell around herself that keeps out reality. She has become an object that needs only to relate to itself. The conquering male, Tod wants to penetrate what he believes is a female unified self: "It was her completeness, her egg-like self-sufficiency, that made him want to crush her" (295). Tod wants to place himself inside of Faye, to make her need him like he needs her, but her self-possession, her "egglike self-sufficiency," cannot be cracked. Tod has "a whole set of personalities, one inside another, like a nest of Chinese boxes" (242), but Faye refuses to see herself as a construct. Her single-minded dreams of being a star someday, and her constant performance of that self, cannot be punctured. In *Miss Lonelyhearts* West writes that Betty's "sureness [is] based on the power to limit experience arbitrarily" (*Novels* 71). The same thing can be said of Faye—and of the movies themselves.

Faye has built herself so thoroughly around the image of the screen siren, an object of male spectatorship and desire that appears available but is not, that it is impossible to pinpoint where the performance begins. When the actress is not pounding the pavement looking for extra work, her favorite activity is lying in bed and mentally shuffling through a pack of vaguely pornographic fantasies. One of her daydreams is a variation of the Cinderella plot; another concerns a muscled man battling a snake. She realizes that her method of artificially selecting what should be natural is a bit mechanical, but is not aware that the "content for a vigorous life of imagination" that she draws upon consists of B movie plots—much like the ones the screenwriter West was called upon to produce for Republic Pictures—filled with Freudian snakes and fat orchids. Faye can laugh at the process, but not at the product.

In this way she is more like Tod, and like the average moviegoer, than he realizes. He laughs at her fantasies, but soon he is constructing fantasies of his own about how he will finally possess her. He sees her artifice, but falls for her anyway. He laughs at his feelings for her but cannot help acting on them. He is lured in by what Walter Benjamin famously dubbed "the phony spell of a commodity" (231). Faye not only wishes to turn herself, but her dreams as well, into commodities. She even has a fantasy of selling her fantasies to a movie studio in order to make some dough until her big break comes. For her the movies are reality.

Faye is "an actress who had learned from bad models in a bad school" (292), and most critics have seen her as a link in a long gilded chain of screendom's "dumb blondes," as West's parody of Hollywood pouring itself into an empty vessel shaped like a curvy woman. Often censure of her slips into to angry misogyny. Stanley Edgar Hyman writes, for instance, that Faye "has a brain the size of a walnut" (31). But Faye is not as dumb as she appears, and West has infused her with more agency than many critics have realized. She knows what genres are in vogue at the studios, and she goes to the movies as often as she can to study. Unlike Esther Blodgett, Faye was not born a star, but she believes she has the raw materials to make herself one.

An important lesson she has learned from "bad models" such as Jean Harlow in the "bad school" of movie theaters is that sex sells. Faye may be a bad actress, but she is trying to lay the groundwork for becoming a good star. She knows that beauty, platinum hair, and sexuality are bankable commodities for a woman in Hollywood, and she will invest them to get whatever she wants. On one level, like a lost member of the Frankfurt School, West is parodying someone copycatting a mass-produced film image of a Jean Harlow copy, adding Faye to a group that includes the early Alice Faye and Fay Wray, but he has also inscribed the character with a strong individual desire to ape them in order to join their ranks.

At one point Faye says that the rumors that fat girls will be in next year is just publicity for Mae West, and the implication is that West is not one of her models. But the two have a lot in common when it comes to attaching value to their sexuality and controlling that value. In this way both women write their own roles. Robert Sklar, analyzing Mae West's screen persona, could also be talking about Faye: "Sex is the only game she can play, and though she disclaims dependence on any man, she depends on her capacity to attract men for her livelihood. What's most astonishing is her lack of sentiment" (185). Faye is not sentimental. She refuses to accept Tod's love because he has neither looks nor power to offer her. His limited value to her resides in his willingness to listen to her dreams of stardom. She will flirt with him, but she will not provide him with a mercy lay. When he meets her, she is a virgin. Sex is all she has in the bank, and philanthropy is not in her nature.

Without regret, as a simple business decision that will allow her to pay her father's funeral bill and support herself, Faye signs up for a tour of duty as a call girl, selling the only thing she has to sell. Tod offers to pay for the burial costs, but Faye will not let him. It has been made obvious to her from his declarations of love coupled with his rape attempt that he wishes to possess more than her body, and she does not want to be in his debt. Her "break" comes when she enters into a "business arrangement" with Homer and makes the transition back from supporting herself by selling sex to supporting herself by selling sexuality. Played as a sucker, Homer gives her the "star treatment," providing Faye with room, board, management, and costumes in exchange for simply being near her. It is a situation Homer has been in before. His other "romance" in the novel is with a prostitute who uses her sexuality to dupe him into paying her hotel bill.

As in Dreiser's *Sister Carrie*, Norman Mailer's *Deer Park*, Émile Zola's *Nana*, and the novels of Alexandre Dumas and Honoré de Balzac, in *The Day of the Locust* the line between prostitution and being an actress is a thin one. West reminds us that prostitutes, like actresses and other performers, have handlers. Tod moves out of his first hotel because it was filled with hookers and "their managers, trainers, and advance agents" (245). Audrey Jenning is a former silent film star who could not make the transition into talkies and chose not to be demoted to bit player. By opening a bordello, she has remained in the entertainment industry elite and has even achieved a measure of highbrow street cred. Claude believes that the movie moguls could achieve respectability by forming a Cinema Foundation and giving some of their money away to "Science and Art. You know, give the racket a front" (255). In this same spirit, Jenning has cemented her place among Los Angeles high society, having tea with distinguished matrons and discussing modernist artists and writers in salons.

MGM's Marcus Loew, a mogul from Hollywood's golden age, once remarked, "We sell tickets to theaters, not movies" (Koszarski 9). In the same spirit, Jenning exhibits silent porno movies in her parlor in order to entice her customers into purchasing the services of the call girls she distributes to wealthy homes across the city. Early in the novel, a group of characters, among them Tod and Claude, go to Jenning's for an evening's entertainment. This episode has either been dismissed or ignored by critics and scholars. George Milburn, in a 1939 review of the novel, faults West for paying so much narrative attention "to an irrelevant visit to a brothel" (qtd. in Siegel 68). But the scene is virtually the entire novel in microcosm.

In an effort to convince the skeptical Tod to come along, studio employee Claude expresses his admiration for the madam's "skillful packaging" of vice and comments that the "dive's a triumph of industrial design." But Tod, whose job as a set designer is to create artifice, says he does not care "how much cellophane she wraps in it," he does not like "natch joints" or any depressing places for deposit such as "vending machines." After telling him that they will only be going there to see a movie, to look but not to touch, Claude extends the vending machine analogy: "You insert a coin and press home the lever. There's some mechanical activity inside the bowels of the device. You receive a small sweet, frown at yourself in the dirty mirror, adjust your hat, take a firm grip on your umbrella and walk away, trying to look as though nothing had happened. It's good but it's not for pictures" (*Novels* 255–56). But it *is* pictures, at least the early ones. Edison's Kinetoscope was designed for one paying viewer at a time, was motor driven, and served a "small sweet" an inch square for about sixty seconds. Furthermore, in comparing sex to a vending machine, Tod and Claude are making the natural mechanized, just as films they work on use a variety of machines to turn the "real" into celluloid.

Film is about seeing, and moviemakers have always tried to figure out what people will pay to see. In 1897, less than a year after the first public screening of a motion picture, the pornographic film *Bedtime for the Bride* opened in France. In the United States, stag films were viewed in all-male bastions like the Elks Club, but in Paris, where West spent some time after college, early porn was associated mainly with brothels. The movie Tod and his friends watch at the whorehouse, *The Predicament of Marie*, is French. The film is closer to bedroom farce or screwball comedy than it is to porn. After a long expositional narrative for a blue movie (members of a family all desire Marie; she just gets started with one; there is a knock on the door; she hides her partner; the next person comes in; there is a knock on the door, and so on; when the whole family is hiding in her room, there is another knock on the door; she thinks it might be a telegram), the projector breaks before any sex happens. The group yells "cheat" and stages a mock riot.

As Linda Williams points out in her book *Hard Core*, the whole reason the brothels showed the movies was to entice the viewers into purchasing the services of the ladies of the house. She writes of the stag film: "Its role seems rather to arouse and then precisely *not* to satisfy a spectator, who must subsequently seek satisfaction outside of the purely visual terms of the film—whether in masturbation, in actual sexual relations, or by channeling sexual arousal into communal wisecracking" (74). Even if the projector did not break, chances are the group would not have been satisfied with the film. One French stag film Williams analyzes ends with the delivery of a telegram saying, "After seeing this picture, rush over to a nice girl and get taken care of." The telegram being delivered to Marie, at the culmination of one frustrated sexual encounter after another, likely contains a similar message. Tod and his friends sit back down to watch the rest of the movie, but there will be no sex in the sex film. The whole thing was a cheat from the beginning.

Perhaps the men in *The Day of the Locust* prefer it that way. As W. H. Auden correctly pointed out, the only type of relation between West's characters is the sadomasochistic (119). Both Homer and Tod experience feelings of guilt and a desire to be punished by Faye. Like Hemingway's Brett Ashley or many of Fitzgerald's women, she is a "bitch goddess," a beautiful woman without mercy. Her power is terrible in its intensity. Tod believes that Faye's invitation "wasn't to pleasure, but to struggle, hard and sharp, closer to murder than to love. If you threw yourself on her, it would be like throwing yourself from the parapet of a skyscraper. You would do so with a scream. You couldn't expect to rise again. Your teeth would be driven into your skull like nails into a pine board and your back would be broken" (*Novels* 251). In *Love and Death in the American Novel*, Leslie Fiedler notes the smooth transition from Fitzgerald's Daisy Fay to West's Faye Greener (326). The green light both women seem to be signaling is not an invitation to possess them; it is an invitation to be destroyed in trying.

At one point the seventeen-year-old actress feigns innocence by appearing in a sailor outfit that makes her look as though she is twelve. Like the United States, she seems young, green(er), and virginal, there for the taking. But appearances are deceiving. As immigrants to the United States and West's heartland starers transplanted to California soon discover, the American dream is not available to all. Everyone cannot perform; some must simply watch and ache. Homer's childlike love for Faye soon turns to violent disillusionment. Like Nabakov's Lolita, and like "Daddy's Girl" Rosemary Hoyt in *Tender Is the Night*, she is a kid who has learned to use her sexuality to get what she wants from adults. As in John O'Hara's *The Big Laugh* or Huxley's *After Many a Summer Dies the Swan*, the actress with the girl's face and the woman's body is a force of sexual destruction.

Faye, as the embodiment of a screen goddess, is a lusted-after object. Her clothes get ripped from her body in the post-cockfight dance/orgy scene. Tod paws her at her own father's funeral. He tries to rape her twice and has long, detailed fantasies of raping her twice more. In *Day of the Locust*, people do not want to worship movie stars from afar; they want to hurt them up close. Funeral scenes are a staple of Hollywood novels and movies about movies. In *A Star Is Born* fans express glee that Norman Maine has committed suicide. In West's novel Harry's funeral is packed with people looking for a show. Faye's landlady has "produced" the performance: picking the flowers, arranging the "star's" costume, picking the exhibition hall. Dead, painted Harry looks like "the interlocutor at a minstrel show" (*Novels* 318). When no movie stars show up and they start getting bored, the cheated start to leave.

West's novel is perhaps more deserving of the name *The Disenchanted* than is Schulberg's book. In fact any of West's novels could fit that title. In the final analysis, *The Day of the Locust* is no more an anti-Hollywood novel than *A Cool Million* is an anti–New England novel or *Balso Snell* is against the bowels of the Trojan Horse. The problem is not place or culture—these are just symptoms. The problem is people. By the time West's mob reassembles at the climactic movie premiere, they are ready to kill someone—anyone. In a section that begins like the movie premiere scene of *A Star Is Born*—but ends very differently—a brokenhearted Homer is ripped to shreds when "the cheated" work themselves into a sexual frenzy of wisecracking and frottage that turns murderous.

For Parker other people were "we"; for West other people were "them." *The Day of the Locust* answers its author's own question about why he could not get uplifting, populist stories about people like Ma and Tom Joad into his fiction—West is scared to death of people like Ma and Tom Joad, or, for that matter, all people. In West, unlike in Steinbeck, gatherings are not about communal solidarity and renewed hopes; they're about violent fascism and death. Jonathan Veitch compares *The Day of the Locust* to two essays by West's contemporary Walter Benjamin:

> The rage to overcome the distance by which cultural objects have heretofore remained sacralized results in a loss of "aura." For Walter

Crowd at the world premiere of *Gone with the Wind*. Photofest

Benjamin, at least the Benjamin of "Art in the Age of Mechanical Reproduction," this is a necessary prelude to the liberation of a populace cowed into submission by the "sacred" status of art. Under this scenario reality at last reveals itself as malleable, subject to human will, and, hence, available to revolutionary action. But Benjamin recounts a less optimistic version of this story in "Some Motifs in Baudelaire," which has much in common with West. There, aura is seen as a lingering repository of the meaning that objects still possess. The loss of aura precipitates a fall into a reified world of dead matter. . . . Instead of the revolutionary action Benjamin envisioned in his earlier thesis, this awakening to a lifeless world provokes a rage closer to fascism. (122)

The Day of the Locust reminds us that *stare* begins with *star* and that there is a *fan* in *fanatic*. Movies, more than any other product of advanced capitalism, helped to shape the way people perceive the world and themselves. Cinema is the most democratic of the arts, but in some ways it is the most dictatorial. To many critics of the first half of the twentieth century, film replaced religion as the opiate of the masses. Robert Warshow in *The Immediate Experience* writes: "The chief function of mass culture is to relieve one of the necessity of experiencing one's life directly. . . . mass culture is the screen through which we see reality and the mirror in which we see ourselves" (38–39). If movies both gave people what they wanted and told them what they wanted, then it stands to reason that people would want life to be like the movies. As the screenwriter Claude remarks, "What the barber wants is amour and glamour" (*Novels* 256). He does not receive it in his everyday life, which leads to the feeling of being "cheated." As Tod says earlier as he watches a crowd of Hollywood's disenfranchised: "It's hard to laugh at the need for beauty and romance" (243). West's jokes, as he told Fitzgerald, were not entirely jokes. In *The Day of the Locust*, the movies feed us fantasies, but we need those fantasies. What West attacks is not so much the evils of the manufactured lies Hollywood dupes us into believing, but a world that causes us to need those lies. It does not do much good to puncture dreams if there is nothing to replace them with.

Tod himself is not immune to the lure of beauty and the need for escape. Caught in the mob, he begins mentally working on his painting, but soon he is constructing a movie in his mind. Authors often choose to write their novels in the past tense, and *The Day of the Locust* is no exception. But film must be present tense. Even in cinema flashbacks, actions are shown happening, not already having happened. *The Burning of Los Angeles,* Tod's static object of art, slowly gains motion by use of active verbs. The boundary dissolves between the riot he is depicting and the riot he is experiencing: "In the lower foreground, men and women fled wildly before the vanguard of the crusading mob." Faye "ran [note that the tense is not *was running*] proudly, her knees held high. . . . Claude turned his head as he ran to thumb his nose at his pursuers. Tod himself picked up a small stone to throw before continuing his flight" (388). Snapped back into reality, rescued from being crushed, Tod lapses back into the artificial. He cannot distinguish the police siren from himself, just as Faye cannot distinguish herself from the screen siren.

The final version of *Day of the Locust* ends here, implying that Tod's descent into madness is total and probably irreversible. Hollywood has destroyed him. Understandably this is the way that most critics have read the novel. But Jay Martin mentions a discarded ending where Tod recuperates at Claude's house and begins to talk sense again (317). And even in the novel as it stands, there are hints that he will be able to begin creating art again, just as Louis Trimble in "The Lost Decade" will design new buildings. Early on in the novel, West's narrator writes: "'The Burning of

Los Angeles,' a picture he was soon to paint, definitely proved he had talent" (*Novels* 242). Again verb tense must be looked at carefully. Here it implies that at some unspecified later date after Tod was taken away in the police car, the painting was completed. The painter's experiences and observations in the land of mass artifice, like West's, have led to the creation of a singular artwork that "proved he had talent" in the opinion of those in a position to judge such talent.

Unfortunately *The Day of the Locust* was not the critical and commercial hit West had been hoping for. Despite his confidence in the novel's content, an early bad omen for West had been the book's red cover, which he hated. In Schulberg's inscribed copy of the novel, West had made a Communist joke: "Dear Budd, When the day comes, we can use this as a flag" ("Two Conversations" 125). In a June 30, 1939, letter to Fitzgerald, West sums up the novel's reception: "So far the box score stands: Good reviews— fifteen percent, bad reviews—twenty-five percent, brutal personal attacks, sixty percent. Sales: practically none. I'll try another one anyway, I guess." On the same day, West wrote to Edmund Wilson that despite the novel's poor sales, "I haven't given up, however, by a long shot. . . . The world outside doesn't make it possible for me to even hope to earn a living writing novels, while here [in Hollywood] the pay is large enough (it isn't as large as people think, however) for me to have at least three or four months off every year" (*Novels* 795–97). Engaged to be married to Eileen McKenney, the subject of writer Ruth McKenney's popular "My Sister Eileen" stories, West needed the money more than ever. If Hollywood could provide him with a steady income and time off to work on his fiction, he, like Fitzgerald, was happy to be there, writing for the big canvas of the movie screen.

6

Put Yourself in My Place

HOLLYWOOD NOVELS OF 1940–1941

Writers aren't people exactly. Or, if they're any good, they're a whole lot of people trying so hard to be one person.

F. Scott Fitzgerald, *The Last Tycoon*

They've let a certain writer here direct his own pictures and he has made such a go of it that there may be a different feeling about that soon. If I had that chance, I would attain my real goal in coming here in the first place.

F. Scott Fitzgerald, after seeing Preston Sturges's 1940 film *The Great McGinty*

Very rarely does victory for the individual writer raise the freedom level of his fellow writers. The fight for freedom of expression in Hollywood is inextricably tied up with the fight for economic security. . . . But the job will not be accomplished in solitude by even the most gifted individual—it will be done by organized writers.

Dalton Trumbo, veteran of the SWG battle

ॐ

On Friday, December 13, 1940, F. Scott Fitzgerald and Dorothy Parker attended a dinner party at Nathanael West's home. One week later, both West and Fitzgerald were dead.

Fitzgerald had been flipping through a Princeton alumni magazine and eating candy when he suffered a massive heart attack and fell to the floor. The next day, December 22, rushing back from a Mexican hunting trip after hearing the news, West ran a stop sign and was killed in a head-on collision near El Centro, California. Both men were waked in Los Angeles before their bodies were sent back east for burial. When Parker viewed Fitzgerald's body, laid out in the William Wordsworth Room of the Pierce Brothers Mortuary, she reportedly called him, quoting Owl-Eyes from *The Great Gatsby*, a "poor son-of-a-bitch" (Meade 386). Fitzgerald was forty-four. West was thirty-seven. Edmund Wilson, who had advised both writers not to lower themselves by writing for the movies, added this 1941 postscript to his essay on California novelists, "The Boys in the Back Room": "West and Fitzgerald were writers of a conscience and with natural gifts rare enough in America or anywhere; and their failure to get their best out of their best years may certainly be laid partly to Hollywood, with its already appalling record of talent depraved and wasted" (56).

But Hollywood did not kill these authors. Bad driving finished West, and years of alcohol abuse took its toll on Fitzgerald. Creatively and professionally, moreover, their last years were not wasted years. In 1940 Fitzgerald continued working on the Hollywood material that would become *The Last Tycoon* and published the Pat Hobby stories. West laid out plans for a new novel on scam "friendship clubs" preying on the lonely, a project that would be financed by his increasing success at navigating the screen-writing system.

At the time of his death, West's established salary was about to go up to six hundred dollars a week (Martin 391). A string of solo credits had something to do with this bump, but West's exploitation of the system was an even bigger factor. He knew that selling originals to the studios paid better than salary work—and if it was a screen adaptation of your own source material, it fetched an even higher price—but it was tough to break into this segment of the market. West realized that a nasty, brutal, and short book such as *A Cool Million* was unfilmable, so he slapped the title on a new idea and sold it as an original adaptation. He knew the system well enough to be confident that no one in the studios would bother to check the content of the actual novel.

West and his writing partner, Boris Ingster, received ten thousand dollars from Columbia for "A Cool Million," the story of a man whose life suddenly improves when people start mistaking him for a millionaire (*Novels* 745–54). Having now sold an original, West and Ingster found it easy to turn around and sell another one. RKO paid them twenty-five thousand dollars for "Bird in Hand," a treatment in which forces contend to possess a turkey with government secrets tattooed on its back. Both projects never reached the screen.

Despite working on film turkeys, West was held in high esteem among the circle of writers in Los Angeles. A fellow habitué of Stanley Rose's bookshop said of him: "He affected writers as Bogart did actors, with his reserve and rock-like integrity" (qtd. in Hamilton 158). As far as the screen-writing game went, other writers had helped West along the way, and he was happy to return the favor. In response to a 1940 letter he received from Bob Brown, a friend back east who was asking how to gain employment in the studios, West advised: "If you do take a crack at it, don't make the mistake so many people do of thinking you have to write down for pictures. Look at some of the better ones and try to utilize the best dramatic situations you can think of. . . . you can absolutely depend on my doing everything I possibly can to help you break in" (*Novels* 798).

As Parker had realized years before, Schulberg had practically been born knowing, and Fitzgerald had learned painfully, an author cannot stoop to what he sets down on paper. Rather than drying them out artistically, Hollywood had infused West and Fitzgerald with the money and inspiration they had needed in order to keep working at their vocations. They had come to accept and even admire the film industry by studying its culture and products; they were no longer among those who turn up their noses at Hollywood "with the contempt we reserve for what we don't understand" (*Last Tycoon* 3).

Mrs. Parker's Second Circle

The Hollywood years were not lonely years for West and Fitzgerald, either. After years of knowing each other mainly through letters and their fiction, they had struck up a strong friendship based on mutual admiration. Traveling in the same circles also helped this process. As Leo Rosten makes clear in his 1941 sociological study of the film industry, *Hollywood: The Movie Colony, the Movie Makers*, social life in Hollywood, for all its global reach and for all its geographic sprawl, resembled that of a small town. Despite popular conception, there was not a glamorous nightclub scene or an abundance of all-night parties held at mansions. As dramatized in Schulberg's *What Makes Sammy Run?*, the transplanted New Yorker Al Manheim (as the Al Manners character had been renamed for the novel) is surprised to keep seeing "the same faces" (50) as he walks around.

To alleviate the boredom and blow off steam, eastern writers, like a cocoon of émigrés, created their own social scene in Hollywood. After days steeped in the pressure-cooker atmosphere of the studios, West, Parker, Fitzgerald, Schulberg, and their large circle of friends dined at the Musso and Frank Grill, drank wine next door in the backroom of Stanley Rose's bookshop, and attended SWG meetings across the street at 1655 Cherokee Avenue. With his companion, Sheilah Graham, Fitzgerald, no drunken recluse, was a frequent dinner guest at the homes of other writers. And according to Graham, Fitzgerald saw West more often than he did his other Hollywood friends (Martin 386). One entry in Fitzgerald's notebook mentions that he could see himself in West's tendency toward "long windedness" in conversation, and another calls the younger writer's novels "doomed to the underworld of literature. But literature" (*Notebooks of FSF* item 1900). Both comments indicate that Fitzgerald viewed West as an important writer who was saying things that people were not paying enough attention to or were not yet ready to hear. But one's peers had a way of sorting things out in time. A few months before his death, Fitzgerald wrote to Scottie: "In the opinion of any real artist, the inventor—which is to say Giotto or Leonardo—is infinitely superior to the finished Tintoretto, and the original D. H. Lawrences are infinitely greater than the Steinbecks" (*Letters of FSF* 73).

Fitzgerald forged a creative friendship of sorts with Schulberg as well. Unlike the West/Fitzgerald kinship, the personal dealings between Fitzgerald and Schulberg appear reliant on mutual opportunism. In the years before his death, Schulberg made a cottage industry out of packaging and repackaging his memories of Fitzgerald, but some critics and biographers posit that the young Hollywood prince was usually more annoyed by the older man than drawn to him. Literary biographer Jeffrey Meyers reports a 1940 episode in Los Angeles when Schulberg blew off a visit from Fitzgerald to go have dinner with some acquaintances (315). Questions linger as to how close they ever really were. Even if we make allowances for Schulberg's justifiable exasperation at Fitzgerald's drinking and poor work habits during their trip to Dartmouth, much of the respect Schulberg claims to have had for Fitzgerald seems to have developed shortly after the older man's death, around the time the *New Republic* was looking for essays for a tribute to Scott.

The two writers read draft versions of each other's Hollywood novels, and while both men voiced praise for each other publicly, each disparaged the other in their more private thoughts. After a look at some of *What Makes Sammy Run?*, Fitzgerald labeled his former partner "Budd the untalented" (qtd. in Turnbull 320). "In Hollywood," Schulberg's *New*

Republic piece, makes clear that during the composition of the Stahr work in progress Fitzgerald was up front about wanting insider Hollywood information from him, and when Schulberg read the manuscript Fitzgerald remarked: "I sort of combined you with my daughter Scottie for Cecilia" (*Four Seasons* 134). In a 2001 interview, however, Schulberg claimed that the book "hurt me a little bit" ("Two Conversations" 122). In the revised edition of *The Four Seasons of Success, Writers in America,* Schulberg recalls his reaction to *The Last Tycoon* material: "It was almost as if I had written the book and then Scott had filtered it through his more tempered and sophisticated imagination. It is still the most uncanny experience I've ever had with another man's work. . . . Scott had channeled off into his book some of my energy, some of my emotion and special insights into Hollywood. The sneak thief of vicarious experience that every writer has to be had taken possession of Scott—probably from our very first meeting" (150–51).

Despite the accusation of metaphysical plagiarism, these words make clear that the relationships among Parker, Schulberg, Fitzgerald, and West were more than social. They were creative and professional as well. In the late 1930s, Parker and Schulberg had both worked on *A Star Is Born* and *Nothing Sacred* for David O. Selznick. In 1941, working from a story and treatment from Schulberg, Parker wrote the screenplay for RKO's *Weekend for Three.* I read a copy of the shooting script at the New York State Archives, and it is one of the shortest feature-length screenplays I've seen. The comedy's plot revolves around the troubles that arise when a married woman's former boyfriend visits for the weekend and appears never to want to leave. It is a variation of the "uninvited guest" stock situation done better in former Algonquin members Moss Hart and George Kaufman's 1939 play *The Man Who Came to Dinner.* Thomas M. Pryor, a reviewer for the *New York Times,* noted "the fine acerbic hand of Miss Parker is only fleetingly detectable in a couple of situations" in *Weekend for Three* (qtd. in Kinney 141). Traces of Parker, sounding more like Henny Youngman or Rodney Dangerfield, can best be found in the lines of the much married, much harried supporting character Stonebraker (played onscreen by Edward Everett Horton), who makes such remarks as "My first wife was different—for a while. Then she became indifferent" and "Lots of men used to look at lots of my wives lots of the time." That same year, 1941, Parker added dialogue to the movie version of her friend Lillian Hellman's play *The Little Foxes.* She was then contacted by Alfred Hitchcock to work on *Saboteur.* Her dialogue appears in the circus freak scenes

(Meade 308), and Parker even has a cameo in the film. She and Hitchcock speed by in a car together.

Parker and Fitzgerald had blurbed West's *The Day of the Locust,* and they performed the same service for Schulberg's *What Makes Sammy Run?.* Both endorsements arrived too late for the first printing and only appeared on later runs. The front jacket copy quoted Fitzgerald, who called the novel "a grand book, utterly fearless with a great deal of beauty side by side with the most bitter satire." Parker, quoted on the back jacket, said of the novel: "It has understanding, pity, savagery, courage and sometimes a strange high beauty. It is written with a pace that rushes you along with it, and a sureness that comes only of great skill. It is good to be present when such things happen." After the publication of Schulberg's book, Parker, who serves as a partial model for characters in both *The Last Tycoon* and *What Makes Sammy Run?,* rose to the book's defense regarding accusations that it was anti-Semitic: "Those who hail us Jews as brothers must allow us to have our villains, the same, alas, as any other race" (qtd. in *What Makes* xv).

West's and Schulberg's Hollywood novels shared a publisher (Random House) and an editor (Saxe Commins), and Fitzgerald had read early drafts of both. Parker's novel had never materialized, and never would, but Hollywood novelists West, Fitzgerald, and Schulberg all influenced each other's books in both form and content. As echoes of *The Great Gatsby* can be heard in *Miss Lonelyhearts,* so too can they be heard in *What Makes Sammy Run?,* and even more loudly. During the composition of *The Last Tycoon,* Fitzgerald boasted to Maxwell Perkins that "there is little published in American fiction that doesn't slightly bear my stamp" (*Dear Scott/Dear Max* 261), but the new novel he was working on included its own traces of other writers. *The Last Tycoon*—with a protagonist blatantly patterned after Irving Thalberg and other characters based on Louis B. Mayer (Brady), Joseph Mankiewicz (La Borwits), and Aldous Huxley (Boxley)—evokes a scene from *The Day of the Locust* and contains sizable chunks of Schulberg's biography and memories (Fitzgerald, *Love of the Last Tycoon* xxvii; Schulberg, *Four Seasons* 134). These three Hollywood novels have different scopes and styles—West's surreal book observes bottom-feeders in the film industry, and Fitzgerald's elegiac manuscript and Schulberg's muckraking novel delve into the world of big fish— but all try to come to terms with Hollywood rather than eviscerate it. These texts do not show the movies to be the brain drain Edmund Wilson would have us believe.

During his final years in Hollywood, Fitzgerald became less thirsty for best sellers and celebrity and more focused on the craft of writing and his posthumous reputation, less interested in making it look like writing came easy to him and more willing to learn new techniques and experiment with different forms. At the end of his life, according to some accounts, he was even becoming a better screenwriter, growing more adept at writing with movie equipment in mind. He had learned that film has a language all of its own, and he was grasping toward a way of saying what he wanted to say within it. Wheeler Winston Dixon, a respected experimental filmmaker and critic, finds that Fitzgerald's last scripts show him learning to create more effective scenes by imagining point-of-view shots. Dixon's examination of an early draft of "Cosmopolitan," the script based on Fitzgerald's story "Babylon Revisited," which focuses on a recovering alcoholic trying to gain back custody of his daughter from his sister-in-law, discusses the effective incorporation of p.o.v. tracking shots that call for the use of eye movements to reflect little Victoria's character, as well as for a series of long shots to express her isolation.

Sheilah Graham speculates that "Scott wanted to be a movie director because of what he thought could be done" (*Real F. Scott Fitzgerald* 183). Fitzgerald himself told Zelda that "Cosmopolitan" was his "great hope for attaining some real status out here as a movie man and not a novelist" (*Letters of FSF* 125), and that "the standard of writing from the best movies, like *Rebecca*, is, believe it or not, much higher at present than that in the commercial magazines" (*FSF: A Life in Letters* 443–44). But Fitzgerald's plans to direct "Cosmopolitan"—or even to get the film produced—never came to fruition. A deal to have Shirley Temple play the starring role fell through, and Fitzgerald never got the solo script in good enough shape for it to go before the cameras. Later in the decade, Schulberg would be hired to rewrite the script for producer Lester Cowan ("Old Scott" 100). This project fell through as well. After years of changing hands and studios, the skeleton of "Cosmopolitan" finally reached the screen as the 1954 MGM film *The Last Time I Saw Paris* starring Elizabeth Taylor.

Schulberg later discovered Fitzgerald's original script in a banker's box containing other's people's screenplays, and it was published, with an introduction by Schulberg, as *Babylon Revisited: The Screenplay*. However, this script is more interesting as a curiosity than as a model screenplay. Nunnally Johnson, without a doubt one of the most respected and successful screenwriters of the studio era, someone who found that his talents were better suited to the film medium than to the stage or the page, wrote to a friend that the "Cosmopolitan" script was "crap" that was "padded with junk and nonsense and corn" (*Letters of NJ* 80). A look at the published screenplay bears this out. Filled with stilted dialogue, a murder-for-hire subplot that smells of the one Fitzgerald was planning for *The Last Tycoon*, and a superfluous love interest for Charlie Wales that takes away from the father/daughter focus that made the short story so powerful, it is not the masterwork Dixon believes it to be (or would like it to be). While Dixon fails in the end to establish Fitzgerald as a gifted screenwriter, he convincingly argues that Fitzgerald grew less reliant on dialogue and exposition and more cognizant of shots and editing in scripts such as "Cosmopolitan" and "Infidelity." Fitzgerald had learned not to "write down" to the screen.

This is exactly the lesson that the producer Monroe Stahr impresses upon the highbrow author George Boxley in *The Last Tycoon*. New to screen writing and not much of a moviegoer, Boxley has submitted a ridiculous scene where a duelist falls into a well and needs to be raised up in a bucket. Pressed to admit that he would not put such a sequence in one of his books, Boxley tells Stahr that "movie standards are different" because films are filled with people "wearing strained facial expressions and talking incredible and unnatural dialogue" (31). Stahr's response shows how far Fitzgerald had come in his understanding of the art of writing *to* the screen instead of *for* the screen:

> "Suppose you're in your office. You've been fighting duels or writing all day and you're too tired to fight or write any more. You're sitting there staring—dull, like we all get sometimes. A pretty stenographer that you've seen before comes into the room and you watch her— idly. She doesn't see you, though you're very close to her. She takes off her gloves, opens her purse and dumps it out on a table—"
>
> Stahr stood up, tossing his key-ring on his desk.
>
> "She has two dimes and a nickel—and a cardboard match box. She leaves the nickel on the desk, puts the two dimes back into her purse and takes the black gloves to the stove, opens it and puts them inside. There's one match in the match box and she starts to light it kneeling by the stove. You notice there's a stiff wind blowing in the window—but just then your telephone rings. The girl picks it up, says hello—listens—and says deliberately into the phone, 'I've never owned a pair of black gloves in my life.' She hangs up, kneels by the stove again, and just as she lights the match, you glance around very

suddenly and see that there's another man in the office, watching every move the girl makes—"

Stahr paused. He picked up his keys and put them in his pocket.

"Go on," said Boxley smiling. "What happens?"

"I don't know," said Stahr. "I was just making pictures." (32)

Hooked by the producer's teasing out of a dramatic, suspenseful scene—caught up in watching Stahr writing out loud—Boxley, brought to the studio for his verbal skill, has just been taught that film is a visual medium. And, it must be mentioned, this film lesson has taken place within the pages of a novel. Fitzgerald's sympathies in the scene are clearly with Stahr, who gets all of the good lines in the exchange, not with Boxley.

One of Fitzgerald's notes for *The Last Tycoon* declares that "ACTION IS CHARACTER" (163), which is also a Screen Writing 101 maxim, and through the use of present-tense verbs, a technique West had used in *The Day of the Locust* when describing Tod mentally working on his painting, Stahr reminds us that film is, in the words of Robert Warshow, an "immediate experience." The repeated use of the pronoun *you* and the peppering of numerous phrases of urgency—"starts to," "just as," "very suddenly"—make the lesson about cinema's continuous present even more memorable.

Like West in *The Day of the Locust,* Fitzgerald hints here at the voyeurism inherent in film going. Boxley, of course, could not be sitting in a small space watching someone watching someone else without either of these people knowing he is there. Unless, that is, he is sitting in a darkened movie theater staring at these figures onscreen, gradually making the transition from "idly" watching the projected images to being sutured into the film as a silent participant/observer. Just as access to consciousness in a novel allows us to see and hear thoughts we ordinarily could not see and hear, motion pictures put us in a position to witness actions we ordinarily could not witness.

When we next see Boxley, he is a man reborn. Instead of getting advice on film technique and focalization, he is giving it. Boxley tells his screenwriting collaborators: "You have the stuffings of a turkey here. . . . It is not pictures. . . . A lot a beautiful speeches . . . but no situations. After all, you know, it is not going to be a novel. . . . Let each character see himself in the other's place. The policeman is about to arrest the thief when he sees that the thief actually has *his* face. I mean, show it that way. You could almost call the thing *Put Yourself in My Place*" (106–7). The lessons Boxley has learned about perspective are more than cinematic; they are also cultural and sociological. By overcoming his condescension, by no longer seeing himself as some sort of highbrow policeman enforcing the laws of writing, Boxley has put himself in a new artistic place, and his excitement is palpable. Call it learning to code switch, call it experiencing double consciousness, or call it, as Fitzgerald might, "negative capability," but there can be no doubt that Boxley has now expanded his creative arsenal.

Like Boxley, Al Manheim in *What Makes Sammy Run?* is a literary man who comes to appreciate the film medium. The producer Fineman tells him the story of a famous playwright charged with writing a film scene establishing that a husband is tiring of his marriage. Twenty pages of brilliant dialogue later, the scene is no closer to being finished. An old hand is brought in, "one of the few men left in the business who got his training in the Mack Sennett two-reel comedy school" of silent films, and the next day the scene looks like this:

INT ELEVATOR MEDIUM SHOT
Husband and wife in evening clothes. Husband wearing top hat.

REVERSE ANGLE
As elevator door opens and classy dame enters.

CLOSE SHOT HUSBAND AND WIFE
Get husband's reaction to new dame. Removes hat with flourish. Wife looks from dame to husband's hat to husband. Then glares at him as we

CUT TO: (159–60)

Inspired by the anecdote, Al cannot wait to get working on his new screenplay. He even begins thinking about writing an original screenplay for a biopic on Czechoslovakian democrat Thomas Masaryk, a project that would dovetail his political and aesthetic interests. "The most exciting way ever invented to tell a story is with a motion picture camera," a fellow screenwriter tells him (160).

Schulberg's novel has often been read as an indictment of the movies. Chip Rhodes writes: "Al's narration makes clear that Hollywood defiles art and the integrity of those who devote their lives to it" ("Ambivalence on the Left" 95). It does no such thing. While Sammy Glick might scoff at art and regard those with principles or integrity as suckers, Al does not wind up feeling this way at all. Under the influence of the novel's love interest, Kit Sargent, like Dorothy Parker a respected eastern author and successful screenwriter who assumes a leadership position in the Screen Writers Guild, he begins to understand the reasons why a creative artist might be drawn to Hollywood and, more important, would want to stay there. It is not always all about the money, as Al explains:

> The trouble with Hollywood is that too many people who will not leave are ashamed to be there. But when a moving picture is right, it socks the eye and the ear and the solar plexus all at once and that is a hell of a temptation for any writer. I felt that when I went back for the fourth time to see *The Informer*. And one afternoon when I happened to catch a revival of the Murnau-Jannings masterpiece *The Last Laugh*. And even when I saw one of my own jobs, a stinker if there ever was one, but with one scene in it that sang because I happened to stumble on real picture technique. That is what held Kit there. Hollywood may be full of phonies, mediocrities, dictators, and good men who have lost their way, but there is something that draws you there that you should not be ashamed of. (234)

It is interesting that Al, a wordsmith, would single out *The Last Laugh* as a masterpiece. The Murnau film is entirely reliant on the visual—not only is it silent; it has no title cards. Similarly *The Informer*, the other film Al praises, is heavily reliant on images rather than words. Screenwriter Dudley Nichols explains his methodology for creating the script: "I sought and found a series of symbols to make visual the tragic psychology of the informer, in this case a primitive man with powerful hungers. The whole action was to be played out in one foggy night, for the fog was symbolic of the groping primitive mind; it is really a mental fog in which he moves and dies. A poster offering a reward for information concerning Gypo's friend became the symbol of the evil idea of betrayal, and it blows along the street, following Gypo; it will not leave him alone" (qtd. in Norman 171–72).

Readers respond to a novel in a conscious way by contemplating what they have read, but a film such as *The Informer*, says Al, "socks the eye and the ear and the solar plexus all at once." Viewers have the immediate experience of responding emotionally to audiovisual stimuli of the moving image. It is a lesson in film criticism Stahr would admire.

What Makes Sammy Run? argues against the misperception that integrity and artistic aspirations must be checked at the studio gates. Despite their bouts of cultural bellyaching, writers in Hollywood were not completely surrounded by philistines. With its deep pockets and global reach, the studios were a magnet for genius. At no other time in history did so many talented people engaged in the same enterprise reside in so small an area. *What Makes Sammy Run?* and *The Last Tycoon* both point toward the fact that just because a piece of work is the product of a bureaucratic organization does not automatically mean it lacks quality or merit. A ballet company divides up labor too. An argument can be made that operas and ballets are put on for art's sake, and Hollywood films are produced to make money. But again, monetary interest does not preclude creative merit, and mass production does not necessarily lead to inferior products. Room for art can be found in the midst of mass production. The economic system of the studios may have demanded standardization of production methods and regulated content, but the nature of the product called for differentiation.

Many people have brand loyalty to their favorite breakfast cereal or toothpaste and will buy a new box or a fresh tube of the exact same thing when the old one is empty, but no filmgoer will give all of her repeat business to just one motion picture. This necessity to make the movies the same but different allows for creative possibilities. As Stahr tells Boxley: "We have to take people's own favorite folklore and dress it up and give it back to them. Anything beyond that is sugar. So won't you give us some sugar, Mr. Boxley?" (*Last Tycoon* 105). Stahr wants his writers to give the people what they expect and a few things they did not even know they wanted.

What Makes Sammy Run? and *The Last Tycoon* both acknowledge that the studio system contains its share of "phonies, mediocrities, dictators, and good men who have lost their way," but they also show that talented artists and visionaries reside there and can thrive there as well. However, dictator and visionary are not mutually exclusive categories, as Monroe Stahr makes evident. As the sole person on the lot who possesses "the whole equation of pictures" (3), he is the only author of his films in that he is the only authorizer. His hundreds of workers, whose job tasks are grouped into divisions and subdivisions, make virtually no decisions during the production process. "I am the unity" (58), Stahr tells the visiting Prince Agge. He is not an artist, but he causes art to happen.

Every movie the studio puts out is firmly guided by Stahr's own hand and bears his imprint, yet he modestly demurs from putting his own name on the screen. He pulls a director off a set and fires him, yet he gives a troubled cameraman another chance. Stahr is honest, creative, handsome, and shrewd. Work is the only thing that matters to him (prior to meeting love interest Kathleen). He is a tyrant, but Fitzgerald loves him almost as much as the narrator, Cecilia, does.

Turning Boxley into a true believer in the power of cinema and counseling an impotent actor are just two of the many miracles Stahr performs in the section of *The Last Tycoon* titled "A Producer's Day." This section of the unfinished manuscript, chapters 3 and 4, is by far the strongest material of the novel. Each interaction with cameramen, directors, editors, actors, and moneymen reveals Stahr to be a singular genius in the midst of a bureaucracy. There are indications that art is more important to him than commerce. He holds up the release of a film to keep tinkering with it. He is even willing to make a prestige picture that he knows will not make back its budget and to "write it off as good will," as the industry's "duty to the public" (48).

In book publishing during the twentieth century, releasing books that would lose money was a common practice. One best-selling beach book could underwrite, for instance, a volume of poems by a respected poet and a second novel by a runner-up for the National Book Critics Circle Award. But the corporation that owns Stahr's studio cannot understand why he'd knowingly release a product that would cost more than it would earn. With block booking, the practice of exhibitors needing to buy all of a studio's crop for the year rather than simply cherry-picking the best films out, there was no such thing as a major studio film that lost money. But Stahr wants to take a short vacation from attaching financial value to creative goods. The more money the "quality picture" loses, the more noble his gesture in having put it on the production schedule. We also sense his glee in this scene in sticking it to his fellow "money men" (45) by separating himself from them.

The characterization of Stahr in *The Last Tycoon* demonstrates that for all the knowledge Fitzgerald had acquired about the movie industry, he still could not let go of the romantic belief that art is the product of a single artist-hero who will inspire and entertain all of mankind. At one point Stahr meets a black fisherman on the beach. The man carries a pail of grunion, some Rosicrucian literature, and a volume of Ralph Waldo Emerson. He tells Stahr: "I never go to movies. . . . There's no profit. I never let my children go" (92). The man walks away, "unaware that he had rocked an entire industry" (93). What has been rocked is Stahr's belief that his films—like the essays of Emerson—can serve a populist function by bridging racial, religious, economic, and class divides and reaching all people everywhere.

By "profit" the fisherman means "edification," but financial profit is what matters most to those in the motion-picture boardrooms of *The Last Tycoon*. Because corporate capitalism is taking over the movie business and by extension, the United States itself, Stahr is the last member of a doomed species. He is not a tycoon in the financial sense of a railroad tycoon or an oil tycoon; he is a tycoon in the original Japanese *tai kun* mold of a noble leader. As a result of his encounter with the black fisherman, "Stahr had thrown four pictures out of his plans—one that was going into production this week. They were borderline pictures in point of interest, but at least he submitted the borderline pictures to the negro and found them trash. And he put back on his list a difficult picture that he had tossed to the wolves, to Brady and Marcus and the rest, to get his way on something else. He rescued it for the negro man" (95). Fitzgerald's outline for the book indicates that the future of the entertainment industry will see the rise of venal philistines such as Brady and Wall Street lawyers such as Fleishacker. Individuality will be crushed under the boot of faceless corporations.

Fitzgerald's outline called for Stahr to meet a tragic end, one befitting a great hero. The author wrote of his novel in progress: "I invented a tragic story . . . because no one has ever written a tragedy about Hollywood. *A Star Is Born* was a pathetic and often beautiful story but not a tragedy, and doomed and heroic things do happen here" (qtd. in Bruccoli, *Some Sort* 462). After foiling Brady's plot to have him killed, Stahr was scheduled to die in a plane crash, a Hollywood Icarus who flew too high. But we shall never know how *The Last Tycoon* would have changed in further drafts. That the novel was unfinished has the effect of deepening the sense of loss and tragedy surrounding the figure of Stahr. After Fitzgerald's death Graham sent the manuscript to Maxwell Perkins, and they, along with Edmund Wilson, decided to publish the work in progress as a memorial to the author. Schulberg claims that he and John O'Hara were asked to shape the material into something resembling a coherent narrative, an assignment they refused because Fitzgerald was too great a writer to tamper with (Beck 27). But Bruccoli notes in his critical edition of the novel that "the testimony is unclear" and quotes from a letter Graham sent to him—seemingly written in all capital letters for added emphasis—insisting that "BUDD SCHULBERG WAS NOT ASKED TO FINISH THE LAST TYCOON. HE OFFERED TO DO IT AND EDMUND WILSON INDIGNANTLY REFUSED" (*Love of the Last Tycoon* xciv). In the end, whatever the case, Wilson took on the editing duties himself, resulting in what Bruccoli disparages as a "cosmeticized text" (xiii).

From Fitzgerald's notes and outline, it appears as if the author had ambitions for the manuscript to be a business novel, detailing the inner workings of how movies get made. He wrote to Zelda that his work in progress was "a constructed novel like *Gatsby,* with passages of poetic prose when it fits the action, but no ruminations or side-shows like *Tender.* Everything must contribute to the dramatic movement" (*Letters of FSF* 128). The novel would be concise and compressed, driven by dialogue, like a movie script. But in the edition Wilson cobbled together, Stahr's psychology, especially where it concerns the love plot, overwhelms the story. In an image salvaged out of West's dream dump, Stahr first sees Kathleen drifting down a flooded back lot on the head of a giant statue. In *The Day of the Locust*, the back lot is a space of decay and disappointment, but here it serves as a locus of renewal. Kathleen is Stahr's dead wife reborn. This is the first push away from a perceptive Hollywood insider novel, and the book floats back toward Fitzgerald's played-out theme of the girl who got away. The author's beautiful gift for description and character is in evidence, but so too, disappointingly, is his familiar problem of controlling point of view.

Like *The Great Gatsby*, the novel concentrates on a great man and the world around him. But Cecilia makes for an awkward narrator. In the beginning pages, she seems to share with Nick Carraway the right mixture of distance and involvement, the correct balance of within and without. She was brought up *around* pictures—Valentino came to her fifth birthday party, as he had come to Schulberg's—yet unlike Rosemary Hoyt in *Tender Is the Night*, she is not *in* pictures. This should make for a good vantage point, but to focus on Stahr's professional life and private life with the degree of detail needed, the third-person-limited point of view would have worked out better.

As in *The Great Gatsby*, the great man is introduced to the reader after the first-person narrator has built him up a bit. But unlike Nick, who is the character most changed by the events he reports, Cecilia has little to do once Stahr enters the picture. Not only does her idealization of Stahr never allow the producer, or the man, to come into focus, but Fitzgerald also has her report on events she could not have witnessed—the scene where Stahr sleeps with Kathleen, for one. Cecilia knows the contents of Stahr's brain and charts his movements with a degree of intimacy a puppy-dog crush could never grant her. Lines such as "This is Cecilia taking up the narrative in person" (77) and "This is Cecilia taking up the story" (98) broadcast this problem. But they also remind us that the manuscript was still in its early stages, and point of view could have changed in revision (as had happened with *Tender Is the Night*). It is possible that, for instance, instead of being bits of Cecilia Brady's narration, these two lines are Fitzgerald's embedded notes to himself.

What Makes Sammy Run? has the advantage over *The Last Tycoon* of being a finished novel built firmly upon the foundation of earlier short stories. Schulberg's book is the insider novel Wilson applauds Fitzgerald for writing in the postscript to "The Boys in the Back Room." Like Nick

Carraway, Al Manheim is honest and genteel. Like Miss Lonelyhearts, he is a newspaperman with a holy-man father. Unlike Nick and Miss Lonelyhearts, he is judgmental and a bit of a square. In the short story version of the novel, Al devolves into a money-hungry hack, but here Schulberg leaves him at the end of the book just as we found him in the beginning: moral, passive, and intellectual. We feel Al's disgust as he watches Sammy Glick's well-plotted, Machiavellian slither up the corporate ladder, but we can also understand why he is fascinated by him. How far and how fast can Sammy go? Can anything stop him? Will he get his comeuppance?

Like Gatsby, Sammy is a show-off and a poseur. Gatsby wears pink suits; Sammy buys shoes that are as loud as Schulberg's "running" symbolism. Gatsby is a beautiful dreamer; Sammy is an ugly schemer. From the moment they meet in the New York newspaper office, Glick can see that Manheim is a chump, but the older writer possesses the education, carriage, and taste that the boy wants to imitate. Sammy is not satisfied with being a lowly radio columnist. Radio, although popular, lacks the glamour of film or the highbrow cachet of the stage. Using Al, Sammy looks to acquire a literary reputation that will increase his cultural capital, which he can then trade in for money and power. Sammy wants Al to help him with his grammar and tell him who Ignazio Silone and Guy de Maupassant are, but he wants to help himself to Manheim's connections even more. At a lunch at the Algonquin, Sammy has Al introduce him to a playwright-critic based on Dorothy Parker's pal George S. Kaufman. The next day's paper carries an item, planted by Glick, of course, that makes the literary man and the young radio reporter seem like bosom companions.

Stahr does not want his own name to appear on screen; Sammy cannot see "Sammy Glick" written enough. Stahr wants power as a vehicle for achieving artistic purity and greatness. Sammy just wants power. Both are workaholics. Stahr organizes the contributions of hundreds of people; Sammy spends all of his effort on self-promotion. In fact he is so good at padding his reputation as a writer that he never has to write anything. He plagiarizes and bluffs and steals. In one episode Sammy composes an entire scenario from scratch by going from table to table in the commissary and having each writer add a small piece to his "great idea," which, like stone soup, gets meatier with each contribution. There is no need for the chef to toss in anything himself.

What Makes Sammy Run? and *The Last Tycoon* both pit a noble producer against an opportunist. Fitzgerald's book focuses on the noble producer; Schulberg's book concentrates on the opportunist. Stahr tries not to fall prey to Brady's treachery; Glick is as treacherous as it gets. Sammy is not the writer as Hollywood victim; he is the writer as Hollywood victimizer. After chewing up other screenwriters, he graduates to preying upon weak and aging executives such as the book lover Fineman, a "fine man" and stand-in for Budd's dethroned father. Manheim chronicles the carnage, and in the process the reader is given a complete tour of the studio system as Glick tears his way through it.

Sammy wants to mentor Al and make him wise up. But Manheim does not want to be coached by the younger writer; he only wants to watch him play the game. In the final analysis, Glick represents greed gone wild. Unlike Horatio Alger's heroes with their pluck and luck, Glick uses shrewd deceit and cold opportunism in his quest for the American dream. He would fit right in with Fleishacker and Brady in *The Last Tycoon*. He is the spiritual godson of Theodore Dreiser's Frank Cowperwood of *The Financier*. To Al, Sammy's story is "a blueprint of a way of life that was paying dividends in America in the first half of the twentieth century" (276). *What Makes Sammy Run?* is not anti-Hollywood; it is anticapitalism. Glick is not a purely Hollywood phenomenon; Al could have stayed home and found a dozen guys just like him on Wall Street.

Glick's rise to producer is quick and savage, but what goes up must come down, and so eventually Schulberg makes sure Sammy is punished. The two things Glick cannot buy, fake, or steal are gentility and an awareness of high culture. Like many an ethnic movie gangster before and after him, he marries a WASP princess. But Laurette Harrington is a beautiful woman without mercy. At a party she mentions Thomas Gainsborough's picture *The Blue Boy*, and Sammy asks if a foreign studio put it out. After stringing him along a bit, it is finally revealed she is talking about a painting. Laurette laughs at his expense, and Sammy cannot conceal his embarrassment (246–47). In *Politics, Desire, and the Hollywood Novel*, Chip Rhodes reads this episode as evidence of Sammy's "preoedipal masochism" (71), but it is also clearly about class striving and cultural reference points that separate one strata from another. Soon after, his wife cuckolds him, and Sammy is left to wander aimlessly through the rooms of his huge, Xanadu-like mansion. In portions of these last chapters, especially when Al goes to the Jewish ghetto to uncover Sammy's origins, discovering that what makes Sammy run is his fear of becoming like his weak father, the plot can lapse into a schmaltzy version of "Jews without Money Call It Sleep"; but the majority of Schulberg's book is the documentary novel, narrated by a pitch-perfect participant/observer, we see only flickering traces of in the manuscript of *The Last Tycoon*.

If the 1941 version of *The Last Tycoon* has been overestimated by well-meaning critics, especially friends and contemporaries such as Wilson ("Far and away the best novel we have about Hollywood . . . and Fitzgerald's most mature piece of work"), Stephen Vincent Benét ("the full powers of its author, at its height, and at their best"), and John Dos Passos ("the beginnings of a great novel"), Fitzgerald's story cycle detailing the misadventures of screenwriter Pat Hobby has been underpraised. Brian Way's comments are typical of the prevailing wisdom that in these pieces the author "shows, as never before, a hard calculated awareness of the exact minimum of effort needed to satisfy his editor and readers" (157). This is unfair—and ahistorical.

It is a well-documented fact that Fitzgerald churned out deliberately subpar stories for the *Saturday Evening Post* during the 1920s, a time when he had a much better feel for the pulse of the popular magazine market than he did later in his career. As Fitzgerald wrote to Perkins: "I just couldn't make the grade as a hack" (*FSF: A Life in Letters* 445). The record shows that Fitzgerald went beyond the "minimum of effort" with the Pat Hobby pieces. The dates of composition for the stories coincide with the composition period of *The Last Tycoon* (Mangum 77), and Arnold Gingrich, the *Esquire* editor who published the seventeen Hollywood tales between January 1940 and May 1941, recalls that the author revised them past the deadline on many occasions and had very definite ideas about the order in which they should appear (*Pat Hobby Stories* ix). Just because they are about a hack does not mean they are hackwork.

Fitzgerald was not selling out with Pat Hobby; he was selling well. Money was certainly a motive in writing the stories. He made $4,500 from the cycle (Bruccoli, *Some Sort* 473), and Scottie Fitzgerald claimed that Pat Hobby "sent me to Vassar" (*Pat Hobby Stories* xxi). But the better pieces—"Boil Some Water," and "Two Old Timers," especially—rise above the status of potboilers. These Fitzgerald stories are smart and funny, like episodes from an existentialist movie serial. While less consciously literary and more baldly commercial than the artier *The Last Tycoon,* on the level of form they are superior to Fitzgerald's unfinished novel. There's no split character focus, and the narrative voice is sharp and direct. There's aesthetic distance from the subject matter, and the plots are simple and sustained. Pat's strength as a screenwriter is structure; the stories themselves are well structured, which is not a virtue of most of Fitzgerald's fiction.

The Pat Hobby stories also do a better job than *The Last Tycoon* at capturing the elements of boredom, routine, and entropy that were a part of Hollywood studio life. Where Stahr spends his days marching across the lot turning scripts and celluloid into golden eggs, Hobby spends most of his time lounging around and thinking up rotten schemes. A writer who "had never written much" (13), Pat is Sammy Glick with less drive and worse luck. Like Glick he is a writer who avoids reading. He advises a pretty, aspiring screenwriter to "give the book to four of your friends to read it. Get them to tell you what stuck in their minds. Write it down and you've got a picture—see" (16). Pat's laziness makes him a target for Fitzgerald's gentle scorn. He has run out of writing ideas, but Fitzgerald had not.

Like Caramel in *The Beautiful and Damned* of twenty years earlier, Hobby represents a type of pandering writer Fitzgerald was consciously trying to avoid becoming. Pat steals ideas, kisses up to the powerful, and even toys with blackmail, but his lack of success and comic degradation save him from coming off as evil. Critics have often called Hobby a failure, but the truth is that he is mediocre. Hobby will never learn. He will never grow. But because he knows how to play the Hollywood game, at least well enough to stay in it, he will always find a way to survive. His plans usually backfire, and his big break never comes, but he always makes a living. Many of the Pat Hobby stories concern his efforts to get on the lot and/or to stay there. In addition to writing (or pretending to), Hobby also conducts studio tours, babysits other writers, acts on camera, poses for artists, and capitalizes on being mistaken for Orson Welles. Although the schemes and plots of the hapless Pat always miss their marks, Fitzgerald's stories about him consistently hit their satiric targets.

Like a Bunch of Plumbers

Hobby barely keeps his foot in the Hollywood door, yet he is a company man who fights to keep outsiders out, especially Communists. In "A Patriotic Short" he rewrites a script written by a "Red" (117), and in "Boil Some Water" he uses a cafeteria tray to flatten a man in a Russian costume who dares to sit at "The Big Table" reserved for executives. At one point Pat jokes about membership in "The Screen Playwriters Guild," conflating the names of the leftist union and the conservative one. According to Pat the union wants Finland recognized and "free pencils and paper" (75).

Before impersonating him for profit, Hobby complains that "Orson Welles belongs with the rest of the snobs back in New York" (44), but the story of the writing of the screenplay for *Citizen Kane* (1941) shows that the boy wonder and the middle-aged hack share not only similar beards but similar schemes. The dirty tricks they play show why a writers' union was necessary. Welles had hired Herman Mankiewicz, Parker's old pal from the Algonquin, to write radio scripts for him, and Mankiewicz had pitched him the idea of writing a screenplay about the newspaper mogul William Randolph Hearst. The two worked together on the script, rewriting each other's drafts. When it was completed, Welles wanted to take all the credit, telling both RKO and gossip columnist Louella Parsons that he'd written the picture solo. Like Sammy Glick, Welles believed his protégé should be content with ghostwriting on salary. Because writers are neither seen nor heard during moviemaking, it is easy to downplay or erase or distort their contributions. Welles even offered Mankiewicz a ten-thousand-dollar bonus if he would stay a ghost and keep his mouth shut (Kael 5–9, 58–67). But Mankiewicz pleaded his case to the Screen Writers Guild, which awarded joint screen credit—with, notably, Mankiewicz's name appearing first. Hollywood writers unions were good for more than dispensing "free pencils and paper."

If politics are treated comically in the Pat Hobby story cycle, Wilson's version of *The Last Tycoon* ends with a scene that hints that the struggle over who would speak for writers in Hollywood might have eventually played a serious role in Fitzgerald's Hollywood novel, as it most certainly does in Schulberg's *What Makes Sammy Run?* Leo Rosten comments: "The obstinacy and indiscretion with which the producers opposed Hollywood writers in their fight for recognition, basic working conditions, and a code of fair practice, is one of the less flattering commentaries on the men who control movie production" (318). Like Rosten's book, Schulberg and Fitzgerald's novels were published in 1941, the year the producers finally sat down with the Screen Writers Guild, which was threatening to strike. A provisional six-month contract had expired, and the studios were in no rush to renew it. The two sides would reach an agreement in May 1941, nine years after the SWG had been formed, but the road to get there had been a rocky one, as these novels chart.

Written by a member of the guild's board, *What Makes Sammy Run?* presents a wide spectrum of writers' responses to unionization and, by extension, their view of themselves as workers and citizens, as professionals and proletarians, and as artists. Sounding like Nathanael West, Al jokes with Kit before a union meeting that he likes seeing other people, "but one at a time, not all bunched together" (130). But Schulberg's novel is clearly on the side of those who align themselves with the group rather than those who advance their own individual interests. While Kit and Al side with the "little guys" (137) of the SWG and opportunists such as Sammy cozy up to the powerful and highly paid screenwriters of the Screen Playwrights (here called "the Association of Photodramatists"), the aesthete

Irving Thalberg. Photofest

Pancake scoffs at the notion of authors getting together to organize "like a bunch of plumbers" (136). When talk surfaces of a plan to have Hollywood screenwriters align themselves with the Authors League of America, a former movie extra who has risen to be a respected writer argues, Pat Hobby–like, that "by God, no bunch of Broadway snobs, who thought they are too good for Hollywood, was going to sit around the Algonquin and tell him what to do" (132). Another red-baiting writer wants to kick out all "the goddam parlor pinks" (137). The producers take this lack of consensus as a sign of weakness and try to break up the SWG through institutional pressures such as graylists and stapling resignation forms to paychecks. When Al refuses to quit the union, the studio lets him go without needing to tell him why. His agent says that if there were a blacklist, he'd certainly be on it: "But they don't need anything like that in this chummy little business. All it takes is a couple of big shots happening to mention it over a poker game—or meeting at Chasen's and passing the word along. That's why you should have played ball" (191).

In *The Last Tycoon*, Stahr prefers to confront the threat of unionization face-to-face and one-on-one. Modeled on Irving Thalberg, a field general during the war to break the SWG, Stahr will fight—with his fists if necessary—to keep labor organizers away from his people and his studio. Stahr believes that "writers are not equipped for authority" (120), and like Fitzgerald himself during most of the 1930s, the screenwriter characters in *The Last Tycoon* seem too self-absorbed—or too self-protective—to care about unionization one way or another. Cecilia arranges a disastrous meeting between the producer and a labor leader named Brimmer. In preparation for the conference, and making effective use of his limited time, Stahr takes a crash course in being an intellectual: he orders a two-page treatment of *The Communist Manifesto* and watches several European movies. Like a father who believes he knows best, Stahr tells Brimmer he is wasting his energy trying to unionize in Hollywood, since writers are "like children—even in normal times they can't keep their minds on their work" (120).

Up to this point in the narrative, the novel has stacked the deck in Stahr's favor by bearing this out. Writer characters do not come off very sympathetically: Wylie White is a "an intellectual of the second order" (38), a jealous and drunken smart aleck; Boxley is a terrible snob; and the Dorothy Parker–ish Jane Meloney is a petite, fifty-year-old, highly paid, highly efficient, witty screenwriter for whom Stahr must "stifle what amounted to a sharp physical revulsion" (38). Stahr believes that he knows writers better than they know themselves. He is not as smart as a writer, the idiot savant of the industry, but as he explains to Brimmer, "I always thought that his brains belonged to me—because I knew how to use them" (125). Whatever went on in a writer's brain—searches for deeper truths? attempts to access the subconscious? interpretations of the universal?— was a mystery to producers, but they knew that most of it was useless.

Brimmer responds that writers are the creative force behind motion pictures. He declares that "they grow the grain but they're not at the feast" (120). To extend his apt metaphor, writers are the farmers who plant the seeds that blossom into motion pictures; their brains are more than crops for Stahr to harvest and take to market. Stahr's studio is not the friendly family farm he believes it to be; it is an agribusiness conglomerate. Brimmer's language makes clear that moviemaking is an economic system and that writers are workers subject to exploitation. After a heated game of ping pong that Stahr treats as a duel, the producer (in a move his earlier characterization has not prepared us for) picks a fistfight with the Communist leader and is knocked to the floor. This is Fitzgerald's way of announcing that the type of Hollywood paternalism represented by Stahr, the idea that everyone at the studio is happy to work under him to fulfill his individual vision, will be, like silent pictures, a thing of the past. With corporations attacking him on one front and unions targeting him on another, the barbarians are at the gates, and Stahr cannot keep them from entering.

Neal Gabler, among others, has written that Jewish movie moguls such as Paramount's Adolf Zukor, Columbia's Harry Cohn, and the Warner brothers lived in constant fear that the empires they had worked so hard to build would suddenly be taken away from them. In the early 1940s the Justice Department was trying to divest studios from theater ownership and was challenging other monopolistic elements of their trade practices. With the "Paramount case," as it was known, set to be heard in courts, labor unrest was an added thorn in the side of the industry. During the 1941 SWG negotiations, Harry Warner had to be led out of the room by his lieutenants when he began shouting that the writers wanted to take away the studio he and his brothers had built: "You goddamn Communist bastards! You dirty sons of bitches! All you'll get from me is shit" (qtd. in Schary 113). The specter of organized labor infiltrating their lots and shaking up the system was just one of the external threats that kept them awake at night. They could also feel Wall Street and Washington constantly breathing down their necks.

Anti-Semitism, whether overt or tacit, whether emanating from the country clubs of their neighbors or from the film-going audience itself, hung over the moguls at all times. When Schulberg's *What Makes Sammy Run?* appeared, a surprise best seller and critical darling that details the adventures of a Shylockian, rapacious Jew who thrives in the environment of the Hollywood studios, the town's power brokers felt betrayed by one of their own. Sam Goldwyn banned Schulberg from his lot. Family friend Louis B. Mayer wanted him deported (Beck 18).

Heat from the studios would have been bad enough, but the Communist Party was also incensed at Schulberg. He had not received permission to print the book, and even with the narrator's name changed from Manners to Manheim—so that the character functioning as the story's moral compass would be Jewish, as was its antihero—the party still found the story anti-Semitic. In addition the Communists denounced the book as too realistic, too depressing, and too decadent. It did not focus enough on the positive force of the workers. Schulberg recalled that one reviewer, under pressure from the party, even retracted a positive review of the novel, claiming that, upon further inspection, "the book was elitist in that it only dealt with the writers; it didn't deal with the grips or the electricians, the workers" ("Two Conversations" 128). The long episodes of Schulberg's book that deal with the SWG repeatedly and clearly make the point that writers and workers are one and the same, but Schulberg was already too fed up with the Communist Party, and with the studio system, even to argue: "I didn't want to stay there any longer and, of course, if I had wanted to, I couldn't, and that was it" ("Two Conversations" 104). He decided to leave Hollywood and concentrate on his promising literary career.

7

The Dust
on the Wings

**REPUTATIONS
AND RECON-
FIGURATIONS
IN THE 1950S**

After all, Shep knew why Manley Halliday hadn't published
in nearly a decade: because he was defeatist, an escapist,
cut off from "vital issues," from "The People," a disillusioned
amanuensis of a dying order. . . . If poor, old Halliday, aware
of himself and all his own friends in their own neurotic little
world, could do what he promised to do in this new work,
wouldn't Shep have to re-examine his own standards? Maybe
ideology wasn't the literary shibboleth he had believed in so
dogmatically.

Budd Schulberg, *The Disenchanted*

A failure now could make—oh with the aid of immense talent of
course, for there were failures and failures—such a reputation!

Henry James, "The Next Time"

လ

As anthropologist Hortense Powdermaker makes clear throughout
Hollywood: The Dream Factory, a 1950 ethnographic study of the
movie colony, the pursuit of money and glory often causes the members of
the entertainment industry to have short memories. Vendettas are put aside,
or close ties are abandoned. Budd Schulberg had sworn off Hollywood in
1941, but after World War II he nonetheless continued to produce articles
and fiction and testimony about Hollywood, and about the writers—such

as Dorothy Parker, Nathanael West, and F. Scott Fitzgerald—he had met while living there. His 1950 novel *The Disenchanted*, for example, is a fictionalized version of the ill-fated screen-writing trip to Dartmouth that he had taken with Fitzgerald in 1939. The year the book was published, Louis B. Mayer—who had wanted Schulberg deported for writing *What Makes Sammy Run?*—approached Schulberg about bringing Sammy Glick to the screen (Beck 71). This seemed like a sudden change in Mayer's attitude, but the mogul was losing his power at MGM, after a long reign, and needed a hit film to rekindle his career. When Schulberg turned down the project, Mayer and the studio simply appropriated many of the book's elements and built them into the 1952 film *The Bad and the Beautiful,* the story of a talented, ruthless producer trying to regain his footing in Hollywood.

Meet the New Boss: *On the Waterfront* and *A Face in the Crowd*

With the studio system on its last legs in the 1950s, Schulberg made an impressive Hollywood comeback of his own. Though exiled from the industry's power center in 1941, he had never really left moviemaking. In 1943, helping out his father, a once-mighty captain of the industry who now could not find a job in the studios, he had helped script *City without Men,* a movie about the families left behind when men go to prison. In that same year, Schulberg had contributed to the screenplay for *Government Girl,* the story of a wartime gal Friday. As a navy lieutenant during World War II and a member of John Ford's documentary unit, he had pitched in to make propaganda films for the armed services. A film he worked on, *December 7,* took home the 1944 Oscar for best documentary short subject. Schulberg also did some rewrites on the 1945 movie *They Were Expendable.* But despite these cinematic achievements, it was with *On the Waterfront* (1954) and *A Face in the Crowd* (1957), projects done in close collaboration with director Elia Kazan in the "new" Hollywood of the 1950s, that Schulberg achieved his greatest film successes.

This was not Schulberg's father's studio system. During an early morning walk through the empty streets of Los Angeles in the early 1950s, David Selznick told screenwriter Ben Hecht that the movies were "over and done with. . . . Hollywood's like Egypt. Full of crumbled pyramids. It'll never come back. It'll just keep on crumbling until finally the wind blows the last studio prop across the sands" (Hecht 467). Forced by the government to divest in their theater holdings, the studios could no longer afford their massive payrolls. Stars, directors, and writers were free to hire themselves out on a picture-to-picture basis, working where they wanted to and when they wanted to. As a result of increasing freedom for increasingly unionized talent, the talent agent suddenly played a major role.

Parker, for instance, was one of the beneficiaries of this new balance of Hollywood power, but also one of the victims of a growing Hollywood climate of political suspicion. In 1950 her name appeared in *Red Channels,* the industry publication that listed reputed Communists. Since Parker was temporarily unable to find any film work because of this red mark, her agent, Leah Salisbury, began aggressively marketing the media rights to her stories and started shaking down organizations—from high school drama clubs to television production companies—that were using Parker's source material without paying out royalties.

Subsidiary rights such as these became increasingly important to authors during the 1950s. This market trend coincided with the Screen Writers Guild being folded into the Writers Guild of America, creating a union that would serve writers working for the stage, the page, and screens big and small. Fitzgerald, a pioneer in collecting subsidiary rights, had known the importance of milking a commodity for all its worth. By 1950 all writers had caught on to these cash cow potentials for their work. In such an environment, the agent replaces the editor as the author's new best friend. Worrying about money so writers did not have to, agents increasingly began advising clients on career direction, on what media or genres to develop, and on what material to exploit. Claiming they had the writer's best interest at heart, they also began to read and critique manuscripts. After all, the thinking went, editors worked for publishers, but agents worked for writers.

Parker later became a client of MCA, where the resident genius was agent Lou Wasserman, the subject of Connie Bruck's biography *When Hollywood Had a King.* In 1950, the year *The Disenchanted* was published and the year Parker was blacklisted, Wasserman had brokered a deal for Jimmy Stewart that had changed the industry. Instead of a straight salary for *Winchester '73,* Stewart had received a percentage of the profits, an arrangement that had netted the actor an enormous amount of money and had paved the way for stars, no longer in servitude to the studios, to become formidable economic free agents who could test their own market value. Bruck argues that Wasserman, a visionary with a photographic memory, was one of the first people in Hollywood to see the potential of television for the film industry. With postwar foreign markets now imposing quotas on the importation of U.S. movies, the small screens in American living rooms were an important new source of revenue.

Television has often been cited as the cause for decreased movie atten-dance in the 1950s (Stuart; Jowett and Linton), but a more likely culprit is the GI Bill. With a subsidy to get a college education came less time to go to the movies. With the education came the additional income to buy a house in the suburbs. This house, miles from city theaters, needed a car in the garage, a dishwasher in the kitchen, and 2.5 children sitting around the dinner table. People started spending less money on the movies because in the 1950s they now had so many other things to spend it on—including televisions. In 1950 four million homes contained televisions. In 1954 there were thirty-two million. By the end of the decade, more than 90 per-cent of homes had one (Balio 315). Still, although a solid case can be made that television maimed radio, it did not significantly cripple the film industry. A company such as Republic Pictures—the Poverty Row outfit Nathanael West once worked for—actually saw a temporary increase in profits after scaling back production and instead focusing on renting out its film library to television.

Looking for new ways to make money, the studios were also investing in technological research. In the early 1950s, one of Republic's divisions, Consolidated Film Industries, introduced a new process called Trucolor that it marketed to filmmakers who could not afford Technicolor. Improved color was only one of many lures the movie industry was using to draw people out of their homes. With Cinemascope, Todd-AO, 3-D, and Cin-erama, the size and dimensions of the big screen were changing, too. So were the films themselves. Scripts and stars and directors were now being packaged *to* the studios, instead of being packaged *by* the studios, and this left an opening for new perspectives and a wider variety of content. With this loosening of studio control came a slackening in the rules of the Production Code, widening the scope of what it was possible to depict. Changes in distribution and exhibition encouraged filmmakers to be hyper-aware of the look, feel, and target audience of each individual film. Be-cause block booking had been abolished, theaters could now order what they wanted from the studios without having to buy the entire bill of fare. Every movie needed to go it alone in the cold marketplace.

In this climate of new freedoms, Elia Kazan approached Schulberg in the early 1950s about doing a film about corruption on the New Jersey docks. Unlike John Ford, Howard Hawks, and other celebrated directors of the studio era, who saw themselves as craftsmen and would stonewall any suggestion of their work as "genius," Kazan viewed himself as a crea-tive artist. His autobiography, *A Life*, casts him as an alienated rebel who resists studio control and fights for creative autonomy in making his controversial, socially relevant films. Yet in what seemed like a radical break from the old studio system, Schulberg as a screenwriter would be given complete authority over the script. Kazan told him: "Budd, if you'll do this I promise to treat it with the same respect I would give to a Tennessee Williams play or an Arthur Miller play or a Bill Inge play. I'll advise or argue with you, but I won't change anything. It'll be your play. I won't change a line of dialogue unless you agree" ("Two Conversations" 111). Hollywood screenwriters were not accustomed to such an offer, one that allowed for a screenplay with such a pronounced artistic stamp on the finished movie itself. While there can be a director's cut of a previously released film, there's no such thing as a writer's cut of a film. The mode of production just does not allow for it. Shot scenes edited out before release can be put back in at a future time; but unshot scenes, images, and words from the script will never make it to the screen. In writing the script, screenwriters "see" the movie before it exists, but once filmed, that screenplay, in a sense, disappears into the maw of the movie created from it.

Viewing himself as a novelist who occasionally wrote for the movies, Schulberg began developing the material as a screenplay and a book simultaneously, angling to have the two projects released at the same time. But writing the novel took longer than expected, and getting the film financed was proving more difficult than Kazan and Schulberg had hoped.

No longer tethered to studios, actors had the luxury of being picky, and Marlon Brando, the star of 1951's *A Streetcar Named Desire*, directed by Kazan, was waffling about doing the picture. Darryl Zanuck's letters show that Fox would not put up the money without a commitment from Brando (Behlmer, *Memo from DFZ* 227). The studio was also feeling pressure from the board to have the films they released be shot in wide-screen color, and the Kazan/Schulberg project, then titled "The Golden Warrior," was shaping up to be too character driven. The project would film on location, strive for a gritty realism, and pull no punches. Zanuck writes: "I felt that since we had overnight committed ourselves to a program of Cinemascope 'spectacles' I had no alternative to back away from intimate stories even though they were good stories" (Behlmer, *Memo from DFZ* 230). After Fox turned the property down, Warner Bros., MGM, Paramount, and Columbia did the same. In the end the film was saved by a savvy independent producer—proving that the new boss in Hollywood often looked an awful lot like the old boss.

Natasha Fraser-Cavassoni's biography of Sam Spiegel details how the producer joined the project, convinced Kazan and Schulberg to change the main character from an investigative journalist to a union member, suggested the title *On the Waterfront*, got United Artists interested in Frank Sinatra starring, dumped both Sinatra and UA when Brando agreed to play Terry Malloy, and brought the package back to Columbia Pictures, where it got the green light. Once a "major-minor," Columbia, which had never owned any theaters anyway, saw its market share—and its cachet—actually increase after the studios were forced to divest. *On the Waterfront*, budgeted at a modest $900,000, began shooting on location in New Jersey in 1953.

Elia Kazan may have sworn not to interfere with the script, but Sam Spiegel had made no such promises. The producer made Schulberg's blood boil by whispering conspiratorially in Kazan's ear during story conferences and trying to take a red pen to some of the dialogue. Despite being barred from the set, throughout filming Spiegel used a barrage of telephone calls to play the director and writer off each other, trying to drive a wedge between them and gain control over the picture from his booth at Manhattan's 21 Club. Fraser-Cavassoni repeats the Hollywood legend that one day Schulberg's wife awoke in the middle of the night to find her husband shaving in the bathroom. When she asked him where he was going, he answered, "I'm driving to New York . . . to kill Sam Spiegel" (314).

In hindsight, however, Schulberg had to admit that the producer had improved the screenplay. He concedes in the foreword to Joanna Rapf's Cambridge Film Handbook for *On the Waterfront:* "To give Spiegel his due, he hammered for tighter structure, and stronger (and what came to be total) focus on my main character. Precious scenes that added texture and complexity were jettisoned to the purpose of keeping it moving. The film asks 'And then? And then? And then.' Often with a pang of regret I had to admit that in the interest of relentless storytelling, my pet sidebars had to go" (xvi). After tussling with Schulberg, Spiegel moved on to pestering Kazan. The producer complained that the film was being shot too slowly, and he tried in vain to enlist Schulberg in getting Kazan to pick up the pace: "Budd, this is serious. . . . We are going to run out of money. You have to make him go faster" (Fraser-Cavassoni 315).

Schulberg, Kazan, Brando, and Spiegel all received Academy Awards for *On the Waterfront*, and all four deserve a piece of the credit for the movie's success. But as usual in a collaborative art, how large a share each ultimately deserves is a subject of debate. Brando, who won the best actor Oscar for his performance, stated in his autobiography that he did more than just act in the film; he also wrote parts of it. With echoes of the attribution controversy over the "This is Mrs. Norman Maine" line of *A Star*

Is Born, Brando claimed that he improvised the "I coulda been a contender" speech, one of the most famous monologues in film history (193–99). But the words were clearly Schulberg's: Tom Stempel's examination of an early draft of "The Golden Warrior" screenplay found the lines of the taxicab scene exactly as they were delivered onscreen (165). Furthermore the published shooting script proves that while Schulberg cannot take credit for Brando's performance, or Leonard Bernstein's score, or the confining and threatening city created by Kazan in collaboration with the film's cinematographer, Boris Kaufman, and art director, Richard Day, he is certainly responsible for the narrative arc of *On the Waterfront* and Terry Malloy's nuanced characterization. It is Schulberg's finest screenplay.

Throughout the shooting script, Schulberg writes *to* the screen, telling the story visually and aurally. Focalization and perspective are handled especially well. As Terry arrives in court to testify against the corrupt union boss Johnny Friendly:

FADE IN

INT   TRAVELING SHOT   COURTROOM   DAY

A courtroom door opens. It is the door out of which the witnesses are brought to testify for hearings of the Waterfront Crime Commission. A counsel is just finishing questioning Big Mac. . . . We don't photograph this. We show Terry walking slowly towards his seat. . . . We hear the dialogue

(o.s) [out of shot]

COUNSEL

(o.s)

You mean. . . . (119–20)

The image takes precedence over the words. It is more vital that we see Malloy than hear the lawyer. During the testimony scene, Schulberg's script calls for the sound of boat whistles, not only for a sense of place but also for the hint that the snitches are "singing."

Read side by side with Schulberg's subsequent novel, titled *Waterfront* (1955), the screenplay emerges as the better-crafted piece of work. The social activist priest's pomposity and moralism, the one weakness of the movie, is amplified in the book version. The novel concentrates more on Father Barry than it does on Terry, and the split focus and sloppy access to consciousness further hurt the book, leading it to wander and get bogged down in Christian allegory. In the script and on the screen (and looking at both in concert reveals just how dependent they are on each other) Terry rightly emerges as the more complex and more interesting character. He

Budd Schulberg in 1955. Photofest

is both sinner and saint; he is both brutal and sensitive; he is a loner who is trying to make a connection to others. His inner turmoil is what drives the narrative. Brando may have brought the character to life, but the DNA is there on the pages of Schulberg's script.

His murderous urges toward Spiegel aside, Schulberg ended up enjoying his *On the Waterfront* experience—a collaboration that would not have been possible under the script-by-committee system during the height of the studio era. Schulberg told an interviewer that working with Kazan made him begin "to feel that, Jesus, you can do the same thing in film that you can do in a book. You can really write what you want to write without any studio interference" ("Two Conversations" 111). But could a writer author a film like he could author a book? During this same time, the mid-1950s, as cinema developed consciousness of its status as art, a body of critical ideas that would come to be called the "auteur theory" began gaining currency in France. Just when screenwriters were in a position to be a stronger guiding vision behind films, American directors—regarded during the studio era as little more than a bunch of interchangeable hired hands—were being proclaimed authors. Out of the muck of industrial production, it was said, could sometimes emerge a singular vision in the high art tradition. The idea of the director as auteur still permeates the way cinema appreciation is taught in classrooms today. Emanating from questions of cultural prestige, it illustrates the tenet that the artistic nature of a product is welded to a belief that it is authored. If film is to be treated as an art alongside painting and poetry, it needs its own version of the solitary genius narrative.

But Kazan always gave Schulberg much of the credit for the movie, and the look and feel of *On the Waterfront* demonstrates the close collaboration between writer and director that went on during every stage of production. Both of their marks are all over the picture. Michael Denning writes that the film's "synthesis of the docks, the waterfront neighborhood, and the gangsters marks it as the culmination of the ghetto pastorals and proletarian thrillers, a combination of the proletarian avant-garde of Kazan and the Hollywood Popular Front of Schulberg" (257).

The movie has also been popularly read as Schulberg's justification of his 1951 testimony as a friendly witness before the House Un-American Activities Committee (HUAC). If this is true, it would prove that screenwriters could now get personal political messages into their studio pictures. But the parallels dissolve unless one believes snitching on murderous gangsters is the same thing as snitching on left-leaning screenwriters. Simply holding beliefs ruined many Hollywood careers. During the studio blacklist, Dalton Trumbo and other writers were able to keep screen writing using "fronts," but no one could front for the actor Larry Parks or the director Jules Dassin.

Perhaps in testifying Schulberg felt, like Shep Stearns of *The Disenchanted,* that turning his back on the ideology and the "literary shibboleth" of 1930s Marxism was a way of demonstrating that he had left his youthful indiscretions behind. In *Naming Names,* perhaps the best account of the HUAC hearings and their aftermath, Victor Navasky reports that Schulberg was sad over having lost some friends over his testimony, but that he did not regret having spoken out (242, 377).

Whether or not Schulberg needed to testify at all is a bone of contention. Parker invoked the First Amendment to the committee, and many others pleaded the Fifth. Schulberg's publisher, Bennett Cerf, told him it would not matter to Random House whether he testified or not (Beck 45). Perhaps Schulberg could have been blacklisted in the film industry, but this is doubtful. He had been getting out of jams his entire adult life. Rich and powerful friends and relations certainly played a part in this, but another part is that Schulberg, like many American authors, perhaps overstated the "danger" of his beliefs and actions. He seldom worked without a net. For example he was fired from *Winter Carnival* for being in cahoots with Fitzgerald, but in his retelling he often elided the part where his father's influence got him rehired. He was persona non grata in Hollywood for *What Makes Sammy Run?* but his "banishment" appears not to have lasted very long. Membership in the Communist Party kept Parker from being granted government clearance to go overseas as a war correspondent during World War II (Schwartz 184), but this same pink mark on Schulberg's record curiously did not prevent him from getting a commission in the U.S. Navy. To hear Schulberg tell it, however, he was more sinned against than sinning. He claimed Ernest Hemingway and John Wayne both tried to pick fistfights with him (Beck 31, 64). Without ever backing down, Schulberg somehow managed to avoid these beatings.

Along these lines *On the Waterfront* contains Schulberg's familiar trope of the powerful bully who eventually gets foiled. This theme pervades the books he published and the films he wrote solo. The backstabbing Sammy Glick, the social-climbing producer Victor Milgrim in *The Disenchanted,* the gangster boss Johnny Friendly in *Waterfront,* the fight promoter Nick Benko in Schulberg's 1947 novel *The Harder They Fall,* and the singing fascist Lonesome Rhodes in *A Face in the Crowd* all crumble, their inner rot revealed. *What Makes Sammy Run?* and *The Disenchanted* had exposed the film business, and *The Harder They Fall* had taken a swing at the business of professional sports. Schulberg's next project, 1957's *A Face in the Crowd,* looks at a third segment of the American entertainment industry—television.

The film is based on Schulberg's story "Your Arkansas Traveler" from the 1953 collection *Some Faces in the Crowd.* Partnering up again with Kazan, Schulberg was even more involved in the shaping of this film than he had been with *On the Waterfront.* In addition to the original story and the original script, he also wrote lyrics for the movie's songs. Kazan's introduction to the film's published script, released before the movie, notes that once again Schulberg was on set each day of shooting and that once again the director promised to be hands-off (xvii). In an attempt to make the script more reader-friendly for the layperson, Schulberg's preface to the screenplay for *A Face in the Crowd* includes his definitions of basic motion-picture terms such as *long shot* and *fade-in* (xxii–xxiv). This glossary, coupled with the fact that the script was published before the film was even released, is Schulberg's attempt to make a case for the screenplay as a stand-alone piece of art. But as with the script for *On the Waterfront,* blueprints, no matter how impressive, only fulfill their promise when we see the objects built from them. A screenplay is always a draft; the film is the finished text.

A Face in the Crowd deviates from the rest of Schulberg's oeuvre in terms of its treatment of the business world. *What Makes Sammy Run?* and *The Disenchanted* are both solidly profilm but staunchly critical of the film industry. *On the Waterfront* is all for organized labor but speaks out against organized crime within the union. Schulberg had his own stable of prizefighters and served as the boxing editor of *Sports Illustrated,* and while the 1956 film version of *The Harder They Fall,* starring Humphrey Bogart in his last screen role, calls for the sport to be banned, the source novel merely pleads for the sweet science to be cleaned up a little bit. *A Face in the Crowd,* on the other hand, reads like an argument for the elimination of television. Other Schulberg works about work call for "the people" to rise up, organize, seize the reins of production, and trample down corruption. In *A Face in the Crowd,* the people have all been narcoticized by their televisions. Lonesome Rhodes (Andy Griffith), a charming hobo turned right-wing demagogue and point man for an arch-conservative senator, has used the idiot box to fool all of the people all of the time.

Rhodes is exposed as a fraud when Marcia Jefferies (Patricia Neal), the woman who gave him his start, flips on his microphone as he begins joking about how dumb his audience is. Marcia follows the character trajectory of Kit Sargent in *Sammy:* she is a strong, intelligent woman who finally wakes up and realizes she is in love with a complete heel. The pipe-smoking, glasses-wearing television writer Mel Miller (Walter Matthau)—whom Rhodes derides as "Vanderbilt '44"—is a more smug and more impotent version of Al Manheim. He wears his lack of success as a badge of honor. When Marcia enters Rhodes's writers' room, entering through a door marked "Classics Adapted While You Wait—We Also Take in Laundry," Mel announces: "Here you see the lepers of the great television industry. Men without faces. . . . They even slide our paychecks under the door so they can pretend we're not here" (186). Screen writing was Shakespeare compared to television writing, which has now claimed the title as basest form of selling out.

With its fear of mass culture, its satire of the false consciousness of cultural elites such as Marcia who blindly idolize the common folk, and its warnings about homegrown fascism, *A Face in the Crowd* seems closer to the pessimism of Nathanael West than to the progressivism of Schulberg. Kit and Al and Shep seek to transform the cinema into an art form for the

Andy Griffith (left) in *A Face in the Crowd*. Photofest

masses. They work toward this end. For Marcia and Mel, however, it is enough to be right about television being a tool of mass hypnosis. Why bother rolling up your sleeves and doing something about it? It is hopeless anyway. After the film's climatic scene, in which Rhodes is alone with his laugh-track machine, Mel tells Marcia that they have not destroyed Rhodes; the cracker-barrel philosopher will be back on a small-market station in no time, selling snake oils like Vitajex and grinning his way back into the nation's living rooms.

After seeing a rough cut of the film, Jack Warner told Kazan and Schulberg: "It's a piece of shit and you two don't know anything about politics" (Kazan 415). The studio released it anyway, thinking it might catch on with a college-educated, sophisticated, urban demographic—the emerging art house audience (Mann 27). Though it opened to a lukewarm critical reception and box office, history has treated it more kindly. When Ronald Reagan came to national power, speaking in the populist rhetoric of the Old Left in the service of the New Right, the comparisons to Lonesome Rhodes started flowing. In its depiction of commercial television, "the greatest instrument of mass persuasion in the history of the world," the film also seems to anticipate *Network* (1976), an overrated movie that shifts from naturalistic to preposterous as it explores the thin line between news and entertainment, and *Bamboozled* (2000), an underrated movie about television's racial politics. Sometimes satire is better appreciated in retrospect, and the dark comedy of *A Face in the Crowd* became more appreciated after a few decades went by, a process that had already begun in the 1950s for Nathanael West's black humor of the 1930s.

The Schoolmasters of Ever After

The films *On the Waterfront* and *A Face in the Crowd* have cemented Schulberg a permanent place in film history. The result of this today is that his renown as a screenwriter has eclipsed his importance as a prose writer. As Manley Halliday makes clear in *The Disenchanted,* an author can only be a first-time novelist once, and Schulberg's post-*Sammy* novels, while healthy sellers, never reached the same level of critical acclaim. Novels such as *Sanctuary V* (1969), about political oppression in Latin America, and *Everything That Moves* (1980), about a teamster boss, have been criticized for their flat characters, predictable plot arcs, and simplistic politics.

Dorothy Parker, no stranger to early success herself, continued to write movies and reviews into the 1950s, but her production of poems and stories was grinding to a halt. She began reviewing books for *Esquire,* but getting her to submit those reviews was often difficult for editor Arnold Gingrich. In the late 1950s and early 1960s, *Esquire* and Gingrich were as generous with Dorothy Parker as they had been with Fitzgerald in 1940. Parker's biographers note that the magazine mailed her a check every month whether she had submitted her column or not. From the beginning of her career, she was a writer who would do almost anything not to have to sit down and write. Hired to compose lyrics for the 1957 Broadway musical *Candide,* Parker managed to write only half a song (Kinney xv).

She did succeed in having two cowritten plays mounted during the decade, *The Ladies of the Corridor* (1953) and *The Ice Age* (1955), but both received negative notices and closed quickly. One favorable review of the former play came from the *New Yorker*: "Mrs. Parker, who is in the habit these days of deprecating her reputation as a wit, is responsible not only for the precise and deadly wit that frequently punctuates the script but also for the acute human understanding" (qtd. in Gill xxv).

She was not writing literature any longer, but in her public role as a literary figure she remained amusingly contrary. Although she liked attention, when asked by her agent to consider an offer from Columbia to make a movie based on her life, Parker "did not dignify the letter with a reply" (Meade 360). At a panel on "The Function of the Writer," to which she had been invited because of decades of vocal commitment to progressive causes, she surprised the audience by delivering a speech claiming that writers should shut up about how badly they are treated by the world and just concentrate on the work of writing (*Portable* 566–68). During a 1959 episode of David Susskind's television show *Open End*—so named because it stayed on the air until the guests got tired of talking—a bored-looking Parker baited young lions Truman Capote and Norman Mailer for more than two hours (Meade 367–68). In the 1950s she had begun getting recognition from artists' colonies such as Yaddo, where she did a residency (but almost no writing) in 1958, and posterity-granting institutions such as the National Institute of Arts and Letters, which inducted her in 1959, and she remained a sought-after speaker in the years before her death in 1967; but today she remains more famous than read or taught.

On the other hand, the critical reputations of West and Fitzgerald—boosted by friends and admirers such as Parker and Schulberg—grew exponentially in the 1950s. In a 1920 advertising leaflet promoting *This Side of Paradise*, the newly minted novelist Fitzgerald had described the path to artistic immortality. It was, he said, to appeal to the youth of one's own generation, "the critics of the next, and the schoolmasters of ever afterward." West's books, and especially his debut novel, had never come close to capturing the imagination and the billfolds of the young (or the old, for that matter). Throughout his career and well into the 1940s, he was judged too morbid and too goofy for the critics on the Popular Front Left and too bohemian and too limited in scope for the group he derided in his letters as the "literature boys" (*Novels* 793).

Influential literary histories such as Alfred Kazin's *On Native Ground* (1942) had ignored West. Franklin Walker's 1950 *The Literature of Southern California* devotes three lines to him, and in a 1951 issue of *Partisan*

Review Isaac Rosenfeld commented that West was an intellectual who succeeded at writing about pop culture by exploring "the secret inner life of the masses" (qtd. in Siegel 16). Later in the decade, W. H. Auden, Daniel Aaron, and James Light wrote appreciations of West, but it was not until Farrar, Straus and Cudahy released the one-volume *Complete Works* in 1957 that West began to enter the literary pantheon as a major minor writer who was ahead of his time. Norman Podhoretz's review in the *New Yorker* declared that the book contained some of the best writing by an American in this century (qtd. in Siegel 16), and other critics were equally laudatory. Parker's "Best Books" column in *Esquire*, the magazine that had also given a late career boost to Fitzgerald, pronounced: "I can think of no book anyone would want to give and to receive more than *The Complete Works of Nathanael West. . . .* Wildly funny, desperately sad, brutal and kind, there is no other like Nathanael West" (*Portable* 555). Like the title character of Henry James's "John Delavoy," an author who was "the most unadvertised, unreported, uninterviewed, unphotographed, uncriticised of all originals" (405), West died unknown. Because his writing was ignored for so long, the exact vocational fear foreshadowed in his debut novel, critics have an even greater appreciation for him now. Posthumously he has reached a level of acclaim of which the frustrated writers who populate *The Dream Life of Balso Snell* could only dream. West's books, like his friend Fitzgerald's, now regularly appear on the syllabi of university schoolmasters.

It was with the expansion of literary studies in higher education after World War II that Fitzgerald's prose began entering classrooms. Teachers trained under the New Criticism belief that texts should be read independently from their biographical or social context were finding much for their students to unpack in novels such as *The Great Gatsby*, with its economy of language and well-crafted spatial design, and in such symbol-laden stories as "Babylon Revisited" and "Winter Dreams." Fitzgerald continues to be a staple of many high school classrooms, where close-reading strategies still reign. Yet it remains Fitzgerald's biography—and especially the biographical fallacies that surround him—that fascinate us most today.

Schulberg expressed pride that *The Disenchanted* helped spark "the popular revival of Scott's work that happily goes on and on" (qtd. in Beck 27). But other canonizing factors, ones more influential than Schulberg's roman à clef, had already been set in motion by 1950. *The Disenchanted* beckons us to gawk at the artist, not to examine the art. In fact, rather than inciting a "popular revival of Scott's work," the book actually fuels the myth of Fitzgerald as a movie industry casualty. During the time Schulberg was composing the novel, Arthur Mizener was putting together the first major biography of Fitzgerald, and the two compared notes. Both works—one fiction and the other nonfiction—are plots of decline. Lionel Trilling's influential essay on a "heroic" (237), hope-filled Fitzgerald in *The Liberal Imagination* (1950) offers a counternarrative to Mizener/Schulberg, along the way making a claim that Fitzgerald's prose voice—a balance between moral judgment and empathy—is the ideal one for a novelist. Trilling demonstrates that Fitzgerald kept his talent until the end, but the legend that he was washed up after the Jazz Age still lingers on.

Tom Dardis writes: "The tradition of seeing Fitzgerald in Hollywood as a suffering man, a failed man, really began with Budd Schulberg's novel of 1950, *The Disenchanted*" (17). *This Side of Paradise* ends with a trip where Amory defends his generation to a middle-aged businessman; *The Disenchanted* offers an artistic debate, begun on a plane, between the 1920s romantic individualism of Manley Halliday and the 1930s social commitment of Shep Stearns: Halliday wants to leave Hollywood and escape back into his boozy, poetic nostalgia for the Jazz Age; Stearns wants to push cinema into the hands of the revolution and create a realist art form made by the people for the people. Much of the early part of the novel is given over to Stearns's attempts to nudge his older partner toward the political Left. Halliday is endowed with an amplified version of Fitzgerald's character flaws, biography, and appearance, yet Schulberg always claimed—never very convincingly—that Halliday isn't based on him (Breit 28).

As Schulberg notes elsewhere, Fitzgerald was his own "prime mover in all this god making and god smashing" (*Four Seasons* 142), something that is equally true of Halliday. Fitzgerald often claimed that he spoke with "the authority of failure," but the nature of this failure is unclear: failure to live up to potential? to find a public who could appreciate him? to be a best-selling author? Even in his darkest periods, Fitzgerald was able to regain faith in his talent and keep his eyes planted on the projects to come. In "The Lost Decade," Louis Trimble emerges from years of drunkenness as a new man. The story shows that Orrison Brown, a Schulberg stand-in, cannot fathom the changes that have taken place in him. In *The Disenchanted* Schulberg forces Halliday to keep playing one note. Despite the fact that the tail end of *The Disenchanted* ultimately reveals the older writer to be a productive artist who is still relevant, the bulk of the narrative is Shep's weekend walk with a zombie. Halliday refuses to let go of his death grip on the past, and throughout the novel he is referred to using terms such as *specter, ghost,* and *shadow.* Listening to Halliday's constant self-analysis of his selfish mistakes, Shep thinks to himself, "is like having a corpse suddenly rise and deliver his own funeral oration, or, worse, perform his own autopsy" (184).

At the time the novel was written, Fitzgerald had been dead for almost a decade, so if anyone was performing a lukewarm eulogy—or, worse, a postmortem dissection—it was Schulberg. At the beginning of *The Disenchanted,* Shep thinks Halliday is dead. He then proceeds to treat him as a relic during the trip and finally sees him dead at the end. Schulberg thus has it both ways. Nostalgia for the writers of the 1920s coexists with an Oedipal relief that they are fading away. Still the novel tries to retain a sort of subjective distance. Unlike Schulberg's first two novels, *The Disenchanted* is written from a Jamesian, third-person-limited point of view. The capitalist joys of Halliday's early career are sung in flashback chapters titled "Old Business." These discordant attempts to mimic Fitzgerald's lyrical style alternate with more sober chapters depicting Halliday's decline during the Depression. Schulberg writes of the older writer's nosedive: "Oh. It was just perfect. It could hardly have jibed more neatly with Shep's theories if he had made it up himself" (74).

As the book goes on, the progressive Stearns comes to change his mind about the nostalgic Halliday. His pity and disgust turn to respect and admiration. On the plane Shep is angry at Halliday's politics, and during the trip he resents him for blowing the assignment, but after reading the master's novel in progress he has an epiphany: "Then it hit him hard: how was it possible for Manley Halliday to write this well in 1939?" (368).

Writing a book about the 1920s and 1930s from a perch in the 1950s, Schulberg can safely have the character of Shep Stearns become disenchanted with the vulgar Marxism of the 1930s and grow to appreciate the timeless artistry of a forgotten writer/competitor. Just as Schulberg thought it a shame that Fitzgerald died before completing *The Last Tycoon,* Stearns pities Halliday for dying before he can finish his masterpiece. In 1939 Schulberg was a certified Communist and an unpublished novelist; in 1950 he was neither. In 1939 Fitzgerald was alive and working on his own Hollywood novel; in 1950 he was not. It is easy to appreciate a stronger voice after it has been silenced midsong.

In a rare bit of loyalty, an angry Ernest Hemingway told friends he hoped Fitzgerald was in heaven working on books titled "Longevity Pays: The Life of Arthur Mizener" and "The Schulberg Incident" (Bruccoli, *Fitzgerald and Hemingway* 222). Stories concerning Hemingway's decades-long, often cruel rivalry with Fitzgerald have been well documented by biographers and critics. What is less analyzed, however, are Hemingway's midcentury statements that praise Fitzgerald's work and defend his fellow writer's posthumous reputation. In the 1950s, as Hemingway made the move in the cultural field from respected writer to American celebrity better known for his life than for his work, he began worrying about his artistic legacy, a shift that resulted in him feeling a stronger kinship toward his dead rival, an author who had struggled with similar vocational issues.

Although Hemingway had spoken to Mizener about Fitzgerald, he was now regretting it. When the January 1950 issue of *Life* ran an excerpt from the biography, an episode titled "Tormented Paradise" that focused on Fitzgerald's drinking problem, Hemingway was appalled. He wrote to Mizener that he'd "rather clean sewers, be a bouncer in a bad whorehouse, or pimp for a living than to sign such an article" (qtd. in Meyers 324). When Schulberg visited Cuba in late 1950, Hemingway refused to see him, passing on the word through mutual friends that Schulberg was "swine." "Poor Scott," Ernest wrote to Malcolm Cowley, "what robe or shroud he had were torn and sold by very strange people. . . . that Schulberg Mizener Axis could well be hanged, head down, in front of any second rate garage" (Bruccoli, *Fitzgerald and Hemingway* 222).

On the other hand, Hemingway also had a thriving side business in making personal attacks on his dead friend's character. He wrote to Charles Scribner in 1951 that "Scott was a rummy and a liar and dishonest about money with the inbred talent of an a dishonest and easily frightened angel" (Meyers 430). Hemingway had been equally critical of Fitzgerald when he was alive, and sometimes had been downright mean to him. He had little patience with weakness or failure. As Fitzgerald wrote: "Ernest would always give a helping hand to a man on a ledge a little higher up" (*Notebooks of FSF* item 1819). Yet the two had remained friends until Fitzgerald's death. There were angry words exchanged, but there was never a falling out.

More than blind loyalty lay behind Hemingway's defense of his late friend Fitzgerald. Intensely competitive, he considered Fitzgerald his territory, and he resented other writers poaching. There is no doubt that Hemingway knew Fitzgerald much better than Schulberg had. But more important, Hemingway was growing worried about his own legacy and the imminent threat of biographers and other writers poking around in his own past.

In the early 1950s, Hemingway, once a wunderkind modernist writer, began transforming completely into Papa—fisherman, hunter, womanizer, boxer, philosopher, and product spokesman. In doing so he became less of an author and more of a celebrity. It was a vocational hazard Fitzgerald had faced decades earlier. Papa was now the most famous and most successful living author in the world. John O'Hara's hyperbolic *New York Times* review of *Across the River and into the Trees* called Hemingway the best writer since Shakespeare. But other critics were not so kind. Although Hemingway thought it was his best book to date, the novel, his first in ten years, received poor reviews. His fame was growing, but his critical reputation was slipping. His beard was more recognizable than the titles of his books.

Although in Hemingway's letters to his friends he scoffs at the elevation of Fitzgerald's literary reputation, the Mizener/Schulberg method of clinically examining an autobiographical writer's character flaws worried him. When Philip Young, a doctoral student at the University of Iowa, approached Hemingway in 1951 about writing a biographical study of his fiction, he was mortified. He had spent decades crafting a relationship between his art and his life, but it gave him the creeps to have someone analyzing the presentation of self he had so carefully crafted. Young's resulting book, *Ernest Hemingway* (1952), is a psychoanalytic study of the inner and outer wounds suffered by Hemingway protagonists, the result of Hemingway's repetition compulsion to relive his war experiences and injuries. Young suggested that the author sought danger not because it increased his fame but because he was so damaged that he simply could not help himself.

A Moveable Feast, the fictionalized, retrospective sketches of his literary apprenticeship that Hemingway began writing in the late 1950s, can be seen as a response to Young's psychobiographical analysis. *A Moveable Feast* is an autobiography that is mainly about what is wrong with other writers. The only aspect of Hemingway's own life he closely analyzes is his epic quest to write one true sentence.

A Moveable Feast, like all autobiographies, shapes people, places, and events for literary effect. For example, although their years in Paris were funded by his wife Hadley's family money and Hemingway's journalism, in this portrait of the author as a young man, he presents himself as an artist starving, literally, for art. Going hungry sharpens his eye for detail and feeds his craft. *A Moveable Feast* is a book about aesthetics, punctuated with potshots at Gertrude Stein, Ford Madox Ford, and other Hemingway rivals.

The sketch titled "Scott Fitzgerald," composed in 1957, was the first piece written for the project and is also the longest. Traditionally "Scott Fitzgerald"—with its references to Fitzgerald's pretty mouth and all—has been read as a jealous smear campaign against a more talented colleague. But a much more central theme is the art and craft of the profession of authorship. Fitzgerald, the more established writer at the time and the one who helped Hemingway hook up with Scribner's, is recast as talented but undisciplined and full of doubts; Hemingway, an apprentice at the time, portrays himself as less artistically gifted but a harder worker who is more dedicated to his craft. The chapter's epigraph sets up the opposition: "His talent was as natural as the pattern that was made by the dust on the butterfly's wings. At one time he understood it no more than the butterfly did and he did not know when it was brushed or marred. Later he became conscious of his damaged wings and of their construction and he learned to think and could not fly any more because the love of flight was gone and he could only remember when it had been effortless" (148).

Good writing is not effortless, Hemingway is saying. It is work. Losing "the love of flight" should not have affected Fitzgerald's writing. Unlike Schulberg, who viewed Fitzgerald as an age rather than an author, Hemingway looks at him (erroneously) as a working writer who had stopped working. Fitzgerald's mistake, according to Hemingway, was relying too much on inspiration and not enough on perspiration. He lacked self-control, gave up when the going got tough, and became too easily discouraged and distracted.

This is also the lesson contained in the related Hemingway sketch of Fitzgerald titled "A Matter of Measurements." Many critics have read this piece as an assault on Fitzgerald's manhood. But as Marc Dolan argues in *Modern Lives*, the issue for Hemingway is not the size of Fitzgerald's penis; it is Fitzgerald's anxiety about its size. These doubts, fueled by Zelda, hampered Fitzgerald's writing. The sketches also express the young Hemingway's disapproval that Fitzgerald brags about how much money he gets for his stories. The work is the only thing that should matter. The Fitzgerald pieces are about not letting anything—like wives, drink, financial return, or fame—get in the way of your craft. The end of "A Matter of Measurements" cuts to the Ritz bar after World War II. The bar chief there does not remember Fitzgerald: "Tell me who he was . . . was he a good writer?" Hemingway responds, "He wrote two very good books and he also wrote some good short stories." It is understated acknowledgment, but acknowledgment nonetheless. The bar chief asks Hemingway to write a memoir, the book that becomes *A Moveable Feast,* "so that I will remember him" (193). Hemingway could be a bully, but he could also give credit where credit was due. He never stopped believing in Fitzgerald's talent. As he wrote to his son Gregory: "Scott's writing got better and better, but no one realized it, not even Scott. That stuff he was writing at the end was best of all. Poor bastard!" (qtd. in Dickstein 88).

Budd Schulberg later in life. Photofest

Seeing Fitzgerald as lost only sweetens the pleasure of rediscovering him. Part of the reason we still remember him now is because he always wrote so well about being forgotten. Viewing Fitzgerald as a study in failure, as do *The Disenchanted* and *A Moveable Feast,* only increases his celebrity. Sometimes, paradoxically, failure can be a success. Schulberg's Halliday, like Hemingway's Fitzgerald, possesses a self-styled, self-actualized, romantic persona, the self-pitying, highly autobiographical writer who drinks himself into stupors and appears to spend his enormous talent as recklessly as the rich in his books spend money. The tragic figure holds great cathartic power for the audience. His flaws are, in fact, what we like most about him.

Like Schulberg's *The Disenchanted,* Sheilah Graham's 1957 memoir *Beloved Infidel* increased interest in Fitzgerald by inviting readers to pity him. Parker dubbed the tell-all book "bone gnawing" and "a possible all time low in American letters" (qtd. in Frewin 556). Just as gossip columnist Graham made a second career of writing volume after volume containing bits of her daily interactions with Fitzgerald, Schulberg remained in the public eye by packaging and repackaging his thoughts on West and Fitzgerald, men he knew sort of well toward the end there. Consisting mainly of pieces originally appearing in *Esquire,* Schulberg's *The Four Seasons of Success* (1972), examines the highs and lows—but mainly the lows—in the careers of several American authors. The book makes the claim that West was "spared by failure" (14) and that Parker and Fitzgerald were ruined by early success. "Put West and Fitzgerald together," Schulberg writes, "and you have a rounded portrait of the artist as a young American strike out victim and home run hitter" (155). In the epilogue Schulberg calls for critics and readers alike to recognize literary authors and support these artists over the long haul, "so that a Nathanael West is allowed to earn his keep while practicing his art, so that a god hurled down from Olympus into the scrubby marketplace is not forced to hack his stories at $250 a crack in order to stitch himself together for a desperate, final assault on the ramparts of self-fulfillment, and perhaps with it, immortality" (203).

West did "earn his keep while practicing his art," but it was not critics and readers who allowed him to do this. It was Hollywood. Fitzgerald had high literary aspirations, but he never viewed himself as "a god hurled down from Olympus into the scrubby marketplace." From the beginning of his career, he was a hardworking professional writer who was savvy about making money on the commodities he produced. Fitzgerald was less successful writing for Hollywood than he had been writing for magazines such as the *Saturday Evening Post* in the 1920s, but both were "scrubby" markets he studied closely. The Pat Hobby stories, which sold for "$250 a crack," were not hackwork; the author saw them as linked stories and had definite ideas on how they should be arranged. And even if we buy that Fitzgerald needed to be financially stitched together, it was Hollywood, not *Esquire,* that had allowed him to purchase the longer piece of thread.

In the new century, Schulberg continued to dole out stories perpetuating the tale of Fitzgerald as a Hollywood failure, a fate he also assigned to Parker. In 2001 he told an interviewer for the *Paris Review* that Fitzgerald was seen as "marginal" in Hollywood and that he was "pathetic, really, because he thought he could be as good a screenwriter as he *had been* a novelist" [emphasis mine] ("Two Conversations" 120,124). Grumbling about the lack of respect his own literary work gets from critics, Schulberg said:

> If there were a literary decathlon, I'd have a shot. Scott Fitzgerald often wished that after *Gatsby* he had never done anything but just stuck to his last. Sometimes at night I feel that way. I have a little bit of that feeling, that I probably would be more respected as a novelist if I had just stayed on that track. Instead, I have this fatal problem of versatility. Because I was raised in such a writing atmosphere, it got so I could write anything. I could write a movie; I could write a novel; I could write a play. I could write lyrics, which I did for *A Face in the Crowd*. Always there were these different strings, so many different ones. I was sort of cursed with versatility. ("Two Conversations" 111)

With his "fatal problem" and talk of being "cursed," Budd Schulberg—a mediocre novelist trapped in the body of a talented screenwriter—sounds like a weakened survivor of a dark plague that attacked fiction writers in studio-era Hollywood. Step out of your genre, and you will be poxed. The more you try to do, the less you will end up achieving. Market-defying novelists who resist the financial and creative lure of Hollywood are the only true authors in such formulations; everyone else is just a hack. By casting Nathanael West and F. Scott Fitzgerald as besieged literary geniuses, Schulberg may have directed some new interest their way after their deaths. But he was also a central producer of the myth that their stars would have burned even brighter, and their brilliance would have been recognized even earlier, if only Hollywood had not dampened their luster.

Works Cited

Aaron, Daniel. "A Note on Nathanael West." In Siegel, 113–17.

———. *Writers on the Left.* New York: Oxford University Press, 1977.

Advice to the Lovelorn. Dir. Alfred Werker. 1933.

Ames, Christopher. *Movies about the Movies: Hollywood Reflected.* Lexington: University Press of Kentucky, 1997.

"Are Film Writers Workers?" *Pacific Weekly,* June 29, 1939, 371.

Auden, W. H. "West's Disease." In Siegel, 118–23.

Austen, Jane. *Letters.* London: Oxford University Press, 1995.

The Bad and the Beautiful. Dir. Vincente Minnelli. 1952.

Balio, Tino, ed. *Grand Design: Hollywood as a Modern Business Enterprise.* Berkeley: University of California Press, 1995.

Bamboozled. Dir. Spike Lee. 2000.

Barreca, Regina. Introduction to *The Complete Stories,* by Dorothy Parker, edited by Colleen Breese. New York: Penguin, 1995.

Beck, Nicholas. *Budd Schulberg.* Lanham, Md.: Scarecrow, 2001.

Behlmer, Rudy, ed. *Memo from David O. Selznick.* New York: Viking, 1972.

———. *Memo from Darryl F. Zanuck.* New York: Grove, 1995.

Behrman, S. N. "Hollywood." *New Yorker,* January 20, 1934, 30–35

Benét, Stephen Vincent. "Fitzgerald's Unfinished Symphony." *Saturday Review of Literature,* December 6, 1941, 10.

Benjamin, Walter. "The Work of Art in the Age of Mechanical Reproduction." In *Illuminations,* edited by Hannah Arendt, translated by Harry Zohn, 217–51. New York: Schocken, 1969.

Berlant, Lauren. *The Female Complaint: The Unfinished Business of Sentimentality in American Culture.* Durham, N.C.: Duke University Press, 2008.

Berman, Jeffrey. *The Talking Cure: Literary Representations of Psychoanalysis.* New York: New York University Press, 1985.

Bloom, Harold, ed. *Nathanael West: Modern Critical Views.* New York: Chelsea House, 1986.

Bloom, Lynn. "Dorothy Parker." In *Critical Survey of Fiction,* vol. 5, edited by Frank N. Magill, 2052–56. Englewood Cliffs, N.J.: Salem, 1982.

The Blue Angel. Dir. Josef von Sternberg. 1930.

Bordwell, David, Janet Staiger, and Kristin Thompson. *The Classical Hollywood Cinema.* New York: Columbia University Press, 1985.

Bourdieu, Pierre. *Distinction: A Social Critique of the Judgment of Taste.* Translated by Richard Nice. Cambridge, Mass.: Harvard University Press, 1984.

———. *The Rules of Art: Genesis and Structure of the Literary Field.* Translated by Susan Emmanuel. Stanford: Stanford University Press, 1996.

Brando, Marlon. *Brando: Songs My Mother Taught Me.* New York: Random House, 1994.

Breit, Harvey. "A Talk With Mr. Schulberg." *New York Times Book Review,* November 5, 1950, 28.

Brooks, Van Wyck. *America's Coming of Age.* New York: B. W. Huebsch, 1915.

———. *Days of the Phoenix.* New York: Dutton, 1957.

———. *The Writer in America.* New York: Dutton, 1953.

Bruccoli, Matthew. *Fitzgerald and Hemingway: A Dangerous Friendship.* New York: Carroll & Graf, 1994.

———. *Some Sort of Epic Grandeur: The Life of F. Scott Fitzgerald.* New York: Harcourt Brace Jovanovich, 1981.

Bruccoli, Matthew, and Jackson Bryer, eds. *F. Scott Fitzgerald in His Own Time.* Kent, Ohio: Kent State University Press, 1971.

Bruccoli, Matthew, Scottie Fitzgerald Smith, and Joan Kerr, eds. *The Romantic Egoists.* New York: Scribner, 1974.

Bruck, Connie. *When Hollywood Had a King.* New York: Random House, 2003.

Bryer, Jackson, ed. *New Essays on F. Scott Fitzgerald's Neglected Stories.* Columbia: University of Missouri Press, 1996.

———. *The Short Stories of F. Scott Fitzgerald: New Approaches in Criticism.* Madison: University of Wisconsin Press, 1982.

Calhoun, Randall. *Dorothy Parker: A Bio-Bibliography.* Westport, Conn.: Greenwood Press, 1993.

Ceplair, Larry, and Steven Englund. *The Inquisition in Hollywood: Politics in the Film Community, 1930–1960.* Garden City, N.Y.: Anchor/Doubleday, 1980.

Charlton, James, ed. *The Writer's Quotation Book.* New York: Barnes & Noble, 1999.

Charvat, William. *The Profession of Authorship in the United States.* Columbus: Ohio State University Press, 1968.

Cheney, O. H. *Economic Survey of the Book Industry, 1930–1931.* New York: National Association of Book Publishers, 1931.

Chipman, Bruce L. *Into America's Dream Dump: A Postmodern Study of the Hollywood Novel.* Lanham, Md.: University Press of America, 1999.

Conroy, Jack. "The Worker as Writer." In *American Writers Congress,* edited by Henry Hart, 83–86. New York: International Publishers, 1935.

Cowley, Malcolm. *Exile's Return: A Literary Odyssey of the 1920s.* New York: Viking, 1951.

Cross, Gary. *An All-Consuming Century: Why Commercialism Won in Modern America.* New York: Columbia University Press, 2000.

Curnutt, Kirk. "Fitzgerald's Consumer World." In *A Historical Guide to F. Scott Fitzgerald,* edited by Kirk Curnutt, 85–128. New York: Oxford University Press, 2004.

Custen, George F. *Twentieth Century's Fox: Darryl F. Zanuck and the Culture of Hollywood.* New York: Basic Books, 1997.

Dardis, Tom. *Some Time in the Sun.* New York: Scribner, 1976.

Denning, Michael. *The Cultural Front.* New York: Verso, 1997.

Dickstein, Morris. *A Mirror in the Roadway: Literature and the Real*

World. Princeton, N.J.: Princeton University Press, 2005.

Dixon, Wheeler Winston. *The Cinematic Vision of F. Scott Fitzgerald*. Ann Arbor: UMI Research Press, 1986.

Dolan, Marc. *Modern Lives: A Cultural Re-Reading of "the Lost Generation."* West Lafayette, Ind.: Purdue University Press, 1996.

Donaldson, Scott. *Fool for Love: F. Scott Fitzgerald*. London: Congdon & Weed, 1983

——. *Hemingway vs. Fitzgerald: The Rise and Fall of a Literary Friendship*. Woodstock, N.Y.: Overlook, 1999.

Dreiser, Theodore. *An American Tragedy*. 1925. New York: Signet, 1964.

——. *The Financier*. 1912. New York: Meridian, 1981.

——. *Sister Carrie*. 1900. New York: Norton, 1970.

Eble, Kenneth, ed. *F. Scott Fitzgerald: A Collection of Criticism*. New York: McGraw-Hill, 1973.

A Face in the Crowd. Dir. Elia Kazan. 1957.

Farrell, James. *The League of Frightened Philistines*. New York: Vanguard, 1954.

Faulkner, William. *Sanctuary*. 1931. New York: Random House, 1962.

Fiedler, Leslie. *Love and Death in the American Novel*. New York: Criterion, 1960.

——. "Some Notes on Fitzgerald." In *F. Scott Fitzgerald: The Man and His Work,* edited by Alfred Kazin, 69–75. New York: Collier, 1967.

Field, Andrew. *Djuna: The Life and Times of Djuna Barnes*. New York: Putnam, 1983.

Fine, Richard. *West of Eden: Writers in Hollywood 1928–1940*. Washington, D.C.: Smithsonian Institution Press, 1993.

Fischer, John, and Robert Silvers, eds. *Writing in America*. New Brunswick, N.J.: Rutgers University Press, 1993.

Fitzgerald, F. Scott. *Afternoon of an Author*. New York: Scribner, 1958.

——. *As Ever, Scott Fitz*. Edited by Matthew Bruccoli and Jennifer Atkinson. Philadelphia: Lippincott, 1972.

——. *Babylon Revisited: The Screenplay*. New York: Carroll & Graf, 1993.

——. *The Beautiful and Damned*. New York: Scribner, 1922.

——. *The Correspondence of F. Scott Fitzgerald*. Edited by Matthew Bruccoli and Margaret Duggan. New York: Random House, 1980.

——. *The Crack-Up*. Edited by Edmund Wilson. New York: New Directions, 1993.

——. *Dear Scott/Dear Max*. Edited by John Kuehl and Jackson Bryer. New York: Scribner, 1971.

——. *F. Scott Fitzgerald: A Life in Letters*. Edited by Matthew Bruccoli. New York: Scribner, 1994.

——. *F. Scott Fitzgerald on Authorship*. Edited by Matthew Bruccoli and Judith Baughman. Columbia: University of South Carolina Press, 1996.

——. *The Great Gatsby*. New York: Modern Library, 1934.

——. *The Last Tycoon*. New York: Scribner, 1941.

——. *F. Scott Fitzgerald's Ledger: A Facsimile Edition*. Washington, D.C.: NCR, 1972.

——. *The Letters of F. Scott Fitzgerald*. Edited by Andrew Turnbull. New York: Scribner, 1963.

——. *The Love of the Last Tycoon: A Western*. Edited by Matthew Bruccoli. Cambridge: Cambridge University Press, 1993.

———. *The Notebooks of F. Scott Fitzgerald*. Edited by Matthew Bruccoli. New York: Harcourt Brace Jovanovich, 1978.

———. *The Pat Hobby Stories*. Edited by Arnold Gingrich. New York: Scribner, 1962.

———. *The Portable F. Scott Fitzgerald*. Edited by Dorothy Parker. New York: Viking, 1945.

———. *The Price Was High: The Last Uncollected Stories of F. Scott Fitzgerald*. Edited by Matthew Bruccoli. New York: Harcourt Brace Jovanovich, 1979.

———. *The Stories of F. Scott Fitzgerald*. New York: Collier, 1986.

———. *Tender Is the Night*. New York: Scribner, 1934.

———. *This Side of Paradise*. New York: Scribner, 1920.

———. *"Three Comrades": The Screenplay*. Carbondale: Southern Illinois University Press, 1978.

Flaubert, Gustave. *The Letters of Gustave Flaubert, 1830–1857*. Edited by Frances Steegmuller. Cambridge, Mass.: Harvard University Press, 1980.

Foley, Barbara. *Radical Representations: Politics and Form in U.S. Proletarian Fiction, 1929–1941*. Durham, N.C.: Duke University Press, 1993.

Fraser-Cavassoni, Natasha. *Sam Spiegel*. New York: Simon & Schuster, 2003.

Frewin, Leslie. *The Late Mrs. Dorothy Parker*. New York: Macmillan, 1986.

Gabler, Neal. *An Empire of Their Own: How the Jews Invented Hollywood*. New York: Doubleday, 1989.

Gill, Brendan. *Here at "The New Yorker."* New York: Random House, 1975.

Gone with the Wind. Dir. Victor Fleming. 1939.

Graham, Sheilah. *Beloved Infidel*. New York: Holt, 1958.

———. *College of One*. New York: Viking, 1967.

———. *The Real F. Scott Fitzgerald*. New York: Grosset & Dunlap, 1976.

Greenfeld, Howard. *Books: From Writer to Reader*. New York: Crown, 1989.

Guillory, John. *Cultural Capital: The Problem of Literary Canon Formation*. Chicago: University of Chicago Press, 1995.

Hamilton, Ian. *Writers in Hollywood, 1915–1951*. New York: Harper & Row, 1990.

The Harder They Fall. Dir. Mark Robson. 1956.

Hecht, Ben. *A Child of the Century*. New York: Simon & Schuster, 1954.

Hellman, Lillian. *An Unfinished Woman*. Boston: Little, Brown, 1969.

Hemingway, Ernest. *A Moveable Feast*. 1964. New York: Scribner, 1987.

Here Is My Heart. Dir. Frank Tuttle. 1934.

Hoffman, Frederick J., Charles Allen, and Carolyn Ulrich. *The Little Magazine: A History and Bibliography*. Princeton, N.J.: Princeton University Press, 1946.

Huxley, Aldous. *After Many a Summer Dies the Swan*. New York: Harper & Row, 1965.

Hyman, Stanley Edgar. *Nathanael West*. Minneapolis: University of Minnesota Press, 1962.

I Stole a Million. Dir. Frank Tuttle. 1939.

The Informer. Dir. John Ford. 1935.

It Could Happen to You. Dir. Phil Rosen. 1937.

James, Henry. *The Figure in the Carpet and Other Stories*. Edited by Frank Kermode. New York: Penguin, 1986.

Johnson, Nunnally. *The Letters of Nunnally Johnson*. Edited by Dorris

Johnson and Ellen Leventhal. New York: Knopf, 1981.

Jowett, Garth, and James L. Linton. *Movies as Mass Communication.* Beverly Hills, Calif.: Sage, 1980.

Joyce, James. *A Portrait of the Artist as a Young Man.* 1916. Oxford: Oxford University Press, 2000.

Kael, Pauline. *The "Citizen Kane" Book: Raising Kane.* New York: Bantam, 1974.

Kazan, Elia. *A Life.* New York: Knopf, 1988.

Kazin, Alfred. *On Native Grounds.* Garden City, N.Y.: Doubleday, 1956.

———, ed. *F. Scott Fitzgerald: The Man and His Work.* New York: Collier, 1967.

Keats, John. *You Might as Well Live: The Life and Times of Dorothy Parker.* New York: Simon & Schuster, 1970.

Kennedy, David. *Freedom from Fear: The American People in Depression and War.* New York: Oxford University Press, 1999.

Kinney, Arthur F. *Dorothy Parker.* New York: Twayne, 1978.

Koszarski, Richard. *An Evening's Entertainment: The Age of the Silent Feature Picture, 1915–1928.* Berkeley: University of California Press, 1990.

Lambert, Gavin. *GWTW: The Making of "Gone with the Wind."* Boston: Little, Brown, 1973.

The Last Laugh. Dir. F. W. Murnau. 1924.

The Last Time I Saw Paris. Dir. Richard Brooks. 1954.

Latham, Aaron. *Crazy Sundays: F. Scott Fitzgerald in Hollywood.* New York: Viking, 1970.

Levine, Lawrence. *Highbrow/Lowbrow: The Emergence of Cultural Hierarchy in America.* Cambridge, Mass.: Harvard University Press, 1988.

Le Vot, André. *F. Scott Fitzgerald: A Biography.* Translated by William Byron. Garden City, N.Y.: Doubleday, 1983.

Light, James F. *Nathanael West: An Interpretative Study.* Evanston, Ill.: Northwestern University Press, 1961.

Lindsay, Vachel. *The Prose of Vachel Lindsay.* Edited by Dennis Camp. Peoria, Ill.: Spoon River Press, 1988.

Long, Robert Emmett. *Nathanael West.* New York: Ungar, 1985.

Loos, Anita. *Kiss Hollywood Goodbye.* New York: Viking, 1974.

Lowenthal, Leo. *Literature and Mass Culture: Communication in Society.* Edison, N.J.: Transaction, 1984.

Madden, David, ed. *Nathanael West: The Cheaters and the Cheated.* Deland, Fla.: Everett/Edwards, 1973.

Mailer, Norman. *The Deer Park.* 1955. New York: Vintage, 1997.

Mangum, Bryant. *A Fortune Yet: Money in the Art of F. Scott Fitzgerald's Short Stories.* New York: Garland, 1991.

Mann, Denise. *Hollywood Independents: The Postwar Talent Takeover.* Minneapolis: University of Minnesota Press, 2008.

Margolies, Alan. "'Kissing, Shooting, and Sacrificing': F. Scott Fitzgerald and the Hollywood Market." In *The Short Stories of F. Scott Fitzgerald: New Approaches in Criticism,* edited by Jackson Bryer, 65–73. Madison: University of Wisconsin Press, 1982.

Martin, Jay. *Nathanael West: The Art of His Life.* New York: Farrar, Straus & Giroux, 1970.

McAlmon, Robert, and Kay Boyle. *Being Geniuses Together.* London: Hogarth, 1984.

McGilligan, Pat, ed. *Backstory: Interviews with Screenwriters of Hollywood's Golden Age.* Berkeley: University of California Press, 1986.

McGurl, Mark. *The Novel Art: Elevations of American Fiction after Henry James*. Princeton, N.J.: Princeton University Press, 2001.

Meade, Marion. *Dorothy Parker: What Fresh Hell Is This?* New York: Penguin, 1989.

Mellow, James. *Invented Lives: F. Scott and Zelda Fitzgerald*. New York: Anchor, 1994.

Menand, Louis. *Discovering Modernism: T. S. Eliot and His Context*. New York: Oxford University Press, 1987.

Mencken, H. L. *The American Language*. New York: Knopf, 1936.

Meyers, Jeffrey. *Scott Fitzgerald: A Biography*. New York: Harper-Collins, 1994.

Milford, Nancy. *Zelda: A Biography*. New York: Harper & Row, 1970.

Mizener, Arthur. *The Far Side of Paradise: A Biography of F. Scott Fitzgerald*. Boston: Houghton Mifflin, 1951.

Moreau, Michael, ed. *Fante/Mencken: John Fante and H. L. Mencken: A Personal Correspondence, 1930–1952*. Santa Rosa, Calif.: Black Sparrow, 1989.

Navasky, Victor. *Naming Names*. London: Calder, 1982.

Norman, Marc. *What Happens Next: A History of American Screenwriting*. New York: Harmony, 2007.

O'Hara, John. *The Big Laugh*. 1962. Hopewell, N.J.: Ecco, 1997.

———. *Hope of Heaven*. New York: Harcourt, Brace, 1938.

———. *Selected Letters of John O'Hara*. Edited by Matthew J. Bruccoli. New York: Random House, 1978.

On the Waterfront. Dir. Elia Kazan. 1954.

One Hour Late. Dir. Ralph Murphy. 1935.

Parker, Dorothy. *The Complete Stories*. Edited by Colleen Breese. New York: Penguin, 1995.

———. *The Portable Dorothy Parker*. New York: Penguin, 1976.

———. "Professional Youth." *Saturday Evening Post*, April 28, 1923, 14, 156–57.

———. "Suzy" Screenplay. N.Y. State Archives. File box 31413-457.

———. "Sweethearts" Screenplay. N.Y. State Archives. File box 36000-666.

———. "Weekend for Three" Screenplay. N.Y. State Archives. File box 41053-906.

———. "When Martin Comes." *Directions: A Publication of the Federal Writers Project*, April 1940, 5.

Pascal, Ernest. "One Organization for All American Writers." *Screen Guilds' Magazine*, April 1936, 13–20.

Pells, Richard. *Radical Visions and American Dreams: Culture and Social Thought in the Depression Years*. New York: Harper & Row, 1973.

Perosa, Sergio. *The Art of F. Scott Fitzgerald*. Translated by Charles Matz and the author. Ann Arbor: University of Michigan Press, 1965.

Piper, Harry Dan. *F. Scott Fitzgerald: A Critical Portrait*. New York: Holt, Rinehart & Winston, 1965.

The Player. Dir. Robert Altman. 1992.

Plimpton, George, ed. *The Writer's Chapbook*. New York: Viking, 1989.

Powdermaker, Hortense. *Hollywood: The Dream Factory*. Boston: Little, Brown, 1950.

The President's Mystery. Dir. Phil Rosen. 1936.

Radway, Janice. *A Feeling for Books: The Book-of-the-Month Club, Literary Taste, and Middle-Class Desire*. Chapel Hill: University of North Carolina Press, 1997.

Rainey, Lawrence. *Institutions of Modernism: Literary Elites and Public Culture.* New Haven: Yale University Press, 1998.

Rebecca. Dir. Alfred Hitchcock. 1940.

Rhodes, Chip. "Ambivalence on the Left: Budd Schulberg's *What Makes Sammy Run?*." *Studies in American Fiction* 30 (Spring 2002): 65–83.

———. *Politics, Desire, and the Hollywood Novel.* Iowa City: University of Iowa Press, 2008.

———. "Raymond Chandler and the Art of the Hollywood Novel: Individualism and Populism in *The Little Sister.*" *Studies in the Novel* 33 (2001): 95–109.

Rosten, Leo. *Hollywood: The Movie Colony, the Movie Makers.* New York: Harcourt, Brace, 1941.

Saboteur. Dir. Alfred Hitchcock. 1942.

Schary, Dore. *Heyday.* Boston: Little, Brown, 1979.

Schatz, Thomas. *The Genius of the System.* New York: Metro, 1988.

Schickel, Richard. *The Men Who Made the Movies.* New York: Atheneum, 1975.

Schulberg, Budd. *The Disenchanted.* New York: Random House, 1950.

———. *A Face in the Crowd: A Play for the Screen.* New York: Random House, 1957.

———. Foreword to *"On the Waterfront": A Cambridge Film Handbook,* edited by Joanna Rapf, xv–xxii. New York: Cambridge University Press, 2003.

———. *The Four Seasons of Success.* Garden City, N.Y.: Doubleday, 1972. Revised as *Writers in America: The Four Seasons of Success.* New York: Stein & Day, 1983.

———. "Government Girl" Screenplay. N.Y. State Archives. File box 44330-1066.

———. *The Harder They Fall.* London: Allison & Busby, 1995.

———. "Hollywood's Second Generation." *New York Times,* July 2, 1939.

———. *Moving Pictures: Memories of a Hollywood Prince.* New York: Stein & Day, 1981.

———. "Old Scott." *Esquire,* January 1961, 97–101.

———. *On the Waterfront: The Final Shooting Script.* New York: French, 1988.

———. *Some Faces in the Crowd.* London: Bodley Head, 1954.

———. *Sparring with Hemingway and Other Legends of the Fight Game.* Chicago: Dee, 1995.

———. "Two Conversations." *Paris Review,* Winter 2001, 86–137.

———. *Waterfront.* 1955. New York: Primus, 1987.

———. *What Makes Sammy Run?* 1941. New York: Vintage, 1993.

———. "What Makes Sammy Run?" in *What Makes Sammy Run?* 283–99.

Schwartz, Nancy Lynn. *The Hollywood Writers' Wars.* New York: Knopf, 1982.

Scribner, Charles, III. Introduction to *Tender Is the Night,* by F. Scott Fitzgerald, vii–xiii. New York: Collier, 1986.

Server, Lee. *Screenwriter: Words Become Pictures.* Pittstown, N.J.: Main Street, 1987.

Shapiro, Julian. "Tired Men and Dung." In Siegel, 46–47.

Siegel, Ben, ed. *Critical Essays on Nathanael West.* New York: Hall, 1994.

Silverstein, Stuart Y. Introduction to *Not Much Fun: The Lost Poems of Dorothy Parker,* comp. Stuart Y. Silverstein, 9–65. New York: Scribner, 1996.

Sklar, Robert. *Movie-Made America.* New York: Vintage, 1994.

Smash-Up: The Story of a Woman. Dir. Stuart Heisler. 1947.

Springer, John Parris. *Hollywood Fictions: The Dream Factory in American Popular Literature.* Norman: University of Oklahoma Press, 2000.

A Star Is Born. Dir. William Wellman. 1937.

Stein, Gertrude. *The Autobiography of Alice B. Toklas.* New York: Vintage, 1990.

———. *Everybody's Autobiography.* Boston: Exact Change, 2004.

Stempel, Tom. *Framework: A History of Screenwriting in the American Film.* New York: Ungar, 1988.

Stillinger, Jack. *Multiple Authorship and the Myth of the Solitary Genius.* Oxford: Oxford University Press, 1991.

Stuart, Frederic. *The Effects of Television on the Motion Picture and Radio Industries.* New York: Arno, 1975.

Suzy. Dir. George Fitzmaurice. 1936.

Sweethearts. Dir. W. S. Van Dyke. 1938.

Swanberg, W. A. *Dreiser.* New York: Bantam, 1967.

Taylor, Dwight. *Joy Ride.* New York: Putnam, 1959.

———. "Scott Fitzgerald in Hollywood." *Harper's,* March 1959, 67–71.

The Ten Year Lunch. Dir. Aviva Slesin. 1987.

Thomson, David. *Showman: The Life of David Selznick.* New York: Knopf, 1992.

Three Comrades. Dir. Frank Borzage. 1938.

Toth, Emily. "Dorothy Parker, Erica Jong, and New Feminist Humor." *Regionalism and the Female Imagination* 2 (1997): 70–85.

Trade Winds. Dir. Tay Garnett. 1938.

Treichler, Paula. "Verbal Subversions in Dorothy Parker: 'Trapped Like a Trap in a Trap.'" *Language and Style* 13, no. 4 (1980): 46–61.

Trilling, Lionel. *The Liberal Imagination.* New York: Viking, 1950.

Turnbull, Andrew. *Scott Fitzgerald.* New York: Scribner, 1962.

Van Gelder, Robert. *Writers and Writing.* New York: Scribner, 1946.

Veitch, Jonathan. *American Superrealism.* Madison: University of Wisconsin Press, 1997.

Walker, Nancy. "The Remarkably Constant Reader: Dorothy Parker as Book Reviewer." *Studies in American Humor* 3, no. 4 (1997): 7–17.

Warshow, Robert. *The Immediate Experience: Movies, Comics, Theatre, and Other Aspects of Popular Culture.* Garden City, N.Y.: Doubleday, 1964.

Way, Brian. *F. Scott Fitzgerald and the Art of Social Fiction.* New York: St. Martin's, 1980.

Weekend for Three. Dir. Irving Reis. 1941.

West, James L. W. *American Authors and the Literary Marketplace since 1900.* Philadelphia: University of Pennsylvania Press, 1990.

———. *The Making of "This Side of Paradise."* Philadelphia: University of Pennsylvania Press, 1983.

West, Nathanael. "Born to Be Wild" Screenplay. N.Y. State Archives. File box 34578-601.

———. *Complete Works.* New York: Farrar, Straus & Cudahy, 1957.

———. *The Day of the Locust.* New York: Random House, 1939.

———. "I Stole a Million" Screenplay. N.Y. State Archives. File box 37213-722.

———. "It Could Happen to You" Screenplay. N.Y. State Archives. File box 33255-540.

———. *Miss Lonelyhearts and The Day of the Locust.* New York: New Directions, 1986.

———. *Novels & Other Writings.* Edited by Sacvan Bercovitch. New York: Library of America, 1997.

———. "The President's Mystery" Screenplay. N.Y. State Archives. File box 31811-475.

Wexler, Joyce. *Who Paid for Modernism?* Fayetteville: University of Arkansas Press, 1997.

What Price Hollywood? Dir. George Cukor. 1932.

Wilde, Oscar. *The Soul of Man under Socialism and Selected Critical Prose.* New York: Penguin, 2001.

Williams, Linda. *Hard Core: Power, Pleasure, and the "Frenzy of the Visible."* Berkeley: University of California Press, 1989.

Williams, Raymond. *Culture and Society.* New York: Columbia University Press, 1983.

Williams, William Carlos. "A New American Writer." In Siegel, 49–50.

———. *Paterson.* New York: New Directions, 1963.

———. *The Selected Letters of William Carlos Williams.* Edited by John Thirwall. New York: McDowell, 1957.

Wilson, Edmund. *Axel's Castle.* New York: Scribner, 1931.

———. *The Boys in the Back Room.* San Francisco: Colt, 1941.

Winter Carnival. Dir. Charles Reisner. 1939.

Wolfe, Tom. *Radical Chic and Mau-Mauing the Flak Catchers.* New York: Bantam, 1999.

Wollen, Peter. *Signs and Meaning in the Cinema.* Bloomington: Indiana University Press, 1969.

Would You Kindly Direct Me to Hell? Dir. Robert Yuhas, 1994.

Wyrick, Debra. "Dadaist Collage Structure and Nathanael West's *Dream Life of Balso Snell.*" In Bloom, 157–64.

Young, Phillip. *Ernest Hemingway.* New York: Rinehart, 1952.

Index

Italicized page numbers refer to illustrations.

Fitzgerald, F. Scott (*continued*)
123–24, 126, 142–43, 144, 152,
153, 164, 176, 177–78, 181, 182,
183, 184–85; and screen credits, 57,
96, 100, 116; as screenwriter, 8, 11,
24–26, 41, 52, 54–55, 56, 59, 60,
63, 69, 70, 86–87, 89, 91, 96–100,
106, 109, 113, 116, 123–25, 138,
141, 145–47; and screenwriters'
union, 64; self-pity, 65, 87; self-
promotion, 13–14, 15, 16, 22, 176,
178; and social support of screen
writing, 9, 116; status as artist, 6, 8,
16, 19–21, 79; and subsidiary rights,
24, 26, 165; and Thalberg, 54, 55,
56–57, 87, 144, 159–60; and West,
2, 39–40, 50, 63, 78–79, 80,
117–18, 119, 120, 134, 137, 138,
141, 142, 144
Fitzgerald, F. Scott, works: "Auction:
Model 1934," 78; "Babylon Revisited," 60, 145, 177; *Babylon Revisited: The Screenplay*, 145–46; *The
Beautiful and Damned*, 7, 16, 19–22,
24, 26, 49, 85, 97, 157; "Boil Some
Water," 156, 157; "The Camel's
Back," 19, 24; "The Crack-Up," 15;
"Crazy Sunday," 7, 40–41, 56–57,
58, 59, 60, 61; "Dice, Brassknuckles, and Guitar," 22; "Financing
Finnegan," 125; *The Great Gatsby*,
24, 33, 40, 56, 63, 78, 79, 80, 118,
119, 126, 140, 144, 152, 153–54,
177, 185; "Head and Shoulders,"
19; *The Last Tycoon*, 4–5, 7, 8, 25,
57–58, 140, 142, 144, 146–57, 158,
159–61, 179; "The Lost Decade,"
124, 125–27, 137, 178; "Mightier
Than the Sword," 1, 3; "Myra
Meets His Family," 19; "The Mystery of the Raymond Mortgage,"
26–27; "The Off-Shore Pirate," 19;
"One Trip Abroad," 60; *The Pat
Hobby Stories*, 1, 3, 7, 8, 20, 140,
156–57, 184; "A Patriotic Short,"
157; "Sleeping and Waking,"
87–88; *Tales of the Jazz Age*, 22;
Tender Is the Night, 7, 40, 63,
64, 81, 82, 83, 84–87, 135, 152,
153; *This Side of Paradise*, 13, 14,
15, 18, 19, 20, 22, 24, 28, 40, 56,
176, 178; "Two Old Timers," 156;
The Vegetable, 24; "Winter Dreams,"
177
Fitzgerald, Zelda: and celebrity, 16,
36; exhibition of paintings, 65; and
F. Scott Fitzgerald's *The Last Tycoon*,
152; and F. Scott Fitzgerald's screen
writing, 145; and Hollywood, 24;
as influence on F. Scott Fitzgerald's
work, 56; lifestyle, 78; mental break-
downs, 40, 87; relationship with
F. Scott Fitzgerald, 182; stabilizing
of, 41; wedding, 15, 16
Flaubert, Gustave, 3, 38
Foley, Barbara, 103
Ford, Ford Madox, 181
Ford, John, 164, 166
Foucault, Michel, 3
Fox, 19, 167
Fraser-Cavassoni, Natasha, 167, 168
Freaks (1932), 57
Freud, Sigmund, 17, 47, 83
Frewin, Leslie, 30, 34

Gabler, Neal: *An Empire of Their
Own*, 33; on movie moguls, 161
Garbo, Greta, 124
Garland, Judy, 111–12
Gaynor, Janet, 107, *112*, 113
GI Bill, 166
Gide, André, 32
Gilbert, John, 57, 109
Gingrich, Arnold, 156, 175
Glyn, Elinor, 32
Gold, Mike, 37–38
Goldwyn, Sam: "Eminent Authors"
project, 18, 25; and Parker, 110; and
Schulberg, 161; and Selznick, 108;
and West, 76
Gone with the Wind (1939), 117, 124,
136
Goodbye Mr. Chips (1939), 117
Goodrich, Frances, 10
Gorky, Maksim, 47, 120
Government Girl (1943), 164

Graham, Sheilah: *Beloved Infidel,* 8, 123, 183–84; *College of One,* 120; and Fitzgerald, 142, 145, 152, 184

Greenfeld, Howard, *Books: From Writer to Reader,* 77

Griffith, Andy, 173, *174*

Griffith, D. W., 18

Grit (1924), 22, 23, 26

Guillory, John, *Cultural Capital,* 27

Gunga Din (1939), 117

Hackett, Albert, 10

Hamilton, Ian, 100

Hammett, Dashiell: as screenwriter, 9; and West, 37, 47, 50, 117

Harcourt, Brace, 76

Harder They Fall, The (1956), 173

Harlow, Jean, 54, 131

Hart, Moss: on Hollywood, 67; *The Man Who Came to Dinner,* 143

Harte, Bret, 38

Hawkes, John, 119

Hawks, Howard, 10, 166

Hearst, William Randolph, 60, 61, 158

Hecht, Ben, 106, 164

Hellman, Lillian: *The Little Foxes,* 143; and West, 37, 45, 78

Hemingway, Ernest: *Across the River and into the Trees,* 181; artistic legacy of, 180–81; and Contact Editions, 40; and Fitzgerald, 2, 32, 41, 56, 65, 88, 179–82; Fitzgerald compared to, 127; *A Moveable Feast,* 181–82, 183; and Parker, 32; and Schulberg, 172, 180; and West, 35, 46, 47, 134

Hemingway, Gregory, 182

Her Face Value (1921), 109

Here Is My Heart (1934), 67–68

high culture: and Fitzgerald, 2, 6, 97, 98; mass culture contrasted with, 4, 5, 6, 7–8, 21, 25, 36, 67; and middle-brow culture industry, 28, 48; and Parker, 67; and Schulberg, 155; and West, 36, 75

Hilton, Daisy, 57

Hilton, Violet, 57

Hitchcock, Alfred, 94, 143–44

Hollywood: Fitzgerald's attitudes toward, 5, 17, 19, 40–41, 117, 120, 141; Fitzgerald's career affected by, 1–2, 4, 6, 12, 16, 91–92, 140, 141, 177, 184, 185; as Fitzgerald's subject matter, 7, 8, 10, 24, 52, 56–59, 83, 84–87, 90, 93, 116, 142, 179; Parker's attitudes toward, 30–31, 121–22; Parker's career affected by, 2, 4, 12, 91–92, 184; as Parker's subject matter, 83, 84, 90, 116; Schulberg's career affected by, 2, 4, 12, 91–92; as Schulberg's subject matter, 7, 90, 93–95, 114, 142, 144, 163; West's career affected by, 2, 4, 6, 12, 91–92, 117, 140, 141, 185; as West's subject matter, 7, 10, 83–84, 90, 93, 116, 118

Hollywood Anti-Nazi League, 104

Hollywood studio system: archetypal narratives of, 26; and blacklisting, 72, 165, 171; changes of 1950s, 164–66; dissolution, 11; as dream factory, 116; and Justice Department, 161, 164, 168; production system, 110, 150; role of authors in, 1, 2, 3, 4–6, 54–55; screenwriters in, 1, 2, 3–4, 6, 54–55, 64, 67, 70–72, 77, 92–93, 97–98, 102; source material warehoused by, 80; structure, 64, 83, 98; and unions, 70–71, 73, 90, 91, 92, 161–62

Hollywood Ten, 101

Hollywood vampire myth, 1–2, 7

Hopkins, Miriam, 78

Horton, Edward Everett, 143

House Un-American Activities Committee (HUAC), 104, 171

Howells, William Dean, 17

Hughes, Rupert, 18

Hunchback of Notre Dame, The (1939), 117

Husband Hunter, The (1920), 19

Huxley, Aldous: *After Many a Summer Dies the Swan,* 135; and Fitzgerald, 144

Huysmans, J.-K., 47, 75

Marx, Harpo, 27
Marx, Karl, 82
Marx, Sam, 54, 87
Marx, Zeppo, 122
Marxism, 78, 81, 171, 179
mass culture: and Fitzgerald, 17, 19, 60, 67, 78, 83, 156; high culture contrasted with, 4, 5, 6, 7–8, 21, 25, 36, 67; Hollywood as symbol of, 4; and Parker, 29, 67, 83; role of artist in, 5, 6, 9; and Stein, 61; and television, 173–75; and West, 48, 49, 61–62, 74, 75–76, 83, 177
mass-market magazines: biographies in, 113; and F. Scott and Zelda Fitzgerald, 16; F. Scott Fitzgerald's stories in, 17, 19, 60, 156; Parker's articles in, 29
Matthau, Walter, 173
Mathieu, Beatrice, 38
Maugham, Somerset, 94
Mayer, Edward Justice, 18
Mayer, Louis B., 144, 161, 164
MCA, 165
McAlmon, Robert, 40, 50–51
McCoy, Horace, 10, 101
McGilligan, Pat, 23
McGuiness, James Kevin, 91
McGurl, Mark, 16–17
McKenney, Eileen, 138
McKenney, Ruth, "My Sister Eileen," 138
Meade, Marion, 28, 31, 114
Mellow, James, 40
Menand, Louis, 47
Mencken, H. L.: *The American Language,* 5; and Fante, 104; and Fitzgerald, 19, 60–61, 86; and *Smart Set,* 29
Menjou, Adolph, 111, *112*
Merriam, Frank, 72
Merton of the Movies (1924), 18
Metro Pictures, and Fitzgerald, 18, 19
Metropolitan Magazine, 19
Meyers, Jeffrey, 142
MGM: and Fitzgerald, 52, 54, 55–57, 96, 98, 100, 125, 127; and hierarchy of screenwriters, 70–71; and Parker,

30–31, 122; and Schulberg, 164; screen writing system, 55, 98
Milburn, George, 133
Milford, Nancy, 15
Millay, Edna St. Vincent, 25
Miller, Henry, 35
Milne, A. A., *House at Pooh Corner,* 32
Mr. Smith Goes to Washington (1939), 117
Mitchell, Margaret, *Gone with the Wind,* 124
Mitford, Nancy, 56
Mizener, Arthur: on Fitzgerald, 1, 17, 19, 178; and Hemingway, 180, 181
modernism: and authorship, 4; and Contact Editions, 40; and *Contact II,* 61; and Modern Library series, 79; and Parker, 28, 66; and West, 36, 42, 46–47, 51–52, 74, 81, 118, 128
Modern Library series, 79
Montgomery, Robert, 56
Moore, George, 46
Moran, Lois, 24
Moss, David, 43, 50
Motion Picture Guild, 118
motion-picture directors: and auteur theory, 170–71; and authorship, 3. *See also specific directors*
motion-picture industry: and adaptations of fiction, 52–53; and American dream, 7, 111; and Depression, 53–54; eastern condescension toward, 67, 90, 106; growth, 5; and illusion of effortlessness, 26, 90; production process, 55–56; role of authors in, 2, 10, 17–19, 54–55; and silent era, 22–23; and sound era, 54; source material from publishing industry, 71, 80, 90–91, 100; and television, 165–66; Wilson on, 7, 144. *See also* Hollywood studio system
motion-picture producers: and authorship, 3; relationship with screenwriters, 1, 6, 55–56, 97–98, 99, 100, 103, 109, 120, 121, 158, 167, 168. *See also specific producers*

Murnau, F. W., 149
Museum of Modern Art, New York, 117

Nabokov, Vladimir, 135
Nathan, George Jean, 19, 29, 60–61
National Industrial Recovery Act, 64
National Institute of Arts and Letters, 176
National Labor Relations Board, 121, 122
Navasky, Victor, *Naming Names,* 171
Nazi Germany, 123
Neal, Patricia, 173
Network (1976), 175
New Masses, 7–38, 121–22, 123
New Republic, 64, 142–43
New York Times, 116, 181
New Yorker: and Behrman, 67; and Campbell, 69; and Parker, 3, 30, 31–32, 65, 176; and West, 37, 177
Nichols, Dudley: and Academy Awards, 103; and screen credits, 56; and Screen Writers Guild, 72, 91; as screenwriter, 103, 149
Ninotchka (1939), 117
No Siree (revue), 29
Norman, Marc, *What Happens Next,* 92
Nothing Sacred (1937), 92, 111, 143
Novarro, Ramon, 56

Ober, Harold, 17, 24, 27, 60, 87, 96, 125
Of Mice and Men (1939), 117
O'Hara, John: *The Big Laugh,* 135; and Fitzgerald, 2, 67, 120, 152; and social support of screen writing, 9
On the Waterfront (1954): production history, 2, 167–69, 171; Schulberg as screenwriter for, 10, 11, 164, 167, 168, 169–70, 171, 172–73, 175
One Hour Late (1935), 67–68
Open End (television show), 176
Ornitz, Samuel, 101

Pacific Weekly, 122
Paramore, Ted, 97, 98

Paramount / Famous Players–Lasky, 22
Paramount Pictures: and Dreiser, 53; and hierarchy of screenwriters, 70–71; and Justice Department, 161; and Parker, 68–69; and B. P. Schulberg, 33, 92, 93
Paris Review, 34, 65, 184
Parker, Dorothy: and Algonquin Round Table, 10, 27–28; attitudes toward Hollywood, 30–31, 121–22; as author, 28–33, 36, 37, 67, 68, 70, 93, 106, 114, 115–16, 121–23, 175; blacklisting of, 165; and Campbell, 10, 68–70, 109, 110–11, 122; collaboration of, 6, 30, 68–69; commercial success as author, 8, 175; cynicism, 58, 68, 110, 122; effect of Hollywood on career, 2, 4, 12, 91–92, 184; financial compensation for screen writing, 2, 30–31, 68, 70, 90, 91, 96, 110, 116, 122; firing from *Vanity Fair,* 27; and Fitzgerald, 2, 15, 29, 32–33, 64–65, 78, 139, 140, 143, 176; on Graham, 184; Hollywood as subject matter, 83, 84, 90, 116; and House Un-American Activities Committee, 171; and leftist politics, 82–83, 90, 91, 103–4, 121–22, 123; persona, 29, 68, 122; photographs of, *69, 105;* and B. P. Schulberg, 34; and Budd Schulberg, 11, 143, 144, 164, 184; and Screen Writers Guild, 9–10, 64, 70, 71, 72, 91, 104, 121, 122, 123; as screenwriter, 10, 18, 30–31, 67–70, 77, 89, 91, 96, 98, 102, 106, 109–11, 114, 116, 121–22, 123, 124, 141, 143–44; and social support of screen writing, 9–10, 142; and status as artist, 6; and subsidiary rights, 165; and West, 37, 50, 67, 70, 102, 117, 120, 135, 139, 144, 176; work on novel, 32–33, 65, 144
Parker, Dorothy, works: *After Such Pleasures,* 65–66; "Best Books" column, 177; "Big Blonde," 32, 66, 84, 121; *Bobbed Hair,* 30; "Bohemia," 35–36; "Business is Business," 30;

Fitzgerald, 124–25; photograph of, *108;* as producer, 107–11; and reuse of plots, 94; and Schulberg, 92, 93, 111, 143

Shakespeare, William, 97

Shapiro, Julian, 46–47

Shaw, George Bernard, 17

Shearer, Norma, 56, 57, 87

Shepard, Alice, 44, 77–78

Sherwood, Robert, 15, 27, 30

Sidney, Sylvia, 34

Silverstein, Stuart, *Not Much Fun,* 122–23

Sinatra, Frank, 168

Sinclair, Upton, 32, 72

Sklar, Robert, 132

Smart Set, 29–30

Smash-Up: The Story of a Woman (1947), 10

Smith, Scottie Fitzgerald: and F. Scott Fitzgerald, 24, 25, 40, 54, 55, 96, 120, 125, 142, 156; *The Romantic Egoists,* 16

Spanish Civil War, 121

Spanish Earth, The (1937), 121

Spengler, Oswald, 82

Spiegel, Sam, 167–68, 170

Sports Illustrated, 173

Springer, John Parris, *Hollywood Fictions,* 1

Stagecoach (1939), 117

Staiger, Janet, 26

Stalin, Josef, 123

Star Is Born, A (1937): and attribution controversy, 168–69; Fitzgerald on, 152; funeral scene, 135; Hollywood as subject, 90; Parker as screenwriter for, 10, 90, 106, 107, 109, 110, 114, 143; production history, 2, 107, 109, 110; scene from, *112;* Schulberg as screenwriter for, 90, 92, 93, 106, 107, 109, 110, 113, 114, 143; and screen-writing process, 107–14

Stein, Gertrude: and Contact Editions, 40; *Everybody's Autobiography,* 48; finances of, 51–52; and Hemingway, 181; and mass culture, 61; on readers, 48–49; and West, 47

Steinbeck, John, *The Grapes of Wrath,* 119, 135

Stempel, Tom, 169

Sten, Anna, 76

Stewart, Donald Ogden, 27, 72, 103

Stewart, Jimmy, 165

Stillinger, Jack, 108–9

Streetcar Named Desire, A (1951), 167

Susskind, David, 176

Suzy (1936), 10

Sweethearts (1938), 122

Swift, Jonathan, 47

talent agents, 165

Talmadge, Constance, 24

Taylor, Dwight, 56–57, 58

Taylor, Elizabeth, 145

Taylor, Laurette, 58

television, 165–66, 173–75

Thalberg, Irving: as cultured man, 34; and Fitzgerald, 54, 55, 56–57, 87, 144, 159–60; photograph of, *159;* and Selznick, 108

They Were Expendable (1945), 164

Thompson, Kristin, 26

Thomson, David, 114

Three Comrades (1938): and Fitzgerald, 116; production history, 2; and screen-writing process, 96–98, 99, 100, 107, 113

Thurber, James, 65

Tolstoy, Leo, 17

Toth, Emily, 66

Trade Winds (1938), 122

Transition, 61

Treichler, Paula, 66–67

Trilling, Lionel, *The Liberal Imagination,* 178

Trumbo, Dalton, 171

Turnbull, Andrew, 56, 116

Twentieth Century Pictures, 78

United Artists, 24, 168

Universal Studios, 76, 117

Vanity Fair, 27

Veitch, Jonathan, 42, 78, 135–36

About the Author

TOM CERASULO is an assistant professor of English and the Shaughness Family Chair for the Study of the Humanities at Elms College in Chicopee, Massachusetts. Cerasulo holds a Ph.D. in English and a certificate in film studies from the Graduate Center of the City University of New York. His research has been published in *American Writers,* the *Arizona Quarterly,* the *Encyclopedia of the Jazz Age, Studies in American Culture,* and other publications.